Teaching English To All

Richard W. Mills

Robert Royce Limited

British Library Cataloguing in Publication Data

Mills, Richard
    Teaching English to all.
    1. English language—Study and teaching
    (Secondary)—England
    I. Title
    428′.007′1242   LB1631

    ISBN 0–947728–21–X

Phototypeset by Input Typesetting Limited, London.
Printed and bound in Great Britain by
Biddles Limited, Guildford and King's Lynn.

For Peter

Contents

Contents

Notes on the Contributors

JUDITH ATKINSON is Head of English at Wolfreton Comprehensive School, Hull, having previously taught in grammar and comprehensive schools.

SHIRLEY HOOLE taught for twenty years in comprehensive schools and latterly was Head of English at Maypole Comprehensive School, Birmingham.

RICHARD MILLS was formerly Head of English at Shenley Court Comprehensive School, Birmingham, and is at present Principal Lecturer and In-Service Co-ordinator at Newman-Westhill Colleges' Academic Association, Birmingham.

LESLIE STRINGER has a number of years' experience in secondary teaching and is now Head of English at Four Dwellings Comprehensive School, Birmingham.

GORDON TAYLOR was formerly Head of English at Blandford Upper School, Dorset, and is at present Senior Lecturer at Chester College of Higher Education.

Introduction

This book has been written for students in training and for secondary school English teachers new to teaching and/or new to, or contemplating, mixed ability grouping or work with wide ability bands. It has, thus, a two-fold purpose: to indicate some of the strategies which might be used with classes of children whose attainment varies enormously, and also to show some of the ways in which English teaching can be tailored to cater for wide abilities, irrespective of the method of grouping.

All the contributors to this book were colleagues for a number of years in the same 11 to 18 comprehensive school English department, where initially streamed and later complete mixed ability work from first to third years was practised. Since that time, we have each gone our separate ways, adding to our earlier experience, but retaining certain basic common beliefs in the theory and practice of English teaching. The book which has been put together should, then, be internally consistent, despite its nature as an anthology. Certainly there are differences in emphasis but nowhere, I think, a downright contradiction.

Much of the material in the book was originally published by Ward Lock Educational as *Teaching English Across the Ability Range*, and does not appear to have dated. However, in addition to some re-writing and some pruning, new material has been included in this version, with extended class libraries, tape-slide information, examples of record keeping, computer sources, small group detail and so forth. I should like to thank my colleague, Keith Barker, for readily taking on the job of checking addresses, telephone numbers, dates and sources.

The first chapter looks initially at the theory behind non-streaming, not in a crusading manner, I hope, but merely to provide some kind of justification for the approaches and practices outlined in the later pages. Some breakdown of literacy and oracy skills is offered so that the challenges facing teachers may be clearly identified.

Part Two of the book moves away from preparation and planning to where the action is – lion's den, chalk face, battlefront – choose your own well-worn metaphor. Some sections are deliberately blow-by-blow accounts of organization and classroom management since we feel such detail could be helpful to inexperienced teachers and students and since, in general, good teaching presupposes good structure. Judith Atkinson describes a kind of English teaching which stresses the integration of experience through form, genre and medium. Shirley Hoole, who is also in sympathy with such thematic work, concentrates on the appreciation of literature, as something of value in its own right and also as an illumination and extension of awareness. Both draw on past and present daily classroom experience for their detail. So, too, does Les Stringer, whose contribution will offer a perspective which will be new to many teachers. His chapter is not the traditional nod in the drama direction, common in such anthologies. It starts with drama but swiftly moves to the specific area of games and simulations showing, with some detailed classroom examples, how such an approach may be integrated into general English teaching.

Next follows Gordon Taylor's chapter on how to incorporate natural objects, artefacts and visual materials into one's teaching, not merely in order to vary the diet but rather because such stimuli are appropriate and effective in all kinds of situations, but especially with small groups. The next section picks this up and attempts to be both theoretical (in its categorization of small group activities) and practical (in the range of possibilities outlined and in the *modus operandi* proposed). Some evidence is presented to show the kinds of learning that may occur in small groups under certain conditions.

Behind Part Three of the book is the notion of the English teacher as prospector or scavenger, hunting anywhere and everywhere for appropriate and useful material and ideas. The days are gone when your provisions for the term were *The Merchant of Venice*, Ridout, Palgrave's *Golden Treasury* and *The Cloister and the Hearth*. Iron rations indeed. You need much more varied fare nowadays in order to cope with the demands, interests and range of your pupils, and the local scrap-metal yard may be as appropriate at times as the City Library. It all depends on what you are trying to do. The final chapters offer a variety of sources and materials for use across the ability range and I hope they will prove to be helpful.

If the methods and materials we describe are appropriate for mixed groups, then they are just as appropriate for streamed forms also, and for any other mode of grouping for learning. Every group is a mixed group; some are more mixed than others.

R.W.M.

Part One: Planning Ahead

1 Mixed Ability English

RICHARD MILLS

Justification

The Oxford Book of Literary Anecdotes has a story about Matthew Arnold which has altered forever my conception of the great man. Lina Waterfield, a narrator, tells how, as a backward child of six, she was unable to read. It was, apparently, a serious case, sufficient to warrant the attention of a family friend, known to be a poet and government inspector. The man was duly sent for and, sitting the little girl on his knee, he spoke to her of books and poetry. Then he ended with these words: 'Your mother tells me that you do not know how to read, and are refusing to learn. It surprises me very much that a little girl of six should not know how to read and expects to be read to. It is disgraceful, and you must promise me to learn at once; if you don't I shall have to put your father and mother in prison.' Within a few weeks Lina could read Grimm's *Fairy Tales*.

I offer this story not as a code of conduct for inspectors or poets, nor as the panacea to reading problems, although the threat did apparently work. Your views of the incident will depend on your preconceptions. You may see it as a very powerful piece of individualized instruction. After all, Lina is sitting on Arnold's knee in a one-to-one relationship. Or you may regard it as yet another Victorian con trick which may have been successful but which probably set up traumas for life. The point is that one person's method is another's madness.

Certainly, those methods which my colleagues and I outline in this book are ones which we believe have been, and can be, efficacious in producing English work of good quality across the range, albeit without penal sanctions, and, since every method or piece of practice is inevitably based on some theory, it is appropriate to put the case for non-streaming, even though the matter seems to be an ideological issue, where argument is unlikely to convince unbelievers. Indeed, it would be strange in a book of this kind if no such statement were to be made. Nevertheless, I am not arguing the case, but rather making the assertions briefly, in no particular order of significance. Eight of these arguments run as follows.

1   Unlike weather forecasting, the system of streaming has a self-validating quality. Children in the A stream behave as such, and those in the D stream (or possibly the fourteenth stream in a very large school) perform according to their label. Teachers' expectations are significant factors in attainment, and such expectations are often conditioned by the streaming process. You walk down the corridor to teach the top fifth year and may well feel stimulated at the prospect of this intellectual encounter. Forty minutes later you travel the same corridor to a low second-year class, wondering just what you'll be able to teach them. There is a sense in which your expectations should, of course, be different if you are to approach your task realistically, but ideally no ceiling on achievement should be contemplated. It may be only natural to prefer lively groups to dull groups, but the terms 'lively' and 'dull' are not synonymous with 'bright' and 'unintelligent'. The labelling process is an insidious one.

2   Ignoring all manner of social skills and such characteristics as commitment to hard work, perseverance and honest endeavour, rigid streaming depends on accurate measurement of ability, but no such infallible measures exist. Even the 10+ selection and rejection procedures, known to be very accurate, were subject to an unavoidable

error of at least 10 per cent which meant that each year thousands of pupils were 'wrongly' allocated. Any selection procedure has a considerable margin of error and any stream, however sophisticated the tests, is far less homogeneous than it is thought to be. Moreover, there is the assumption that intellectual capacity does not alter: it merely has to be assessed and then treated accordingly, rather like the diagnosis of some incurable illness. Such a notion is now out of favour.

3   Such selection is, in any event, strongly affected by additional factors such as social class, by birth dates (i.e. amount of time spent in infant school), by language background and parental attitude.

4   A stream of water generally flows in the same direction, over the same ground, at the same speed. A stream of children, it is implied, is expected to pursue activities corporately. The class generally works on the same material at the same speed. In other words, streaming is an organizational device and promotes a teaching style which minimizes individual differences. Under this system children should be dealt with *en masse* and, indeed, if this doesn't happen, then one argument in support of streaming automatically disappears. It's only when we don't know children particularly well that we feel they have a lot in common: the more we get to know them, the more they diverge. Imagine your own son or daughter to be one of your pupils and you will realize just how little you know of the other twenty-nine in the class, however conscientious you may be. Mixed ability grouping forces us to notice and take into account the specific strengths and weaknesses, interests and idiosyncrasies of individual children, and treat each according to need.

5   Streaming promotes a competitive and hierarchical ethos. Top streams have high status, bottom streams virtually no social standing. Children may strive to be promoted but movement is inevitably a two-way process and few, if any, benefit by being demoted. If there is too much movement between streams then, it could be argued, the original

division was inaccurate. If there is too little, then, presumably, the system ossifies and those who have aspirations give up hope. Similar problems apply to banding and setting, which is a more sophisticated form of streaming. Whatever ideological stance one takes here, there is no denying that, logically, mixed ability grouping precludes competition. Non-swimmers and Olympic swimming medalists may do many things together, but they will not compete in the same swimming race.

6   Not only does streaming act as a divisive academic influence within a school but it also has other undesirable social effects. While A streams show high morale (and are often believed by their contemporaries to contain 'snobs'), low ability groups have a bad self-image which they may seek to deserve. Such images may be strengthened by teacher expectation. Certainly, there is evidence that mixed ability grouping may have considerable beneficial effects so far as discipline is concerned.

7   Some opponents of mixed ability grouping maintain that, under such a system, the bright pupils will be held back and the less academic will struggle to maintain progress. (What of the majority of 'average' pupils?) Such evidence as is available would indicate that this is an ungrounded fear and that the bright do as well, whereas the weak ones may improve significantly. Perhaps in a *streamed* situation the bright weren't stretched and the weak were under-achievers? There is an obvious need for much more research here. Certainly, no professional person would support a system which manifestly led to a lowering of standards and to a general mediocrity of attainment. To oppose streaming is not to oppose high standards. However, behind the misgivings mentioned above, there seems to lie the assumption that in mixed ability work there will continue to be comparison of pupils with each other and the group will be moving along a common path, with the leaders striding out in front and the stragglers dawdling at the back. Such a notion is a hangover from streamed thinking. In fact, pupils are following a variety of trails, perhaps not all towards the same destination. Each pupil

should be engaged on work which is appropriate, relevant to needs and interests, and in such a class atmosphere that each is valued, irrespective of strengths and weaknesses. A very tall order. No attempt should be made, I believe, to disguise differences and to pretend they don't exist: that would be a useless attempt at deception, fooling no one. Rather, a mature awareness of difference, in a non-competitive atmosphere, seems more desirable, and teacher attitude is clearly crucial. Teachers involved in mixed ability work, as in any other system of grouping, must want it to succeed.

8   Points 1–6 are arguments *against* streaming and only by implication *for* mixed ability grouping. We now move away from points of principle, some of them based on notions of equality of treatment and attitude, to the question of subject suitability. Whatever the appropriateness for mixed ability work of other subject areas in the curriculum, it can be strongly argued that English, by its very nature, is particularly appropriate.

Subject suitability

There appear to be five main models of English teaching, none of which is entirely discrete.

(a)   **Basic skills** with its stress on a minimum competence in reading and writing so that all school leavers should at least be able to read a daily newspaper and cope with the literacy demands of a bureaucratic and industrialized society.

(b)   **Cultural heritage** which argues that all pupils should be acquainted with work by the great writers of their country, and the myths and legends and cultural foundations out of which such writing grows.

(c)   **Sociological stance** where the stress is on English as a study of contemporary national and international social issues and the individual only in relation to local and more wide-ranging contexts.

(d)   **Language communication** which, for our present

7

purposes, could be defined as seeking to replace the previous notion of grammatical correctness with the more ambiguous, and perhaps at times subjective, concept of appropriateness, and which endeavours to examine and promote genuine language in a variety of real contexts.

(e) **Personal development** where the individual, with his/her own needs, beliefs and experiences, is at the centre of the stage and where, to use the old terminology, the intention is 'to develop persons according to their full potential.'

These then, very baldly, are five possible approaches to the teaching of English. Any school English syllabus or, more pertinently, the actual teaching which takes place, will show a bias towards one or two of these approaches. However, there can be strengths and weaknesses in each, unless some kind of balance is achieved. Let us assume that we make an amalgam of the strengths of each. Then, in this best of all possible worlds, we shall be endeavouring to develop a range of literacy and oracy skills and an adequate technical competence; to impart some appreciation and knowledge of the prose, poetry and drama of our own and other cultures; to consider and explore matters of immediate and lasting human concern; to look at language 'such as men do use' in a variety of contexts and to attempt to ensure that our pupils can operate well in a range of situations; to assist, above all, in the intellectual, aesthetic, moral and spiritual growth of each boy and girl we encounter. It is this last model, that of personal growth, which, in its ideal form, can subsume all the strengths of the other models and it is, for me, synonymous with mixed ability teaching since it places the emphasis firmly on the individual child in all his/her uniqueness. This approach to English teaching is the premise which underpins the thinking of all the contributors to this book.

Although they possess no monopoly on promoting personal growth, many English teachers often lay great stress on the development of individual perceptions and insights and on the maturing understanding of each person. In dealing closely with social and individual concerns of morality, relationship, taste, personal experience and so forth, through literature and the mass media and by virtue of regular contact with pupils throughout the week, English and Humanities staff are often able to develop strong relationships based on mutual trust and understanding. Let me add, many 'non-English' teachers may also achieve such understanding, and perhaps some 'English' teachers do not. I suspect that the role of say, boys' and girls' craft teachers in this respect has been underestimated. After all, such teachers often work with small groups and individuals who are performing different tasks at varying speeds. These teachers have an ideal opportunity to foster mutual understanding on a one-to-one basis. In any event, whatever the specialism, the cause of staff unity is hardly served by polishing one's badge of understanding too vigorously.

Transition

In his short story, *Dead Men's Path*, Chinua Achebe tells of the ambitious young Headmaster, Michael Obi, who, in order to fulfil his great plans for Ndume Central School, is scornful of the village's traditions and sets out to destroy them overnight. Such unilateral action is a recipe for disaster, not because the long-term aims are unacceptable, but on account of indecent speed, a lack of respect for the views of others, and a contempt for older ways.

The moral seems to be: 'Make haste slowly' and it's one which a school changing from streamed to unstreamed teaching might well adopt. Innovation has a threatening quality: it poses a challenge to status, role and previous experience. Like a new friendship, it is often better when allowed time to mature than when embraced too early and too indiscriminately. Moreover, there are so many imposed changes in the educational maelstrom that any additional upheaval needs careful scrutiny in order to measure certain turmoil against possible benefits. The words of Gaius Petronius, 66 AD, have a curiously modern ring:

We trained hard – but it seemed that every time we were beginning to form up into teams we would be reorganized. I was to learn later in life that we tend to meet any new situation by reorganizing – and a wonderful method it can be for creating the illusion of progress whilst producing confusion, inefficiency and demoralization.

One way of avoiding this trinity of undesirables is by constant department discussion, formal and informal, and I want now to identify some of the areas which might concern an English department contemplating a move to mixed ability teaching. I am assuming that the move has not been forced on them from the top, since there is plenty of evidence that innovation of that kind has little chance of lasting success. The fruit may grow rapidly, but it soon withers. Instead, let us take the case of a department where a majority professes a belief in mixed ability grouping but has little or no experience of it, and where some highly successful and respected colleagues are very sceptical. It's an ideological confrontation where care should be taken to avoid unhelpful stereotypes such as:

Supporters = progressive – child centred – modern
Opponents = reactionary – subject centred – old fashioned

One way in which a department might proceed is to contemplate the tremendous variety of literacy and oracy skills which any teacher of a mixed ability class might expect to encounter. What ranges might we find in a first-year mixed group of eleven year olds, and what are some of the teaching strategies we might adopt? Let us look at the areas of reading, listening and speaking, and writing.

Reading

We could well encounter a span of measured reading age from 7 to 14 years and a tremendous diversity of interest and taste. Some children cannot read a daily newspaper, nor much else for that matter; some can cope with *The Times* if they wish. Some are hooked on the Famous Five's adventures; others prefer the exploits of Mr Pickwick. Some read no books at all; others devour several a week. The main point is that whatever written material we are thinking of – whether it is fiction or factual information, notices on the board, instructions on work cards, newspapers or magazines – there are some boys and girls who will have difficulty with reading matter of any kind. It is probably the inability of some children to read reasonably well which is the biggest problem facing the teacher of mixed groups, since so much energy, time and attention have to be devoted to ways and means of either remedying the deficiency or circumventing it.

In order to do either of these two things satisfactorily, we need to have as much information as possible about the weak reader. Ideally, he/she would have a full medical examination which would involve audiometric, ophthalmic and neurological tests. That ideal is rarely attained, except in the case of children with severe learning difficulties or those with parents who are determined to be as fully informed as possible. Here is one example (Gray 1976) of the sort of information which could come from a thorough examination:

My younger son Peter (aged 7 years) was assessed by a paediatrician, a neurologist and a psychologist. The three visits were spread over nine months, and we were given no information until the last visit. The centre (a dyslexia clinic) appeared grossly overworked and understaffed.

At our final visit, the neurologist summed up their findings. Peter had a full-scale WISC IQ of 121, verbal 140, but performance below average. He had very poor visual perception, that is, his brain did not interpret correctly what his eyes saw. This explained his constant confusion of 't' and 'f', 'm' and 'w', 'e' and 'g', 'p' 'd' 'b' and 'q', and his trying to walk through the closed halves of doors when smaller! His hand/eye co-ordination was poor, and he had difficulty with fine finger movements. Regular scanning of straight lines, needed in reading, would be difficult for him for some time to come. They did not consider he had brain damage, but was suffering from a 'maturational lag'.

All children can be tested for reading age and reading level, and this can be done objectively and subjectively. *Objectively*, you will find a *group* or *individual* reading test which can be administered by a *teacher* (some can only be used by trained psychologists) which is applicable to the *secondary* range, which will either *diagnose* and/or show *attainment* and which, at the same time, is relatively *inexpensive*. The most commonly used tests are those of word recognition (e.g. Schonell and Burt), but they are of limited usefulness. More helpful are those by Neale (1957), and the GAP (1970).[1]

Here is part of an educational psychologist's report on the reading ability of fourteen-year-old Brian:

> An assessment of his reading showed this to be slow. On the Neale Analysis of Reading Ability he had scores of 10 years and 2 months for accuracy and 11 years and 2 months for comprehension . . . He used phonics quite well and although his reading was halting, there were few words which he did not attempt at all. The English Picture Vocabulary Test produced a below average score, showing he had a low level of listening vocabulary. On the Wechsler Intelligence Scale for Children (Revised) his general knowledge score was above average. Two non-verbal tests on picture completion and coding had average scores. From this assessment I would suggest that verbal skills are below non-verbal skills. I looked at his spelling and started him off on a word collection of regular digraphs and endings. (Phinn 1984)

It is for you to look at the tests available, if you wish, and to decide on the most appropriate for your purposes.[2] The children could then be tested early and late in the academic year. There is nothing incompatible between the practice of mixed ability grouping and the use of diagnostic tests. However, the tests described above have their origin in some kind of medical model and it may well be that they are being superseded by the practice of building up a detailed profile based on regular contact and work done. In other words, process as well as product.

I believe we should treat any results which purport to measure attainment with respect certainly, but also with a healthy suspension of judgement, being aware of the perils of too dogmatic a stance in this area. Diagnostic information is, in my view, much more valuable. However, what of subjective judgements? What of the teacher's own continuous assessment? Here, I believe, good infant and junior school methods should be used. You can hear children read aloud, making a mental, and later written, note of the kinds of errors they make and deducing categories of errors from the clues provided, questioning them on what they read or asking about a passage just read silently, constantly building up and revising a detailed record which monitors strengths and weaknesses, interests and hobbies, books they have read and ones they have failed to read. Open University material offers considerable help in this area of reading and interest inventories.

Perhaps it all sounds a little formidable, but what I have in mind is a simple yet useful cumulative record which should not become a burden for the teacher, nor for the children. No child should be required to write about every book read. It will only made them read less and there are other, more imaginative ways in which you can check progress.

When you are aware of attainment levels and interests, look again at your departmental stock to see if it is appropriate and adequate. You will, presumably, have the examination texts you require, but can you offer good factual material as well as satisfying fiction? Are there any useful play texts for first and second years? Can you cater for the weak third-year readers? Here you will, no doubt, come up against the old dilemma: should you be happy if the really weak or poorly motivated ones are reading anything at all, whatever it might be? I'm not just thinking of Enid Blyton. I visited a school and happened to see at lunchtime a group of five second-year girls sitting on the lawn, one of whom was reading aloud to the other four. It was an idyllic scene and I don't recall seeing it before or since. Then, as I walked by, I noticed the title of the book – *The Exorcist*.

As you're inspecting your stock, look carefully at the questions in your text books and on your work cards. Are they clear? Have you included a translation of any difficult phrases, so as to accommodate a wide range of children? Let me emphasize that I'm not arguing for a lowering of standards. Quite the contrary, I want standards to be higher than ever, but don't let us correlate incomprehensibility with academic excellence. Colleagues from other departments should look carefully, too, at the language of their questions and their subject and their teaching. The phrase 'a language policy across the curriculum' might then begin to become a reality. Here's one example I came across of a question addressed to eleven year olds based on a prose passage: 'What does Moorehead wish us to understand when he compares the animal's dignity and majesty with that of the prophets?' I'm sure there are better ways of saying that. Perhaps that was a fairly obvious candidate for attention, but we can easily be caught unawares by much simpler constructions. An acquaintance of mine included on a word card the instruction: 'Give the definition of "amphibious"', and discovered that, while a particular girl knew the meaning of amphibious, she was fooled by the injunction 'Give the definition of'.

Please be clear that I am not arguing for a reduction of all written language to monosyllabic Anglo-Saxon grunts. That way illiteracy lies. Often we must help weak readers through difficult text, but equally we should be sensitive to the problems posed by awkward constructions as well as unfamiliar vocabulary.

Let us assume that we now know the children's levels and interests and we know our stock quite well also. How do we match the stock to the children? I will make some points briefly here, since Shirley Hoole deals at length with the subject and, in fact, offers a different emphasis.

Traditionally, we have had class readers and no doubt there are some appropriate for mixed groups, but to expect thirty boys and girls regularly to maintain interest in the same book for the same amount of time is probably unrealistic. The short story, if chosen with care, is a much more appropriate form for this kind of treatment and some sets of short stories could be kept together, precisely for the purpose of class teaching lessons, in order to develop skills of comprehension and appreciation and to ensure that all children are introduced to various techniques involved in prose reading, as well as using such stories as springboards for creative activities.

Another method of organization is to have four or five titles in a class (six copies of each book) chosen and distributed on the basis of interest, rather than reading age. Otherwise you are in danger of streaming within your mixed class. Any one small group of six children would work, at times corporately and at times individually, reading their books and completing a variety of tasks based on work cards. One advantage of such a system, apart from the element of choice which it may permit, is the more flexible use of stock involved.

Better still, I believe, is a class library where individual informed choice can be made and this means dividing up your departmental stock into, perhaps, sets of thirty separate titles with two copies of each title, i.e. sixty books. in all, or more if you have them. If you ask pupils to donate used books to the class library, as I did on one occasion, I would expect you to pick up some useful material within the lumber. You may also develop a school bookshop and/or develop one of the existing schemes for encouraging children to buy their own books.

Class libraries, alongside school libraries, do mean that more children read more books, but there are still problems to be solved and you do have to devise adequate ways of monitoring what is read, whether it has been understood, and so on. However, we should take care not to kill the habit with pedantic insistence on complete understanding. In an excellent chapter entitled 'Making Children Hate Reading', John Holt (1967) wrote:

Unfortunately, we English teachers are easily hung up on this matter of understanding. Why should children understand everything they read? Why should anyone? *Does* anyone? I don't, and I never did. I was always reading books that teachers would have said were 'too hard' for me, books full of words I didn't know. That's how I got to be a good reader. When about ten, I read all the D'Artagnan stories and loved them, it didn't trouble me in the least that I didn't know why France was at war with England or who was quarrelling with whom in the French court or why the Musketeers should always be at odds with Cardinal Richelieu's men. I didn't even know who the Cardinal was, except that he was a dangerous and powerful man that my friends had to watch out for. This was all I needed to know.

I remember reading those stories about the same age as Holt and being mildly baffled by those same questions, but not sufficiently for it to inhibit my enjoyment. That's probably the key: only enjoyment and high motivation will really develop the reading habit. Recently I came across eight-year-old Wayne reading these words:

She sat on her eggs to keep them warm. She sat on them for days and days. The only time she went away was to get some food. She came back soon.

Then he said to me: 'I save eggs, you see. I've got a raven, a woodpigeon, a golden pheasant, tree creeper, a house sparrer, a hedge sparrer, a quail, a coot, a moorhen, a swan, a blackbird, a starling, a thrush, a duck, a hen, a pochard, a twite.' He was, in fact, an expert on the subject, collecting and swapping eggs like stamps or marbles, as a hobby, and he said that he always chose reading books about birds and eggs. His own knowledge was clearly far in advance of the text of his reading book, *Gertie the Duck*, but the mere subject held his interest.

A last point about class libraries. It's very useful to have suitable reference material in your classroom so that it becomes a natural activity, both in the class and the school library, to look up information, thereby developing a range of reference skills. You might think about the following reference sources as a basis:

a good dictionary
Roget's *Thesaurus*

Bible (with a concordance?)
an atlas
Pears Cyclopaedia
Whitaker's Almanack
Radio Times and *TV Times*
a newspaper
a telephone directory
a dictionary of quotations

Mentioning the school library leads me to consider in passing its modern development, the Resource Centre. Such a development is directly in line with mixed ability teaching, where you often need to draw on as many kinds of stimulus as are available, and it should be remembered here that some excellent resources are human – pupils, teachers, other adults – and that we should explore this potential as well as any other. All teachers will develop their own personal materials, but in the additional central collection one would eventually expect to find a range of books, photographs, charts, work sheets, newspapers, magazines, colour slides, film, film strips, objects, tapes, cassettes, records, computer programs, and folders (produced by pupils). This does not mean that poor readers should be for ever looking at photographs, drawing pictures, or listening to tapes, but such material and methods may be used to develop a range of language skills in the weak and the strong, as Gordon Taylor indicates in a later chapter.

Time and again we return to the weak readers. What do we do about them? The first thing is to recognize that the school exists as much for them as for the external exam candidates. In fact, probably more so, but there are no easy answers and I have known weak readers ·who have improved only marginally despite great efforts by very hard-working staff. Ideally, after the screening and testing which I mentioned earlier, all kinds of strategies will be used, including:

1   Interest based work – with a boy like Wayne this is no problem, but there do appear to be children who obscure their interests remarkably successfully.

2   Extra tuition – possibly in some of the time allocated to a subject other than English, if all parties are agreeable. In one school where I worked, the Head of Modern Languages permitted such an arrangement.

3   Devices to build confidence, including encouragement, success at short-term goals, enthusiasm and conviction on the teacher's part and an awareness of the possible value of counselling and of the virtue of building on strengths rather than stressing weaknesses. In other words, an attempt to deal with the whole person.

4   Use of multi-media materials mentioned above.

5   Use of various kinds of hardware, including the Language Master,[3] the Audio Page,[4] the cassette recorder with junction box,[5] and, as it develops, interactive video.

6   Above all, perhaps, good systematic infant and junior method, without infantile material.

Finally, let me end this section on reading with an unusual testimony to the enduring quality of literature. These are the words of a seven-year-old boy as he compares comics with books:

> I don't like comics. Comics rip too easily, but books are tough. You try to break them, but you can't. I sawed through my book. I tried to sell it, so I sawed through it, in half. My saw was ever so sharp. I couldn't even get through it.

Listening and speaking

Reading and writing are often regarded as the high status skills among the language arts, but much recent research has focused on the need for good foundations in listening and speaking, and it is to these areas that we now turn our attention.

Whatever results may be obtained from listening tests we can never be wholly certain of any child's listening thresholds in the day-to-day classroom activity. We can't legislate, mercifully, for what goes on between the ears. However, our experience indicates that some children can apparently concentrate for lengthy periods of time and subsequently act upon what they heard, even after long intervals. Others hear our words and those pearls of wisdom sink like stones into cotton wool, provoking no discernible response. Between these two extremes there is every level of listening skill and somehow we must try to provide for such range within our groups. Bullock gave useful advice:

> People listen best when they have to take some action upon the information they have received. Where they have the opportunity to reply or to participate through action their attention is stimulated.(10.19)

So, although I am sceptical of Listening Laboratories of the SRA variety since these tend to isolate the skill and try to develop it in a vacuum, nevertheless it does seem sensible to plan for some amelioration in listening skills within the normal daily work in school. Certainly, many teachers are increasingly anxious about the quality of listening and, despite any hard evidence, attribute a supposed deterioration to the deleterious effect of television.

As with listening, so a similar range of skill with speaking may be discerned in our wide ability group. One or two may be highly articulate and virtually able to enter into Socratic-type dialogue. Some may speak several languages but not be particularly proficient in English. Some children, not unlike some adults, will utter many words with no thought. One or two may remain absolutely silent, as did one boy I met, for over a year. Many will not understand particular words or constructions which we use. If you, as a teacher, use a sentence such as 'Presumably you will be familiar with the contextual constraints involved', then you need to translate it in the next breath into something like 'You'll probably know a bit about how the situation you're in affects what you say'. Then you follow up with some examples. However, in the unlikely instance I've just given, there are obvious difficulties of construction, vocabulary and concept. Our language could be much simpler and still pose many problems for our pupils and we need constantly to listen to the words we speak and provide, in a subtle and discreet manner (unlike my example), a running commentary or translation. Sometimes such a translation may be supplied by a pupil. Shirley Hoole tells me she once participated in the following exchange with some fourth-year pupils:

S.H.	Don't assume that a boy with an upper-class accent is necessarily effeminate. Don't equate class with femininity or masculinity.
Pupil	What does she mean?
Another pupil (Karen)	She means, 'Don't think because he talks posh he's a puff.'

Apparently they then had a very profitable discussion on why the teacher couldn't (or felt she couldn't) use such language herself, and on the differences between teacher and pupil language.

Listening and talking are two sides of the same coin. Perhaps we have all too readily tried to develop the former skill in our pupils by exercising the latter skill ourselves. 'Who needs the most practice talking in school?' asked John Holt (1967). 'Who gets the most?' Bullock, less pithily but with no less concern, stated:

There is research evidence to suggest that on average the teacher talks for three quarters of the time in the usual teacher-class situation. It has been calculated from this that in a 45-minute period the amount of time left for a class of 30 to contribute is an average of some 20 seconds per pupil. (10.4)

As it is, we know that the time in a class lesson is never evenly apportioned in this way, as a wedding cake might be. When we speak of having had 'a good discussion', what we often mean is that we were able to conduct an interesting dialogue between ourselves and three or four articulate pupils, while the other twenty-seven were good enough to be passive, listening or not listening. At least we may have advanced a little from the time when a pupil of primary school age, questioned as to the worst things he could possibly do, replied 'Murder, and talking in the corridor' (Widlake 1971).

Other problems spring to mind. How do we continue to stretch highly able and articulate pupils while, at the same time, helping them to become sensitive enough to avoid rejection by less fluent contemporaries? How do we encourage in some children more thought and less talk? How do we develop such a climate that silent people will feel able to say something with comparative confidence, thereby developing a grasp of ideas which they as yet dimly perceive? How do we grapple with the two or three pupils in the class who need to be taught English as a second language, and for whom there is no peripatetic help? How do we provide such a variety of contexts and situations that pupils have the opportunity to use language in a number of different ways and for a number of different purposes? The questions almost ask themselves, and the list could easily be continued, but let us now consider briefly some of the areas in which the answers may lie, with more detail of strategies in ensuing chapters.

A major requirement is for us all to become more sensitive to language, both our own and that of our pupils and students. One of the ways to do this is, on occasion, to tape-record ourselves and the children in the classroom and produce a transcript of part of the lesson. You probably can't do a great deal of this, but an occasional analysis will, like a long week-end, act as a refresher. For example, you will be able to remind yourself of proportions of teacher-talk and pupil-talk; of the pros and cons of open and closed questions; of the virtues of encouragement and praise; of the kinds of language the pupils are called upon to use. Here is a short excerpt for you to analyse. What would you say to (or about) the teacher who figures in this extract? He is working with 42 ten year olds.

Teacher   One, ONE, one good sentence that describes you eating a meal. It, it, it might be, it doesn't have to include the er thing you're actually eating.

	No. Put up your hand and tell me one. One good sentence that describes what you're eating.
Pupil	Munching, crunching all the chicken away.
Teacher	Munching, crunching all the chicken away. That's good, Paul. Can you think of anything, Clare?
Clare	No, sir.
Teacher	Er, well. Come on, think, Clare. Use your brain. Dominic?
Dominic	Shloshing chips and beans in your mouth, sir.
Teacher	Shloshing chips and beans in your mouth. Can you think of a better word than 'shloshing' 'cause you're, you're tending to get a bit slangy? Dominic?
Dominic	Stuffing.
Teacher	Stuffing. That, er, that's still a bit slangy. Can you think of . . .
Dominic	Piling.
Teacher	Yes, er, that's a little better. Can you think of something, well . . . write down the sentence now that you've now thought of . . . quickly . . . that describes . . . how you're eating a meal . . . describe what . . . go on, say what you're doing. Can you think of some good describing words, to describe the meal? What can you think of one quickly?
Pupils	(*unintelligible*)
Teacher	Yes. Delicious. Yes, that's a good one. Can you think of er, er a better word than 'delicious'?
Pupil	Luscious.
Teacher	Luscious.
Pupil	Scrumptious.
Teacher	Scrumptious. Can you think of anything else?

I can only speculate on whether you and I would make the same points about that short exchange. It's certainly a salutary experience for teachers to see their fleeting words frozen in print and assuming a status which they would not have wished for them. But there are compensations, too. We may find some gems. My wife was in a class of infants, listening to a music programme on the radio.

Towards the end of the programme one of the·participants ran his fingers across a harp. The children hadn't been told it was a harp, and a girl in the class, whose command of English was very limited, said, 'It's like water, dingley, dingley.' That seems to me a splendid comment; what you might call 'creative speaking'.

Such tape recording and transcription, then, is one of the ways in which we can learn to listen to language, our own and other people's. We must also devise ways in which pupils can exercise their language in differing contexts so that they become practised in adapting to differing language expectations and able to operate effectively in a range of situations. The arrangement of furniture within a traditional lesson – ranks of single desks facing the teacher – promotes a boomerang style of dialogue where virtually every comment from a pupil is mediated through the teacher who redirects it either to the whole class or to an individual, often having passed judgement on it or modified it in some way en route. There is undoubtedly at times a place for this kind of activity, but let us be clear of its language limitations. It is not suitable for promoting inter-action between the pupils; it merely sustains action and reaction between pupils and teacher. Hence the need, on occasions, to move to a kind of regrouping which will encourage children to talk.

The most obvious method is to work in pairs and in small groups. Good small group discussion can occur spon-taneously, and when that happens it's very satisfying for the members of the group and for us as teachers. More often, it has to be worked for and I favour a fairly fixed kind of control early on. The sort of thing I'm thinking of is where a group of no more than five is given a poem, or a piece of prose, or a short story, or newspaper article, or photograph with several questions they have to answer within a limited amount of time (say, fifteen minutes, but obviously extended at your discretion). This is followed up later by one from each group acting as secretary and reporting back, or by whole class discussion, or by written work. In other words, the small group discussion has a clear purpose in view. It's an activity intended to train children to focus their thoughts, and I like to think it will lead to the situation where they may be given the poem itself to grapple with, or the short story to relate to their own experience, or the current problem to try to resolve, or the contemporary issue to explore and open up. At this stage *process* is more important than *product*. They are, we hope, learning that it's a rational thing to try to bring order out of the chaos in one's mind, and to discuss matters with other people, agreeing perhaps on occasion to differ. There is no virtue in spurious consensus. At the same time, all being well, *process* is refining *product*.

Naturally, there will be times when they 'go off the subject', but that could sometimes be valuable. If the talk merely becomes the loose kind of general chat about Liverpool or Manchester United that they could have in the playground (and that you and I may have in our staff rooms) then, generally speaking, that is lesson time wasted. However, because that *can* happen on occasions, I don't think it invalidates the general view that small group discussion is a very valuable strategy. After all, in a traditional class lesson, the pupils may be merely *dreaming* of Liverpool or Manchester United or Wimbledon. To sum up and develop this point, let me quote James Britton (1970):

At the secondary school stage, the educational importance of good conversation in small intimate groups can hardly be over-emphasized. It paves the way for class discussion, which in the informative subjects may be a principal mode of learning, but it has its own value as a mode of learning, particularly in English lessons, where the main stream of activity will be the handling of experiences in the spectator role. This will be no unfamiliar occupation for adolescents, whose own conversations are likely to be a traffic in what D. W. Harding has called 'considered experience' – things that have happened to themselves or to other people, offered in such a way as to involve direct or implied evaluation. But they will need a good deal of help in moving to general inferences. Left to themselves they tend to oscillate between particular instances and vast generalizations taken over at second hand, leaving a gap that needs to be filled by intermediate generalizations they must make for themselves.

So much then, at this stage, for small group work, and I will return to the subject at greater length in a later chapter. What else can we do to encourage awareness of spoken language and to develop oral skills?

1   Children can listen to and discuss tape-recorded speech from radio and television and real life.

2   They can go out into the school and the community and interview people, possibly using cassette recorders as well as notebooks.

3   They can become accustomed to recording material on cassette as well as on paper. At my last school we were in the habit, at one stage, of having fortnightly radio programmes produced by a different second-year group each fortnight and relayed to the other eleven second-year groups. Such programmes could be exchanged between schools. One school which I visit sends out regular radio programmes to the local hospital.

4   They can engage in all kinds of drama – Les Stringer tackles this later. At times, the really shy ones will participate in a type of drama where they can speak within a group but not be exposed individually. Occasional choral speech, which can easily be linked with mime, offers this kind of safety, as do crowd scenes. Hand puppets, too, may offer an outlet for shy children and I well remember the liberating effect on a timid child of having stage make-up put on her face along with others, in an ordinary classroom drama lesson.

5   They can experience all kinds of language games.

I don't rule out two-minute lecturettes, what someone once described as 'female lectures'. They can have their uses but they often take place in a forced context and I don't think they generally develop natural speech rhythms. Such talks can be of great value where they are spon-

taneous or semi-spontaneous, arising out of real interest
and expertise and building on personal anecdotes in the
most natural way. The kind of thing I'm thinking of is, to
use a fictitious example, Billy Caspar's talk in Barry Hines'
book *A Kestrel for a Knave* (film titled *Kes*) about how to
train a wild kestrel. I have found, as I'm sure you have
too, that children often talk very well about their pets,
particularly when they bring them into school and demon-
strate to the rest of the class. Gerbils, hamsters, rabbits,
tortoises are obvious convergent candidates, but I wouldn't
rule out the more divergent, such as snakes or skunks,
or indeed any animal which is under control. Similarly,
photographs and objects from home are often good stimuli
for a short talk and more acceptable, to some, than skunks.
Each object has its own story. One girl, Ingrid, once brought
into school her deceased granny's suede gloves which, I
noticed, had three sets of numbers inked on the inside
cuff. Two had lines through them and the third remained
distinct. This was, in fact, the current doctor's telephone
number and Ingrid's granny, so I was told, had never gone
anywhere without that information. It was a fascinating
insight into another person's life.

What is needed, above all, for good talk to flourish, is a
non-judgemental kind of atmosphere where pupils can say
whatever they genuinely believe to be true, provided we
don't get involved in being unprofessional. Most children
readily understand a teacher's loyalty to colleagues when
the convention is made clear to them.

Let me stress, too, that encouraging talk in the classroom
does not automatically lead to the disorder of a market place
or rabble. Good talk necessarily involves good listening and
should be as disciplined an activity, according to its own
conventions, as any other work in the classroom.

Writing

Having briefly considered the sort of situation a wide ability
English teacher faces in the areas of reading, listening and
speaking, let us now move on to perhaps the most
traditional activity of the classroom, namely writing.

Differences between children when talking or engaged in drama may not be particularly noticeable, despite the wide range of skill, but when they hand in written work, the variations in attainment and proficiency are plain. We meet some who sprinkle punctuation marks like confetti, others so sparing that they never use any; we meet some who observe accepted spelling conventions, others who invent their own but change them line by line; we meet some who cannot transfer the thoughts in their head to intelligible marks on the page and others whose written fluency we ourselves may envy.

Here are four pieces of work which were written by two boys and two girls on the same occasion in the same first-year mixed ability class. I include them not because they represent the work of the most and least able children (they don't), but because they exemplify work which forces the teacher to think of their authors as individual people who need to be guided in different ways. Here is the first piece.

Snow

The snow was ridged thickly on the forked twig,
And hear and there the plump snow falls in sudden
   mounds,
The air is silent and eeire with the stillness of everthing
Where some early footsteps had been made the snow
   was drifting over them,
The snow creaked beaneath my feet as I walked
   through a field heavily shod with snow,
The robin lay there his song choked in his throat,
This marved glittered in the cold sun such a place
   where paradise was.

Stephen

It has a stylistic control but is derivative and strives after a literary effect which takes Stephen away from his own real experience. He needs to be handled with care, so that when advised that not every noun needs an adjective he doesn't regard this as a rejection of his undoubted feeling for words. His strength lies in his observation rather than his literary borrowings and this is something to build on. He might even be able to appreciate the notion of pathetic fallacy, and this can perhaps be explained with examples from Walt Disney.

Patricia also writes of snow, and of rain too.

Snow

SNOW
Cold and
soft white
and
light, iciey,
and creystal, wet,
Smoth refreashing
and clear, sour
smell, Gaive

RAIN
Wet and cold, pittering
on the window pain soggey
Shoses, cold hands, wet-hair
Sharp and Jagged, terrible tast

Patricia

She has produced an interesting word list which lacks development. With the help of judicious questioning, she could extend some of these single words into whole phrases and sentences which mirror her own experience of snow and rain. Whereas Stephen develops too many of his words into phrases, Pat develops none. Spelling errors also could be pointed out to her and phonic help given, particularly in relation to the 'e' sound.

Denise's work reads as follows:

The Snow

One day my mom said to me can you go down the shops for me please and I said yes I will. But put your boots on because it is snowing and put your coat on and your hat on I got out side the door.

Denise

She writes in a very low level, blow-by-blow, narrative style which, in my experience, takes a long time to remedy. She needs to hear and read a lot of good writing, including that of other children in the class, so as to be clear of the focus for the task. Practice at selecting significant detail, possibly starting with an exercise on the composition of telegrams, should help. All this could only be accomplished over a period of time. Individualized teaching of this kind, when you're dealing with large numbers of children, is very demanding indeed, but certainly made more possible in a workshop context where at times you move from person to person.

The fourth piece is by Barry, who produces something extraordinary, but which can hardly be deciphered.

Storm

Now it is almost nigt from the bron Zesofisk jug full ofrer jug full of pure white ligal Fire, bright white tipples over und spillsdown and is gon.

Barry

Perhaps you might start here by asking him to write a fair copy for your own collection. This would give him useful handwriting practice as well as providing you with a remarkable piece of writing for your records. He could develop his skills with practice in more writing of a similar kind, and you might select appropriate snippets from Gerard Manley Hopkins for him to hear or read, since both he and Hopkins have something in common. Obviously your aim is to improve his technical control, while building on his divergent strength.

What considerations should guide the marking of written work? Certainly, there should be departmental discussion to establish a coherent policy. I think you will find that a numerical mark is inflexible, a grade gives a little more leeway but is still inhibiting, and that detailed comment, oral and written, is most valuable if you can persuade the children to act on it. This is the ideal. In practice, you are so pressed for time that often all you can do is to indicate very briefly that you have actually read and responded to the piece that the child has written. Over a period of time I do believe it is possible to convince children that you are very concerned with what they actually write, not with the mark or grade they might get; that you don't wish to measure them against anyone else since there's really no point in this; that you are looking for positive virtues rather than merely spotting technical errors, and that your main intention is to encourage them to write as well as they can. It's a long business, but it can be done with most pupils.

Let me be autobiographical for a moment in order to develop this point. In learning to play the piano I have so often been reminded of useful educational points that I'm inclined to feel that any teacher should also constantly be a learner of a specific skill, not only in order to respond to the Victorian ethic of self-improvement, but also to be reminded of what life is like as the underdog. As a piano learner, I can testify that encouragement is a great boost, that practice at what I *can* do is satisfying, and that the foundations of the civilized world don't crumble when I hit a wrong note. Indeed, I've been told several times that *technique* is more important. Moreover, it's been evident that a sense of structure and sequence and making progress is helpful, and there is great pleasure in successfully playing a small but tricky item, such as a run of five or six difficult notes. I have yet to be criticized for not doing enough practice, even though there have been weeks when I've hardly touched the piano. And so on. I could make many more teaching points from this example, but these are sufficient for you to appreciate the classroom equivalent and, even allowing for differences in maturity and motivation between my learning the piano and school pupils learning English, I don't see why my responses in a learning situation should be so very different from theirs. Indeed, I think they are parallel and should be remembered when we act in the role of teacher as critic and mark a piece of written work. Such acts of empathy may affect our teaching behaviour more radically than trying to respond to results of research.

Let us now move on to the setting of written work. I feel we should more often than not offer a choice to the children, sometimes of topic but always of range within a topic. It doesn't mean that they will inevitably opt for the easiest task, although this is a danger which the teacher must guard against. One hopes they will choose tasks which are potentially interesting and challenging to them and to which they would like to respond, given the constraints of the situation.

Here is an example of a number of assignments on an extract from Philip Larkin's poem *Whitsun Weddings* which might be used by individuals at fourth/fifth-year level. I've included nine questions and would expect the pupils to do several of them, but only after a close reading, and re-reading, of the poem.

---

1 Is Larkin a snob?
2 What impressions of England does he convey in the first two verses? (Some of you might try to represent parts of the poem in painting, drawing or collage.)
3 Write the wedding speech of one of the broad-belted fathers.
4 Continue the conversation from 'I nearly died . . .'
5 The poem starts in sunlight and ends in rain. Is the poet being pessimistic?
6 Draw up four columns and list the arguments for and against weddings in church and at a registry office.
7 Is the image of the bride in the drawing the same one that Larkin has in mind?
8 Which is the best wedding you have ever been to? Why was it the best?
9 'Marriage is for fools.' Are you one of the wise?

What I have tried to do here is to offer a mixture of creative and critical responses; to offer a range of written possibilities from a speech, to conversation notes, continuous prose and also other responses of a non-verbal kind; to encourage a judgement on the relationship between visual image and written word, and to get the pupils to reflect on their own experience and also consider more general implications of the issues. I am not suggesting we do all of this all of the time; the material itself will always impose constraints on the kind of questions asked. Nor am I suggesting that the example I have just given is without flaws, but it is an attempt to encourage what one might call 'disciplined freedom', i.e. to permit choice within a framework dependent on some detailed study and reflection. If you merely say to your pupils, 'You can write about anything you like', on most occasions you will get very poor-quality responses. However, if some of them want positively to work on something they have thought up, you would be foolish to suppress this.

They can, then, often choose their own assignments from a number of options and also, I believe, their own form of written expression – free verse, prose, a play, notes, conversation. They won't always choose free verse on the grounds that it frees them from some conventional writing restrictions. However, in order that their choice be informed, they need to know precisely what is involved in writing a play, or conversation, or free verse. They all need to be shown in the fairly formal manner of traditional class teaching, I believe, how to cope adequately with each form before they can be expected to exercise a proper choice and produce good-quality work. This cannot be done at a stroke, and without careful initial and on-going guidance many will produce rubbish. However, when a choice is given, make sure it is a real one. You may remember the *Peanuts* extract (Reimer 1971):

I learned something in school today.
I signed up for folk guitar, computer programming, stained glass art, shoemaking, and a natural foods workshop.

I got Spelling, History, Arithmetic and two study
  periods.
So what did you learn?
I learned that what you sign up for and what you get
  are two different things.

Bear in mind that, as with small group discussion, you
can have small group production also, as when a group
scripts a play, or a pair of children work together to produce
a piece of writing. Pupils can be encouraged to read each
other's work and suggest improvements.

A more individual activity is involved in the use of work
cards and I can hardly discuss writing in wide ability
classes without mentioning them. You can, of course, use
professionally produced sets such as SRA[6] despite any reservations you may have. Five reservations which I would
want to express are the following. I am not convinced that
they develop skills which will transfer out of the work card
situation, although they do focus attention on reading for
information. They are invariably unrelated to anything else
in school and exist in a vacuum. They have no real audience, other than the teacher as judge or umpire. The focus
may fall on completing as many cards as possible rather
than learning from them. (In one school I overheard a girl
say to herself as she looked at her neighbour's card, 'Bloody
hell, I'm only on orange'.) They have an American origin
which shows itself occasionally in some of the assignments
and uses of language, and in the predominantly trans-
atlantic context.

Against such points one must set the strengths of SRA
and its equivalents.[7] These are chiefly five: they cater for
children of all abilities; most children and many teachers
like them; they offer a sense of progress, to teacher and
pupil; they provide the opportunity for independent work
and self checking; they free the teacher to go round and
work with individuals. All these are attractions which
teachers do not lightly throw away, as sales of the material
will testify.

Apart from professionally produced cards, and there are
many on the market in addition to those I've mentioned,
you can, of course, make your own. It's time consuming and

often hard work, but the big advantage is that you can produce particular cards to suit particular children whom you teach, and to reflect local conditions and circumstances. There is a danger that even home-produced materials can themselves take on the status of a textbook and become as inflexible. However, they are rarely so attractive as good books, and to replace a colourful, professionally produced, well-illustrated book by an anaemic banda copy, apparently written in invisible ink, seems a poor exchange. Attractive and well-constructed work cards can be useful but, like all other methods and materials, must be kept in their place.

What of the weak writers? What can we do for them? Again they need careful remedial attention which first diagnoses the precise problems and, with any one child, there will be several. They also need good primary school method which may have to go right back to basics. We have all met secondary school children whose chief writing problem was their inability to form letters correctly. In addition, any confidence boost is welcome and here are two suggestions: a weak writer could, on occasions, produce a photo essay, i.e. a series of photographs or pictures stuck in a book with captions underneath (which you might perhaps write first, on instruction, for the child to copy) to tell the story. One advantage of this is that it can look very attractive. A polaroid instant camera is very appropriate for this kind of activity and Gordon Taylor mentions other possibilities later.

Another possibility is for the child to record what he or she wants to say onto a cassette. You or another child can transcribe it and type it out. This is very time-consuming and you couldn't do it often, but it can be the means whereby a child who normally produces no writing at all can, overnight, produce an extended piece. Here is an example. It's the work of a nine-year-old boy, Michael, living in a dilapidated city suburb. His writing ability is so severely limited that he can only manage two or three lines of indecipherable scribble, but here he is describing into the tape recorder the experience he has just had of visiting a demolition site near his school.

And we seen lots of bombed down houses. We seen a

dustbin lid full up with dirty, dirty cans. And then we went and took a photo inside of one house. Then we carried on walking and then Miss said, 'Would you like a piece of paper?' and we said, 'Yes'. 'Would you draw a picture of an 'ouse, bombed down house?' and we said, 'Yes'.

There was lots of bricks and lots of slates. We seen a man pulling slates out of roofs and then we seen a man carrying planks of wood. And then, later on, a few days ago, we seen bombs. All the houses. And a tractor came in and bombed down all the houses. All the houses was burnt. Then we seen a fire. And then a boy went over and he pulled a stick from the fire and he was playing with it and he was scaring people with the fire. And then he soon got told off by the teacher.

Then we drawed a picture of the inside. It was very good. We seen a man on the roof knocking a brick through the ceiling. Ceilings were fell through. The chimneys fell off and a whole lot of walls were fall down. All all the toilets was broken. No roofs. Broken chains. Broken toilet tops. And then we saw a dirty old bath and we seen lots of mud. We seen lots of bombed down houses and we.

One day we seen a man carrying planks and he fell in a pile of bricks. He hurt himself. And then he got up and carried the plank and then he burnt it. And then a man on the roof shouted, 'Are you all right?' 'Yes, yes,' he said. 'Come and help me.' 'I, I can't. I have to do, knock the ceiling through and throw and throw the bricks all down.'

And then we seen lots of chimneys fell off, falling off. Then we seen a man on a roof knocking slates through. The slates, when they hit the bottom, they went crash.

That's all I've got to say for today.

Despite obvious weaknesses, the strengths of such a spoken utterance are evident: clarity and vividness of recall, power of cumulative detail, interest of personal incident, above all, vitality. Michael has something worth saying, based on real experience, and says it quite well. He can't write about his world so he talks about it. If the student teaching him hadn't appreciated the validity of the spoken word, then we should never have known his responses to what he saw, and he would not have seen his piece on the wall for the first time ever.

Such ploys obviously cannot constitute the whole answer, but they might offer a way in. Certainly, display and presentation of work should not be neglected. If you're using a multi-media approach in your group and if you're working in a thematic kind of way which, as Judith Atkinson points out later, is often very appropriate since children can be involved in different activities related to the same overall theme, then you'll probably find that exercise books are very limited instruments for this purpose. They're not flexible enough and you need to think in terms of folders or envelopes of material, which overcome the problem of having scrappy bits of paper floating about. I like the idea of children producing folders of material which can be displayed when a theme comes to an end and even, on occasion, donated to the school library or resource centre. Secondary school teachers can learn a lot from junior school colleagues about presentation of children's work in folders, on the wall, and in exhibitions.

Alongside this I favour the idea of children having a private exercise book. I'm not thinking of what some people call a 'graffiti book', but rather a kind of personal anthology. The book would only be written in when the child wanted to record something or make a copy of someone else's work. It would remain private unless the child wanted to show it to the teacher. It would not be marked and it would not be forced.

The advantage of such a private record is that it provides a spontaneous but regular opportunity for boys and girls to grapple with their experience for their own satisfaction and for the sake of the activity itself, in a non-judgemental context. They are not writing for the teacher as critic and final arbiter of good taste, but merely for themselves. It is personal writing unprovoked by an artificial stimulus or an external command.

Any occasion on which a boy or girl can write for an audience other than that of teacher as judge should be welcomed since, as recent research has indicated, the constraints upon a writer are, in certain circumstances, enormous. Pupils may constantly find themselves writing what they think teacher wants to read, or merely echoing the teacher's language, at the expense of developing their own views and style. There must be constraints acting upon any writer, as I can testify at this very moment, but if we ring the changes in our demands, then the pupils should be better placed to operate in a variety of contexts. I've already mentioned the circumstances in which pupils may write for themselves. They can also on occasions write for other pupils, or for a display or exhibition, or possibly for their parents. Some could also be encouraged to write for specialist magazines, comics and newspapers. I'm not thinking merely of letters to the editor, but factual articles and fiction too. Clearly, any pupils proposing to operate in this way would need to study the style, format and demands of the publication they were hoping to contribute to, and that in itself would be a useful exercise. Addresses are to be found in the *Writers' and Artists' Yearbook*, published annually by A. & C. Black. I am not suggesting for a moment that this idea could ever be realistically adopted on a large scale, but it might be an avenue worth exploring with a few of your pupils, one of a number of strategies scattered thoughout this book for extending the most able boys and girls.

Effects

Such, then, are some of the problems and some of the strategies which may be adopted with a wide ability class.

I want now to end this chapter with a circular model which may, depending on your point of view, call to mind either Dante's circles of Hell or Heaven, if not Purgatory. What I've tried to show in this model, which for convenience and in deference to Dante I'll call 'The Singing Spheres', are some of the wider implications which may be faced by the whole school when one of its major departments moves to mixed ability work.

At the centre is the non-streaming innovation. This has certain departmental ramifications and these are shown by the inner sphere. Each of these may lead to more far-reaching changes and, ultimately, to modifications in the whole ethos of the school. 'The Singing Spheres' model begins from actual changes experienced by the contributors to this book, when the department in which we were working moved from streamed to mixed ability grouping. However, the diagram, as it appears here, has moved on from the actual to the possible and indicates other effects which might reasonably follow.

The Singing Spheres

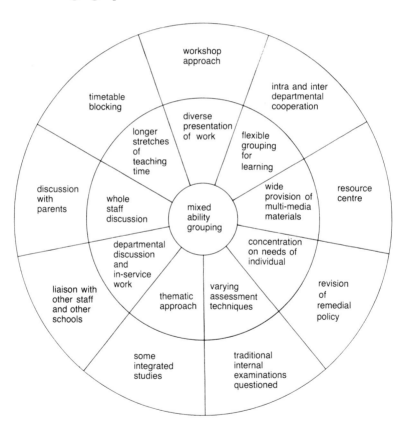

Modification of Whole School Ethos

I am aware of certain internal inconsistencies which are almost inevitable in an educational Aunt Sally of this kind. For instance, no segment should be regarded as discrete; one often merges into another. An outer sphere segment is not inevitably produced only from its adjacent inner sphere segment. Thus, a workshop approach may develop rationally from a diverse presentation of work, but equally it could also develop from wide provision of multi-media materials, or concentration on the needs of the individual. So it may be helpful to think of the circle almost as consisting of independently moving spheres in a kind of spinning top or roulette wheel. The developing changes aren't so haphazard as that gambling analogy might suggest, but neither are they fixed and inevitable.

Just how far the mixed ability innovation by one department is allowed to affect other areas in the school will depend on many factors. It might be possible to regard it as a departmental aberration, an oddity within an otherwise normal family, to be tolerated like a mild Early Church heresy rather than encouraged. In these circumstances, the chain of events mirrored in the diagram would merely remain interesting theoretical possibilities, to be discussed but not pursued, and inevitably there would be dysfunction within the school, with incompatible aims and procedures coexisting uneasily. To give one example, the English department may have replaced traditional end-of-year examinations by a series of periodic attainment tests and constant diagnosis of strengths and weaknesses; the remainder of the school may still be wedded to formal examinations, intended not only to give children exam practice but also to grade them in rank order. Such incompatibility is undesirable but not unknown.

Any innovation within a school – a new style of report book, a system of merit marks, a ten-day timetable, a new course in child care – will have some effect outside its immediately apparent boundaries. Certain of the effects may be considerable, but only if the original innovators find kindred spirits elsewhere among the staff whose own interests may be promoted or, at least, not harmed.

There is no compulsion to develop any of the innovations indicated in the model but, in the situation envisaged, such issues will almost certainly become staple ingredients in staff room discussion. Mixed ability teaching constantly forces upon us consideration of weighty educational dilemmas. The model could be regarded as a summary of the practical implications of the transition over a period of time, and while each of the segments would merit its own chapter at the very least, I want finally to look merely at one part of the school's organization or policy which can hardly remain unaffected. I'm referring to so-called 'remedial provision'.

Under the labelling system which streaming promotes, certain pupils are designated 'remedials' and hived off into a remedial department. Some such departments are even called 'opportunity' or 'challenge' units, in an effort to avoid the pejorative overtones of the word 'remedial'. The apparent function of a remedial department is to restore its pupils to normality as soon as possible and send them back into the mainstream, having recovered lost ground. The notion that they 'catch up' implies, of course, either that they have been moving faster than the more able or that everyone else, meanwhile, has been standing still. It's another of those unhelpful sporting metaphors which bedevil educational debate. Very occasionally a formerly weak pupil goes on to university, but more often than not 'once a remedial always a remedial' and, reflecting this doom-laden inevitability, a teacher said to me on one occasion 'Remedials ought to be kept with their own kind.'

This is the language of the isolation hospital, as if those with learning difficulties had a contagious disease and had to be kept apart. In fact, if the very weak pupils are all grouped together, then the problems involved in teaching them are enormous, even if the group is half the normal class size.

It seems preferable to me to try to cope with two or three of the weakest pupils in each mixed ability group rather than permanently hive off twenty or so and group them together. This is not to deny or undervalue in any way the daily efforts of many excellent remedial teachers. However, best of all is a flexible policy where pupils are treated as individuals and regrouped on occasion for a variety of purposes, with the composition of those groups regularly changing. Under such a system, small groups of children with common problems and common strengths would be withdrawn at times *from across the entire ability range* for special tuition or attended to in the class itself, perhaps by someone other than the usual class teacher. Such groups could sometimes be self-chosen and sometimes directed. Given the right kind of school ethos, such discriminatory treatment would be acceptable to everyone, particularly since it would be seen to apply to children of all abilities. Under a flexible system, pupils would be regarded not as competitors to be measured against each other but as individual people with their own integrity. All staff would share the responsibility for developing a range of talents and ameliorating a range of weaknesses, and those staff with special expertise and experience in the difficulties faced by slow learners would become advisers to their colleagues, rather than members of a separate department. Such an approach is in line with the thinking of the Warnock Report.

The logistical, administrative and communication difficulties of a withdrawal system should not be underestimated. In an ideal and well-organized system, members of staff take small groups in time-tabled classrooms as part of their normal teaching load. Often, however, willing staff seem to lose their free time and have to teach in the foyer, corridor, library or dining room. You need agreement over the time and extent of withdrawal, since to extract pupils from mixed ability English for additional help in reading seems illogical and would suggest failure (of the mixed ability system) to cope with poor readers. You need to know whom to withdraw and how to do it unobtrusively, and when to change clientèle. Above all, you need to know what to do with your pupils and how to link your activities with their normal class work. This presupposes good channels of communication and time in which to discuss individuals, whereas most secondary teachers would claim, with justification, to be very hard pressed indeed.

Some schools, too, positively adopt the policy of withdrawal not to remedy weaknesses only but to extend strengths. To some degree this has operated for years in most schools with academic clubs and societies, and with activities such as athletics, drama, dance and music. This was not withdrawal in the strict sense of the word, i.e. a taking out from normal timetable, but extra-curricular activity, with the odd period or two stolen just prior to a school production or event. When we speak of identifying pupils at risk, perhaps we should not exclude those who, though academically very competent, are under-achieving. Perhaps additional sessions and/or substitute periods should be arranged for pupils such as these.

One inventive school I visit quite often responds to this challenge on several fronts, withdrawing good mathematicians occasionally from the form or 'pastoral' period, as it is called, providing alternative arrangements for non-PE types and for conscientious objectors during assembly time, and permitting art and craft pupils access to the workshops at almost any time. None of this is done with the aim of keeping everyone on an academic treadmill, but rather with the intention of providing what the customers want and need. This same school has introduced Punjabi and statistics options, with two sessions in school time and one in the early evening for each subject.

Provided there are equal opportunities for all, any provision of additional help for those who are already gifted does not seem to me to be at all incompatible with the philosophy of comprehensive education. All pupils need help at different levels. The non-reader must become literate; the highly able scientist must be extended. Some schools are, apparently, able to get round all the formidable organizational barriers and provide a withdrawal service which operates effectively and sensitively to the benefit of the children and, no doubt, the school community.

NOTES

1   *Neale Analysis of Reading Ability*, Macmillan. Age 6 to 12. Scored for comprehension, accuracy and speed. It takes up to thirty minutes per pupil. *GAP Reading Comprehension Test*, Heinemann. Age 7½ to 12½ years. Missing words to be supplied (i.e. cloze procedure) in seven prose passages in fifteen minutes. Readers might consult Vincent, D. et al (1983) *Review of Reading Tests*, NFER-Nelson.

2   The Reading and Language Information Centre, School of Education, London Road, Reading RG1 5AQ, Berkshire (Tel. 0734 866879) is a most valuable source of information and for advice on reading. Visitors are welcomed to the permanent book exhibition; short courses for teachers are available; and many small but useful and practical publications are on sale.

3   Made by Bell & Howell A/V Ltd, Alperton House, Bridgewater Road, Wembley, Middlesex, this is a kind of tape recorder which uses professionally produced and homemade 'talking cards'. Oblong cardboard pieces carrying magnetic strips, with visual and/or written material on them, are fed through the machine which 'speaks' the appropriate words. It's easily operated by children (and adults) of any age.

4   Produced by Arnold-Wheaton, this is basically a tape-recorder which enables the text of a sheet fixed to the machine to be heard aloud by a pupil who is following that text.

5   A junction box (Bell & Howell) is a simple device plugged into an ordinary cassette recorder and enabling up to six children to put on headphones and hear what has been recorded, without outside interference and without causing any noise. It's ideal for a small group listening to a story, for example.

6   Details are available from Customer Services Department, Science Research Associates Ltd, Newton Road, Henley-on-Thames, RG9 1EW (Tel. 04912 5959).

7   Such as the *Reading Workshops* and *Remedial Reading Workshop* which may be obtained from Ward Lock Educational.

BIBLIOGRAPHY

BRITTON, J. *Language and Learning*, Allen Lane, The Penguin Press, 1970.

BULLOCK REPORT *A Language for Life*, HMSO, 1975.

GRAY, L. 'My Children and Dyslexia' *Where*, ACE No. 115, April 1976.

HOLT, J. *How Children Learn*, Penguin, 1970.

The Underachieving School, Penguin, 1972.

Reimer, E. *School is Dead*, Penguin, 1971, quoting Charles Schultz.

Widlake, P. 'Deprivation' in *Teachers for Tomorrow* K. Calthrop and G. Owens, Heinemann, 1971.

APPENDIX

Record keeping

Assessment and accountability are two current watchwords. Nothing wrong with that, provided we remember that they are both slippery customers. In this context I take assessment to be by the teacher of the pupil's abilities and attainment levels, and accountability to be of the teacher to the children/the parents/the school/the education service. And that is only the beginning of the problem, for grading children and their work is not like grading common market apples, and the accountability concept seems to derive from an industrial model which measures higher productivity by graphs and expenditure. English teaching is not like that. It is more subtle, more sensitive, more humane.

So any matrix, checklist of skills, statement of criteria which I am now about to offer, should be regarded as an *aide mémoire* to the development of that sensitivity, not as the ultimate product of it. We keep records in order to enable us to do our job better, not because salvation lies in record keeping, not because we wish to promote slavish adherence to checklists.

The documents which now follow are, then, chopping blocks for teachers and students to mull over and improve upon and be prodded by.

(a) *Checklist of skills*

(against which teachers may measure their own units of work and syllabuses)

44

Reading

To provide:

1 Material for enjoyment and pleasure.
2 Experience of a variety of genres (e.g. books, magazines, pamphlets, forms, reports, poetry, plays etc including fact and fiction).
3 Material requiring a variety of reading approaches: skim/scan/scrutinize.
4 Material to read aloud, read silently, hear read.
5 Material relevant to age and interest and capable of extending horizons.
6 Material from a variety of cultural backgrounds.
7 Material to develop imagination and insight into character/motive etc.
8 Material to develop appreciation of style and structure.
9 Material to extend vocabulary and develop comprehension skills.

Writing

1 To provide a variety of writing tasks in a variety of genres and in a variety of contexts.
2 To write, where possible, for real audiences and to be conscious of the reader's needs, particularly in relation to content, tone and structure.
3 To offer opportunities for describing, recording, informing, persuading, comparing, exploring, narrating, for writing personally and less personally.
4 To stress writing to learn, in addition to learning to write.
5 To provide opportunities for drafting, editing, proofreading, publishing.
6 To encourage the development of technical skills (e.g. traditional orthography, spelling, punctuation, paragraphing).
7 To become aware of the views of some professional writers about their work.

Visual Study

1 To encourage scrutiny of a variety of media carrying

visual information (e.g. hoarding, post card, photograph, magazine, newspaper, TV, signpost etc).
2 To explore a variety of signs, symbols, logos, codes.
3 To develop skills of comprehension, association, interpretation, discrimination.
4 To develop an appreciation of composition skills.

Listening
1 To give experience of listening to a variety of genres from a variety of media.
2 To provide a variety of listening contexts, a variety of voice ranges and a variety of accents, dialects, and languages.
3 To develop powers of discernment and discrimination.
4 To develop concentration span.
5 To encourage patience/perseverance/tolerance of opposed viewpoints.

Speaking
1 To give opportunity to speak in a variety of settings and contexts, formal and informal.
2 To develop the ability to convey information/express and explore feelings/explain/describe.
3 To develop a variety of qualities, including fluency, clarity, coherence, honesty.
4 To stress speaking to learn, as well as learning to speak.
5 To recognize the value of the anecdote from personal experience as a useful and valid starting point for further exploration.
6 To encourage the kind of technical skills (e.g. pronunciation, tone etc) which lead to effective communication.
7 To be constantly conscious of the needs of the listener(s).
8 To encourage confidence not confidence-tricksters.

(b) *Assessment of writing*

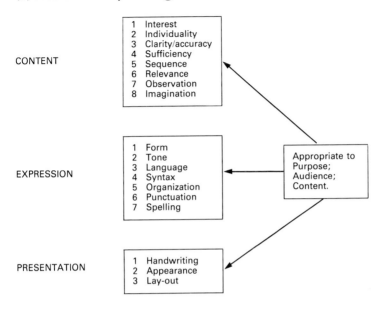

CONTENT

```
1  Interest
2  Individuality
3  Clarity/accuracy
4  Sufficiency
5  Sequence
6  Relevance
7  Observation
8  Imagination
```

EXPRESSION

```
1  Form
2  Tone
3  Language
4  Syntax
5  Organization
6  Punctuation
7  Spelling
```

Appropriate to
Purpose;
Audience;
Content.

PRESENTATION

```
1  Handwriting
2  Appearance
3  Lay-out
```

(c) *Pupil's English profile*

Speaking

A   Can converse with interest and liveliness, clarity, fluency and confidence on a variety of topics in a variety of contexts.

B   Can converse reasonably on some topics and in some situations.

C   Can converse with friends in basic language.

Listening

A   Can attend with understanding for substantial periods of time on a variety of topics and in a variety of contexts.

B   Can attend with reasonable understanding for a limited period of time on some topics and in some contexts.

C   Can attend to short utterances with reasonable response.

Writing
A Can write well on a variety of subjects and in a variety of genres and for a variety of audiences.
B Can write reasonably on some subjects in some genres and for some audiences.
C Can copy and write short legible pieces.

Reading
A Reads widely and with understanding.
B Reads adequately with sufficient understanding.
C Reads basic text with adequate comprehension.

Study skills
A Can use to advantage a wide range of texts and techniques.
B Can use some reference books and techniques to present straightforward report.
C Can follow alphabetical order and make use of one or two reference books (e.g. dictionary).

(d) *Group self-assessment*

A Members of your group (first names and surnames)
i
ii
iii
iv
v (maximum)
B Year and class
C What was your task?
D On what date was it set?
E Date to be handed to other group?
F Date to be handed in?
G Briefly describe how you went about your task (i.e. what did you do and who did what?)
H What problems did you face and fail to solve?
I What pleased you most?
J Are you completely satisfied with what you did? Why/why not?

K How do you assess your work? (Give a grade: A, B, C, D, E, with comment.)

L How does another group assess your work? (Grade A-E, with comment).

M Teacher's assessment, with comment.

(e) *Individual self-assessment*

Think about the work you have done recently in English (i.e. within the last six weeks). Complete the right-hand column to show what you did in each area.

	Speaking	**What topics or tasks?**
i	Discussion in pairs	i
ii	Discussion in small groups	ii
iii	Discussion as a class	iii
iv	Acting	iv
v	Tape recording	v
vi	Film making	vi
vii	Talking to a stranger	vii

	Reading	
i	To yourself	i
ii	To a partner	ii
iii	To a small group	iii
iv	To a class	iv
v	To younger pupils	v
vi	To find out something (e.g. in a library)	vi

	Writing	
i	essays?	i
ii	stories?	ii
iii	poems?	iii
iv	letters?	iv
v	plays?	v
vi	any other?	vi

A i Which of each of these activities

(Speaking/Reading/Writing) did you like best and why?

ii Which of each of these activities did you dislike most and why?

B i In what ways have you improved over the last six weeks?

ii What things do you still find difficult?

iii What could help you most to improve?

(f) *One teacher's comment (on 11 year old boy)*

Language

Ranjit rarely speaks voluntarily and then it is usually in one-word answers. To almost every comment of the teacher he says 'Yes Miss', as a kind of defence mechanism to escape further questioning. He will communicate with younger peers in Punjabi, although other children in the class say he is always swearing and using bad language in his mother tongue. His progress in spoken and written English has been slow over his two years in this school and remains at a basic level.

Relationships and behaviour

He has a problem with relationships generally. He has formed no relationships in his class and indeed is sometimes teased gently by bigger boys. This he appears to resent but he does not defend himself in any way. The other children on his table are only too ready to show him how to do his work, to comment 'Ranjit can't do this' and to treat him as an aberration. It was noticeable that Ranjit was much happier in his small E2L group with children two years younger than himself. His language ability was superior to theirs and he obviously enjoyed this and was more relaxed in this situation. Moreover his physical immaturity (he looks like the average nine year old) was not so apparent in this group. Ranjit appears to despise girls and will not sit by them. He barely tolerates the attention of any teacher, however much care is taken to make the atmosphere relaxed and to win his confidence. He is very tense and uneasy in any close teaching situation, yet needs this to complete any work satisfactorily. Otherwise, he will sit and do nothing as far as possible. He often 'loses' his pen/pencil and his attendance is irregular. Ranjit shows no sign of interest in any school subject, he rarely smiles, shows no enjoyment and no interest in group activities.

English as a second language
Ranjit is operating at just above basic level. That is to say he understands the gist of discussions, but has gaps in understanding normal rapid speech. He can cope with a simple sequence of events or instructions, direct and indirect objects, some passive constructions. His pronunciation is still influenced by his L1 but clearly intelligible. His range of expression is limited to simple sentences, often lacking in inflexions, e.g. 'She's knock she's door'. 'The dog behind the tree'. 'The man fall of the bike.' His range of vocabulary is limited, e.g. he uses 'gets' rather than fishing/catching and other descriptive language. He rarely takes the initiative in conversation and requires support and prompting from the teacher. He often pauses, searching for the right words, or says 'I don't know'. He has difficulty with auditory discrimination, confusing certain English phonemes e.g. 'fruit' for 'food', 'went' for 'want'. This affects his reading as he distorts meanings by substituting incorrect phonemes.

Part Two: Inside the Classroom

2   Theme and Topic Work

JUDITH ATKINSON

Thematic work

Thematic work has always been at the centre of my
teaching with mixed ability classes in the 11 to 13 age
range. As a way of looking in depth at a chosen subject, it
involves the class in a shared exploration; as a way of
organizing a series of English activities, it provides a framework for the variety of work I want individuals and groups
to explore.

One of the chief claims made for mixed ability teaching
is that it allows individuals to progress at their own rate,
and clearly one of the teacher's first aims is to provide work
which will ensure this. A second, and to me very important,
claim is that children will learn from each other in many
different and often unexpected ways. When a class works
on a given theme together, both these aims can be achieved.
Individual writing, reading, drawing, recording and planning can go on alongside shared activities because the
whole class is focused on the same area and the members
of the class are consciously sharing their experiences.

From the point of view of organization, following a theme
gives the teacher the opportunity to plan a block of work
which lasts a reasonable length of time, perhaps for a month
or half a term. This has several advantages. I can, in
preparing assignments, ensure that the varied activities

which come under the title of 'English' will be covered, and that the balance of these activities will be right. Through giving plenty of choice I can provide work for different levels of ability. I can also give myself, and the children, the feeling of continuity and purpose which a series of 'one-off' lessons will not.

This way of working is sometimes criticized by those who suspect that the theme chosen by the teacher is merely a convenient organizational aid. They argue that the link between given assignments is often tenuous and contrived, and that the children will rarely see these links and will come to the end of the theme without having gained any greater insight into the subject. It is true that if a subject is wrongly chosen for the age level or character of a group, it will not engage their interest, despite the organization which went into it. Equally, children will gain little from a month spent on a theme which was not sufficiently thought out, with materials haphazardly chosen and presented, and the structure of which was not carefully planned.

With successful theme work, though, a sceptical observer would only need to watch a mixed ability class at work to see and feel their involvement. The kind of classroom scene I'm thinking of has an atmosphere of purposeful activity. In one corner, individuals are writing, sometimes breaking off to read each other's work, or to try out an idea on someone before they use it, or to ask for help with spelling or the choice of a word. A group of four in another corner is preparing 'speeches' for a class discussion the following day. Two children are collecting a cassette recorder to take into a stockroom where they will record the play they've been writing together. Two more children are pinning up the mounted work they have finished. Another group is talking to me about an idea they've had for their next assignment: it isn't on the work sheet but they think it's a good and workable idea. It's at a stage like this, when the children begin to interpret and explore the theme for themselves, that the teacher, and the observer, must realize that the theme has 'taken off'.

Another misgiving expressed is that the informality I've described is often, in reality, sloppiness. With so many different activities going on, with so much emphasis put on children directing themselves, won't the result be unfinished or unfocused work, children who achieve nothing, noisy confusion and limp, exhausted teachers? Again, all this could be true, and only thoughtful preparation and organization will ensure that it isn't. I hope I can show how this can be done by describing in some detail the preparation and working of two different themes I've used with mixed ability classes. They could equally well have been used with loosely banded or streamed groups.

Other Worlds was a theme which a group of 13 year olds used in the second term of the third year. The work lasted for a month. I spent two lead lessons providing stimuli which I hoped would give the class an imaginative grasp of worlds other than their own. In the first lesson I read to them an extract from *First Men in the Moon* by H.G. Wells, the passage which describes Cavor and his fellow astronaut making their first steps on the Moon. As a whole class we then discussed the sights and sensations the two men met. In pairs the children then compared Wells' imagined Moon with the real Moon as seen in a series of space photographs in *Things Working* (Ward Lock English Project, Stage One) and the lesson closed with me listing on the blackboard, following the pupils' suggestions, the experiences and sensations which astronauts must have had.

In the second lesson I asked the class to think of other, different worlds and, as I played them a tape, to write down what kind of world the sounds suggested to them. The tape contained three extracts: the first from the second movement of Shostakovich's Cello Concerto, an eerie cello solo; the second from Debussy's 'La Mer'; and the third a sound-effects passage of dripping water and voices echoing and resounding in an underground cavern. After listening and writing, we compiled a list of suggested other worlds. I then asked the children to choose from the list a world to study for themselves.

At the beginning of the next session I seated the children in groups according to the world they had chosen. There were some difficulties, since the dreamworld group had to be split into two, whereas the underwater group had only three members, which was just workable. Eventually we had six groups studying five topics: dreamworlds, underwater worlds, underground worlds, space and other planet worlds, and explorers' worlds. I handed out work sheets to each group, two for each child.

Creating and wording work sheets like these obviously requires particular thought when they are to be used with wide ability groups. There are, I think, two alternative approaches. The first one is to provide several different sheets graded in difficulty and either colour-coded so that children can pick one in 'their' colour, or handed out to appropriate children by the teacher. The second is the method I more often adopt, which is to create open-ended assignments which can be treated by children at different levels, and worded clearly and simply so that weaker children can grasp the basic meaning and can begin work without needing the teacher to start them off. Although I provide several choices for work, I limit the number I give, as I think that a long list of suggestions overwhelms even the most able. This is one of the weaknesses I've found with commercially produced workcards; the list of possible activities is often bewilderingly long.

Here are two of the writing work sheets I used for the Other Worlds theme. I structured the work so that all the children could start with a visual stimulus. Abler children would then move on more quickly to other assignments while those with more limited vocabulary or initiative could spend longer with the pictures to provide them with initial ideas.

Underwater world

1 Before you start work, look at pictures of the underwater world. Read the story called *Through the Tunnel* or the extracts on pages 19, 23 and 26 in *Thoughtshapes*.
2 With the help of the pictures, imagine yourself underwater. Make a list in rough of words and phrases for the following:
  (a) colours and lights under water
  (b) the difference between sound above and below water

(c) movements of humans and of sea creatures
(d) things and shapes seen under water

Then, choose one long or two or three shorter pieces of writing.

I   Write a poem or short story called 'Underwater World'. Use the words and phrases you've collected to help you.

II   Write the daily journal of someone who is a member of a team in an underwater lab, or investigating the reports of a monster, perhaps the Loch Ness monster, or exploring the wreck of a ship, perhaps a treasure ship or a Viking ship.
Remember to include descriptions of what you do; the new and strange things which happen to you; what you see; what it feels like to be diving and swimming; the dangers; how you feel about everything that happens.

III   Write a fantasy story about a human discovering a kingdom underneath the sea. (Ask me for a poem called *The Forsaken Merman* to give you ideas.)

The world of space and other planets

Study the photographs in *Things Working* of the Moon's surface and the astronauts in space and on the Moon. In rough write down words and phrases to describe what you see and what you imagine the astronauts feel like as they move. Think also about their fears, their excitements. Remember television films of their life in the space capsule.

Then, choose one long or two or three shorter pieces of writing.

I   Imagine that you are an astronaut on a Moon mission. Write your daily journal, starting from 'blast-off' day. Remember to include descriptions of what you do; the new and strange things that happen to you; what you see; how it feels to be weightless in the spaceship and lighter on the Moon; how you feel about everything that happens.

II Write a poem or short description called 'Moonworld'. Use the words and phrases you've collected to help you.

III An astronaut has returned from the Moon or from a previously unexplored planet and he is interviewed on the radio. Write the interview and, if you wish, borrow a cassette recorder and with another person record the interview.

IV Ask me for the copy of *Other Worlds* and read the story about Mars. Think about it. Think also about the H.G. Wells story we read. Then write a story about humans on an unexplored planet. Remember to give your reader a vivid impression of what the planet looks like.

The materials I provided in the classroom were a book box containing six copies each of:

Other Worlds English Project Stage One, Ward Lock Educational
Things Working English Project Stage One, Ward Lock Educational
The Nightmare Wang Yen-Shou in *Voices II*, G. Summerfield, Penguin
You be the Judge Brian Peachment, Arnold
Through the Tunnel Doris Lessing in *Spectrum I*, Longman
Thoughtshapes Barry Maybury, OUP
Ernie and his Incredible Illucinations Alan Ayckbourn in *Playbill*, Heinemann

In addition to these texts there were library books on sea creatures, space and exploration, colour supplements and *National Geographical* articles and pictures on remote tribes, space, Jacques Cousteau etc., and cassette tapes of three BBC *Listening and Writing* broadcasts.

Instructions to the class were that, as individuals, they were to choose a minimum of two written assignments and a minimum of one group activity. Once each group and individual had started work, my next concern was to keep a hold over the activities of the class as a whole. I let the work continue for a week or so, and then had a class lesson in which the Underwater group introduced facts and opinions about the Loch Ness monster and then directed a class discussion. At a session a week later one of the Dreamworld group performed part of *Ernie's Incredible Illucinations* to the rest. Although these sessions meant that some individual writing had to be interrupted, they achieved the aim of involving the whole class, giving groups an audience, and providing variety. The completed written work was eventually presented as an illustrated display. The following extracts should give some idea of the range of work produced.

Astronaut's diary
(extract)

Jan 1   Everything went well so far. The lift off felt strange straped up to the seats the pull of the gravity agains you. We had a sleap and dinner it was mixed veg and spuds gravy, and for dissert it was rice pudding suposed to be any way.

Jan 2   Then in the morning music wok us up. We did our exercises they was quite simple we then had breakfast which was grapefrute and coffee. Just after eating we ran into a meteorite storm it sounded like a bome going of but time after time, we was in it for about 5 minutes then silence again, nothing but space when we looked out of the portholes. I then sat and read for a while my mate played a mouthorgan.

Jan 3   Slept badly as if I was being suffocated.

Jan 7   Orbiting the moon now looked as if as soon as we land on it, it will swallow us up. We landed. I opened the hatch and started two walk down, then I jumped and I went about 5 feet across the surface.

Neil

Underwater

It was a very hot day, the sun was shining very brightly, so me and my companions rented a boat to go out and explore under the sea. On the way out me and one of my companions put on our diving outfits so that we would be ready when we arrived at the spot that we wanted to be. When we arrived at our spot we both dived in, and started to explore the undersea world. The things that we so was brilliant, everything was very quiet and still. The colour of the water was dark blue. Then we went deeper down to the bottom of the sea, all of a sudden a scole of fish came swimming by us, they looked like spadefish but I wasn't show. Then all of a sudden my companion pointed behind me to warn me that there was a shark going to attack us. When I saw it coming it looked like a great monster coming to get something to eat, its razor sharp teeth was sparkling like diamons. So we had to swim for our lives, just then we so a holed out coral so we hid inside it until the shark got fed up of chasing us. Then we got out of the coral and made our way back to the boat because our oxygen was running out.

Nicky

Colours and light under the sea

Seaweed a field of green,
specks of colour of tiny fish,
glowing fins and tails,
reds, orange and yellows,
bands of greens, blues and blacks.
Shiny vicious teeth,
beading, staring eyes,
the murky rocky kingdom.
Shining stones and shells,
transparent creatures,
greeny, black eels,
delicate feelers of anemones.
The screen of light resting on the top,
speckles, stripes and spots flash past,
dull camouflages,
trailing stream of bubbles,
slight swaying of the plants,
dazzling couloured coral.

Sylvia

I felt pleased that all three writers had made imaginative efforts to enter the 'other world' they'd chosen. Neil and Nicky clearly needed help with technical mistakes in their writing. It was interesting to me that Neil spelt 'meteorite' and 'suffocated' correctly, obviously because these were important but also difficult words which he recognized the need to check. In this case I therefore pointed out to him the careless errors like 'sleap', 'grapefrute' and 'two' and he corrected them before copying the work out for display. Nicky's problem was different. I pointed out and corrected the spelling of 'diamons' as this was obviously a word he'd chosen with care. He made mistakes which are common in the area of the school, such as the phonetic spelling of 'saw' as 'so' and 'sure' as 'show', so I directed him to the appropriate work card on common errors. Here it is:

---

so/saw/sew/sore

These words are often confused because they sound similar, but it's important to spell them correctly because their meanings are so different.
Fill in the gaps in the following sentences with the right words, then correct your own work.
1 It's impossible to   without a needle,
         I asked her to   this hem for me.
2 They   many ladybirds during the summer.
3 The bathers   the shark's fin gliding smoothly through the waves.
4   when the doctor   that the boy's toe was   he agreed to help him quickly.
5 When Robert had finished his work on the chair, his hand was   from putting pressure on the

---

Friends, Enemies, Fans and Gangs was a theme I used with a second-year mixed ability group for four weeks in the summer term. The title was rather unwieldy, but I wanted the children to think about their relationships with other people, both in personal friendships and in larger groups.
   I introduced the theme with three whole-class lessons. In

the first I played a tape of one of the BBC *Listening and Writing* programmes and the class followed this in the accompanying pamphlets. It was the first part of a trilogy by Peter Fieldson called *Another Saturday*, in which the central character, an unemployed boy straight from school, has his only excitement of the week, his trip to watch his football team play an away game. The form of the play suited my purposes particularly well, because most of it was first person narrative with individual short scenes, for example, at home, on the train, at the ground, threaded into the story. This meant that the hero's comments on, and explanations of, his own and his friends' behaviour in the crowd provided good starting points for later discussion. As the tape lasted twenty minutes I followed it with a class discussion, first of the play itself and then of the children's own experience of crowd behaviour at football matches. This discussion continued in the following lesson, widening out to include the behaviour of fans at pop concerts, and I drew it together to prepare for a piece of writing to be done by the whole class, a description of their own experience of being part of an excited crowd. This was begun in the lesson so that I could go round and talk to most of the children about their ideas and help the weaker writers to plan their work and find the words they needed. The writing was completed at home so that I could move on to the next stage with the whole class.

Next lesson I handed out three work sheets to each individual. Here they are, reflecting the range of choice of assignment and mode of expression advocated in chapter 1. These were:

1 Writing for yourself
2 Reading and writing
3 Talking and reading.

---

1 Friends, enemies, fans and gangs
Writing for yourself

Stories and descriptions
1 Choose a picture. Study it carefully and discuss it

with me or a neighbour. Write the story or poem the picture suggests to you.

2 How you made a friend or lost a friend.

3 A portrait of a good friend of yours – first discuss what you'll include in your portrait.

4 Our gang – the story of a gang you were in when you were younger, or now. How did you join? Where do you meet? How do you spend your time together? Are there any rules? Who is the leader? Are there any disadvantages in being in the gang? What are the advantages? Any memorable incidents?

5 Write a story in two or three chapters about the forming of a gang, or fan club – include some of the ideas from question 4. You might write the story as though you are a member of the group, perhaps the leader or a new recruit.

6 Write an account of a memorable day spent with a few of your friends, perhaps a day last holiday. Remember to include conversations in your story.

7 Write about a time when, either in order to be accepted by a gang or because you were a member of a gang, you did something which you know to be wrong.

8 The good and bad things about friends.

(Several of these ideas could be expressed in poems.)

Explaining things

1 First discuss in pairs, then write down your ideas as lists and explanations. How would you find or build an ideal gang headquarters? Equip it? Keep it secret? Use it?

2 Find out about the different 'uniforms' gangs and groups have worn since the 1950s. Draw and describe them, then try to explain why you think people have worn clothes in this way.

3 Discuss in pairs the problem of football hooliganism – talk about why it happens, what you've seen happen and the remedies you would suggest to the Minister for Sport. Then write a report of your discussion.

2 **Friends, enemies, fans and gangs**
Reading and writing

There is a list of stories, extracts and poems about the topic in the box of books. Try to read several. Choose one that interests you particularly and ask for suggestions for further work.

BOOKLIST
Thoughtshapes B. Maybury
Wordscapes B. Maybury

Goalkeeper's Revenge B. Naughton
Imagine R. Protherough, J. Smith

Late Night on Watling Street B. Naughton
First Choice M. Marland

Explore and Express 3 R. Adams, J. Foster, R. Wilson
Listening and Reading

Listening and Writing

Listening and Writing

Scene M. Marland

NOVELS
Magnolia Buildings E. Stucley
Gumble's Yard J.R. Townsend
The Balaclava Gang George Layton

STORIES AND EXTRACTS
The Dress
The Fight
Lovejoy and Tip

In the Forest of the Night
Red Lights
City Boy
Childhood stories

Through the Tunnel
One of the Virtues
Section *Gangs and Victims*

The Dog with a Million Fleas
Tuppenny Rush
Joby and Gus
The Otherday
The Gang

PLAYS
Julian
The Chicken Run
The Car
Last Bus

The Twelfth of July J. Lingard
One Hundred Million Francs P. Berna
The Outsiders S.E. Hinton
Tom's Midnight Garden P. Pearce
The Children's Crusade I. Serraillier
Louie's SOS E.W. Hildick
Birdy and the Group E.W. Hildick
Sell Out R. Maddock
The Cave R. Church
Joby S. Barstow

BOOKLIST
Loneliness and Parting
A. Adams

Wordscapes B. Maybury
Things Being Various
S. Clements et al.
Songs of Innocence and Experience W. Blake
Themes – Conflict R. Jones

POEMS
Evening in the Park
Acquainted with the Night
The Boy Fishing
Dennis Law
My Parents Kept Me

The Poison Tree

Section *Misfits*

---

3 **Friends, enemies, fans and gangs**
Talking and reading

1 In a group of four or five read the play *Julian* together. Then choose one part of the play for recording. Rehearse it, record it and follow it with a recorded discussion about the play, particularly about Finch and Julian. Whom do you sympathize with? Why? Would you have followed Julian out? What do you think of Sandra? And about her action at the end of the play?

2 In a group of four or five record your discussion about *one* of the following topics:
(a) Being a fan (b) Being a supporter (c) Making friends.

3 In a small group write, rehearse and record a play about a gang and an outsider. (You could get some ideas from *Julian*.)

4   Make up a programme of reading about the topic –
    your own and poems and stories you have read. (*The
    Fight* on p.33 of *Wordscapes* is a good one to choose
    – you could read it as a pair.) Then rehearse the
    readings and record them.

5   Imagine that you and two or three other people are
    experts on different aspects of either soccer hooli-
    ganism or pop group fans. With one person as an
    interviewer, record a programme in which the
    experts argue about one of these subjects.

I read through the assignments with the children, adding
further information and answering questions, then
explained that each individual should complete a minimum
of one assignment from each sheet, so ensuring that three
kinds of work would be covered by each child and that all
would take part in at least one group activity and at least
one individual assignment. The material I'd prepared for
the class included a book box referred to on the work sheets,
containing individual copies of novels and sets of six copies
each of short story collections, plays and source books.
There was a folder of picture work cards, made from newspaper and colour supplement photographs. In another folder
were newspaper cuttings about hooliganism, gang warfare
etc, and, from the school library, a *Socio Pack* which
included useful historical material about gangs and fans
during the fifties and sixties.

I find that I can rarely predict how children will take up
a theme and interpret the ideas I give them. This theme
was no exception. As the class enjoyed reading plays in
groups, the play *Julian* was soon being read by nearly every
child in the room. After the first reading (which takes about
twenty minutes) several children wanted to write about the
play rather than record and discuss it, so I had to make my
first additions to the work sheet. One able boy became so
interested in the characters and the ambiguous situation
left at the end of the play that he decided to write another
play of his own as a sequel. I underestimated, too, the
amount of interest shown, particularly by the boys, in the
history of gangs and of their characteristic 'uniforms' and

this showed up the lack of factual material I'd provided for this assignment.

After about a fortnight it was clear that, although work on fans and gangs was progressing enthusiastically, only a few thoughtful girls had given any attention to reading, thinking and writing about individual friends. As this seemed an important element to me, I drew the class together for an input of new material. We read together the extract from *Joby* by Stan Barstow, in which Joby and his new 'hard' friend Gus get caught shoplifting and Joby realizes Gus's unreliability as a friend. This had the right effect of reawakening interest in this aspect of the theme, and sparked off new written work and, for some, an enthusiastic reading of *Joby*.

When I finally drew everything together at the end of the fourth week, most children had completed four or five varied assignments. Written work was either on display or collected together as booklets, and several cassettes made by the children had been played or were still to be heard. Not surprisingly with a theme about communicating with other people, a lot of good work was on tape. Some groups were familiar enough with tape recorders to have been able to discuss friendship and crowd behaviour with great sense and thoughtfulness. The following pieces of children's work should give some impression of the different kinds of writing attempted during the theme. The titles are as follows:

1 My Views on Football Hooliganism by Philip
2 Head Quarters by Paul
3 The Good and Bad Things about Friends by Susan
4 The New Reckrute by Kevin
5 A Portrait of Jane by Alison

My views on football hooligisim

Some examples of football hooligmism. I myself have not seen football hooliginism but I suppose thats because I haven't been to many football matches. But I have heard a lot of stories about it. For instance the main reason hooliganim starts is becaus of a goal or from losing.

The crowd just go mad such as when a goal is scored for one side, the opposid teams fans turn around and just start scraping. Thene there is retaliation from the winning side.

At Derby matches which is teams from the same area such a a London Derby which involves clubs such as West ham, Arsenal, Fullam, Spurs Chelsea, and Q.P.R. In these sort of matches it doesn't matter which team is at home or away because the support is about eaqull because they dont have far to come. In these matches win, lose, or draw there is always a riot.

Usualy when a team loses they go on the rampadge. There was an incident at York an old man had a lot off to the hooligans who were on the rampage and they threw his car into the river Oose.

Resons for hooliganism

People who go to soccer matches in a gang just go to fite hard with their friends.

But if they were on their own they would most probrably behave.

If a side looses they go looking for trouble and usualy find it. On a TV programe a few months ago there were boys talking to an interviewer and they seemed very pleased with themselves because they had to got a fine of £80 for damages.

This is my way of showing that fines wont help.

I think that every supporter should have a special pass with their name, a photo of themselves and the main details about themselves. These passes can only be bought from a special office where there is a file on every supporter. If this supporter does misbehave he can have his pass taken off him for the rest of the season.

Philip

Head Quarters

It was a monday morning, me and my gang where going to find anew Head Quarters. So we split up and went to look for a new one. As I was scrambling along a back of ariver I suddenly noticed a cave in the side. I quickly ran back and group the gang up. We set off with shovels and bags so we can make bigger. I toke all morning to make the hole big enough for us all. In the afternoon we took boxes and old stools to sit on. We managed to take a table in and a chest of drawers. We dug a small a hole and layed our secret information in and then buried it. Then we found a big round stone in the ditch. We was just about to move it when I came up with an idea. We could use this as a door way. The next thing was to bring the rest of the stuff from the old Head Quarters. We did not have to bring much because the day before someone burnt most of the stuff. We then decided we better camoflage it because by now it was getting dark. We finished the Head Quarters at about 9.00. All that was need to be done now was to make traps for the enermys. The main gang was the Bashers we were always fighting them. So we had to make traps so we were show that their was nobody their. We had several devises to show were the bashers where. One was to have cans tied to gether so when erybody walk that way they could hit a can. The second one was to have sheets of metal along all the paths and put soil over them. The way was to have trip wires laided in the grass. The most important was was to have spys in the trees to spy out the Bashers. The most sucseful by miles was a trap we called the death Trap, which was hole bedded in the ground and straw put over. So when some one walk over the hole they would fall in. The only danger was a attack from the stream end. The only way was to protect it was by fighting we had a old drain pipe which we used as a perascope to scan the area.

Paul

The good and bad things about friends

Friends are people who you can trust. You need friends to talk to, and turn to. They should understand problems, or if you are in difficulty be able to talk and understand the problem. Its no good having a friend if you don't understand their problems as well as them understanding yours. Friends are for helping you if your boyfriend has packed you in and you darnt ask your mother or father about it because you get unbrassed.

You may find that your friend will like you to go places with them. Such as town, Fair, School. I sometimes ask my friends about homework and school problems. These are good things about friends, but you may find that there are many bad things about them as well.

The good and bad things about friends

Some friends like to climb apple trees and play at ringing doorbells and running away I agree this is fun but it is also cruel and silly.

Some people use a friend for school. There are many people who do this. They play and mess around with them and then when the home time bell goes they usually say. 'Get lost or Clear off'. This is cruel. You must tell your friend, well I'm your school mate but I have another friend for playing with at night and out of school. I like to have friends, some for the class and some for night, I like to be friendly with every one instead of leaving someone out.

Susan

The new reckrute

now you say you want to be a member of the gang o yes thats right who told you about this gang my Brother did i see and who is you Brother? Alan has alan told you anything else about the gang? No good. Now if you join the gang you will have to be excepted By the cormity and you wont have to say a word to anyone about the gang understand. yes i under stand allright Blindfold him you understand why we are doing this dont you? Yes it is for I dont know where the den is untill i have been swarn in. all-right in the car to the den driver. very well Sir allright, get out now take him inside lads now befor we start you have to fill this form in i have sent for you to come here today, to say that your qualfications are right, i here By sware you in as, a member of the gypsyville gang.

Kevin

A portrait of Jane

This is a portrait of my friend. She is called Jane. Jane has blue eyes, brown hair and her skin is fair. She has a face covered with freckles. Jane's height is 4ft 4 inches. She is quite chubby. Jane's family is not very big. She has two sisters the youngest is 7 years old her name is Debra thee other girl is called Dawn she is 11 years old. Her father is very good at jodo and her mum is very good at wakling backwards on her hands. Her mum and dad are quite big her mum is chubby and very funny. I go down to Janes on saturdays and some-times sleep the night. She has a dog called patch. She is called patch because she had some different colodired patches. Jane's disslikes are people who swear theif and lie. So are mine. The things she likes are ridding houses and swimming. The food she eats is mostly meats and vegetables. She likes sweets as well also fruit.

Alison

There are several general points about the handling of theme work in the classroom which will not have emerged from the particular examples I've described. The success of a theme depends as much on the organization of the work in progress as on the preparation for it. To describe an English classroom as a workshop has become something of a cliché, but I can think of no more appropriate word. What the teacher has to aim for is a classroom environment where children can start or continue work without needing the teacher to switch them on. English work in secondary schools is always fragmented by the subject-based timetable and the continuity of theme work will be completely lost if children cannot pick up easily and in an independent, businesslike way from where they finished in the previous lesson.

This workshop environment can't be created immediately. The first consideration is the room itself and the furniture the school puts into it. Very few secondary school English classrooms are naturally right: most are too small, have heavy, unwieldy desks, no blackout, no shelves, and little display or storage space. Many teachers have the even greater misfortune of having no rooms of their own and of roaming the school followed by bearers with boxes. In an ideal situation, a room which lends itself to this kind of work should be large enough to allow children and teacher to move about and talk quietly without disturbing others. The desks or tables should be light enough to move into different blocks according to the activity. There should be shelves or a cupboard where books and materials are clearly displayed and easily obtainable and there should be a well placed table where materials particularly relevant to the theme can be looked through. Even more ideally, the room should black out easily, and there should be an adjoining stockroom, broom cupboard or corridor alcove where small groups can make recordings without disturbing others or being disturbed. Very few English teachers will have rooms like this and probably have little hope of achieving them, but reorganization of existing facilities and some persistence in asking for more can help.

Even with ideal facilities, though, confusion can still reign if the children's attitude to the work is wrong. Children unfamiliar with mixed ability classes and theme work will not automatically work responsibly at their own pace, choose appropriate assignments, plan out their own work to keep the right balance when they make their choice. They have to learn to work in this way, and it will probably take at least half a term to teach them.

As the teacher obviously cannot supervise each individual's work programme all the time, it is important, particularly during the first term with a group, that the work should be structured in such a way that children are steered into making the right choices, both according to their ability and to their individual needs. For instance, I usually build in conditions about the choice of assignments. I stipulate that a certain number of individual and group topics should be covered, or that a minimum amount of different kinds of writing should be done. Alternatively, as children finish work at such different times, I ask that they should consult me each time they intend to move on to something new. I soon know the group well enough to be able to anticipate where difficulties will arise, so I keep a particular check on children like Kevin, a boy of limited ability and enormous ambition, who would always choose work far too difficult, or Vanessa, an intelligent, lazy, dreamy girl, who would always choose the first assignment on the list, whatever its suitability, because that would take less energy.

Even when children have the habit of moving on responsibly to the next activity, there will still be situations – for example, near the end of a lesson or when an individual is waiting for others in his group – in which time could be wasted or in which the quiet, lazy ones could escape notice as they sit 'waiting to get on'. For times like these the classroom needs to be equipped with a class library of novels chosen with different abilities in mind, with stories on cassette, and with boxes of graded cards, preferably made by the teacher, on dictionary work or common errors, an example of which I included earlier.

To help both the teacher and themselves, children should be aware of their own programme. I ask children to make a checklist, in their folders, of work to be covered, which they tick off as they complete assignments. For example, this would have been Alison's checklist during the Friends and Enemies theme:

1 *Talking and reading* 4 – recording a programme of poems and extracts with Jane
2 *Writing for yourself* 3 – a portrait of Jane
3 *Explaining things* 2 – about fans' uniforms
4 *Reading – Joby* and writing about Joby's first shoplifting adventure.

A regular reporting-back session could replace or add to this. I've often been pleasantly surprised by the responsible way children explain to the rest of the class what they're doing.

Children's work does not fit conveniently into the compartments imposed by a timetable, and theme work could become disorganized if one piece of work were left unfinished because the lesson came to an end, or because the other three children in a group were ready to start a shared assignment next lesson before a child had finished his individual work. It's at moments like these that I use homework during a theme. I rarely set homework in the traditional way for a mixed ability group, but I very often ask children to finish work at home. Many do this willingly, and make the suggestion before I do. When the work is done with enthusiasm there's no need to check it in the following lesson. I make a mental or written note of lazy children who have been given work to do at home and ask to see the results the next session.

The collecting in, marking and handing back of written work could be a problem when a theme is underway. I keep a folder on the front desk in which children put work they wish to be marked. I hand back and discuss work with individuals and, when it's necessary, direct them to the appropriate work card if I think the correction of a technical mistake needs reinforcement at that moment.

I put no numerical mark or grade on written work, but always try to write a full comment, including enough constructive criticism to be helpful to the child, if I can't discuss the work for any reason when I hand it back. I mark recurring technical mistakes and give the correct spelling of words which children have either struggled with or which are newly acquired. I discuss basic punctuation mistakes with individuals and ask them to rewrite part or all of their work for display. For example, Kevin, the author of *The New Reckrute*, rewrote his story, correcting spelling and setting out the conversation correctly. The dialogue in the story seemed to me to have considerable style and was worth improving. Kevin saw the need to improve it when a friend found the story impossible to understand.

In my mark book I give a grade indicating effort so that I have a record of each individual's attempts to achieve his best. Alongside this, on another page, I keep a record of each child's attainments and problems in writing, reading and oral work. For example, this was the entry during the autumn term for Paul, the author of *Head Quarters*.

Written work Competent. Careless spelling mistakes through haste: was/were/where sure/show their/there. Paragraphs.

Reading Fluent and lively.

Oral Work Logical and alert. Better in small groups than in class.

This picture of the child is, of course, built up gradually during the first few weeks with a group and I keep it up to date by, for instance, recording if a child has mastered a particular technical problem like the proper use of capital letters or of paragraphs.

Some activities can't be 'marked', so I make sure that there are regular sessions in which we play and discuss the recordings children have made, read work out, perform prepared plays and draw attention to work which has been displayed.

When habits and routines have been established and a theme is in progress, classes organize themselves at the beginning of each lesson. I lay out the work in progress, the paper, book box and other material beforehand or as the class come in. Without waiting for me, they collect work and pick up where they left off. If some are working in groups they assemble themselves, perhaps with the need to rearrange furniture. Although I usually say nothing at the beginning of the lesson, I always speak to the whole class after a few minutes, once everyone is established in their places, and remind them about the level of noise, the amount of time the theme still has to run and the import-ance of setting themselves an aim to achieve in that particular lesson. I find that to achieve the right level of noise, when group work is going on alongside individual concentration, requires practice and training. Groups are rarely larger than four or five and, once discussion is an accepted way of working and not a safety valve from strict silence, as it could be in some lessons, then children soon realize that they can work more satisfactorily with quiet talk than with raised voices. I don't find that individuals concentrating on reading or writing are disturbed by a working buzz of noise going on in the same room. Many children find this a natural environment. If a group has chosen an activity which is noisier than usual, for example, rehearsing a short play, I move them into an empty class-room, a stockroom or the corridor. With some schools and some pupils this would not be possible, in which case I would ask the group to postpone this activity until a session when most of the class are doing work in groups and the noise level would be naturally higher than normal.

Another element of classroom organization which needs to work smoothly is the forming and maintaining of small groups. As group work is characteristic of all the work I do in English, classes soon become used to it. Sometimes I organize the groups. For example, if I hand back a piece of writing to the whole class at the same time, I might form groups of children with similar technical problems who will work on them together, or I will form groups according to aptitude or interest to look at a particular short story toge-ther. When children choose a group work option from a work sheet, I generally leave them to arrange their own groups. These are usually friendship groups and are nearly always small mixed ability groups in themselves. Once a group like this has been established in the first term, it often works together efficiently for much of the year.

Perhaps it sounds as though my chief objective has been to organize myself out of a job. When most children in a class have become independent and responsible, aren't I redundant? In one sense, I am. When I started teaching, in nearly every lesson I was the focus of all eyes. I read, performed, steered class discussion, questioned, gave infor-mation, played to the gallery. Now I find my role is very different, less taxing in one way, much more so in another. It will only be in the lessons which introduce and spark off a theme, and in the later input sessions, that I will be at the front of the class and in the spotlight. In many ways this is a relief, but I exchange this for the equally demanding role of peripatetic adviser, corrector, exhorter, and resource centre. It is the role which for years many primary school teachers have taken for granted. For me it has become one of the chief pleasures of mixed ability teaching.

The social and educational benefits of mixed ability learning seem to me to be very closely intertwined. When a group is thoroughly involved in work of the kind I've been describing, the atmosphere produced in the room by the blending of such a variety of abilities and personalities is very different from that produced by a streamed group. The sense of sharing learning together is strong, and the teacher in the midst of the room becomes part of it in a direct and close way.

At the end of the summer term a group of five children from a third-year mixed ability class I'd taught for a year taped a discussion about English and English lessons. They were a mixed ability group in miniature, and they talked by themselves with some questions to prompt their thoughts. What surprised me about the talk was their consciousness of the learning process they'd been taking part in during the year. I think some of their comments will illustrate the teaching and learning approach I've been describing.

Andrew is an alert, intelligent boy who is 'good at English' in the conventional sense. These were his comments on the variety of work within English and on working together. 'You learn more things. You go in different directions instead of just going on writing and reading ... You know more, because you've been talking to them all.'

Julie, a lively, noisy, bright, careless writer, enjoyed English lessons because 'they're more friendly'. She also recognized that the friendliness had a positive learning value: 'You all muck in together and sort things out together.'

The most perceptive comments came from Mark, a very articulate boy whose writing never succeeded in being an adequate vehicle for his considerable insight. His comments included these: 'It's like all the subjects in one, really, isn't it? ... You can discuss it without the teachers going on at you ... You work as if you want to get on with it, you work so that you can enjoy it ... In History it's by yourself. It seems to be a more sociable lesson, English.'

Topic work

English teachers and writers of books about English teaching all seem to use the phrase 'topic work' in different senses, so it seems sensible to begin this section with a definition or explanation of practice. For me, topic work is an inquiry into a given subject by a class of children. It is very close to theme work, but there are differences in choice of subject and approach. I choose subjects for theme work which are general, wide ranging, and capable of being interpreted in several different ways. Subjects for topic work cover a more closely defined area and are more factual in nature: for example, the production of newspapers, the development of the local neighbourhood, dialects, school buildings, television. Inquiring into topics like these requires a particular range of language skills. In theme work, children use language in a wide variety of ways. A single work sheet, as part of a theme on 'water', may ask a child to write a poem about the sea and to design and explain a canoe. In topic work, language is used mainly to interpret and present facts and opinions. The written source material children use will be mostly factual: reference books, pamphlets, maps, newspapers. They are likely to spend time collecting evidence for themselves, studying their school buildings, interviewing local inhabitants, making up and filling in questionnaires. During a theme, individual children complete several pieces of work; during a topic, they will probably complete for themselves, or contribute to, a single 'product' like a magazine, a survey, a debate or a recording.

Topic work, as I have described it, plays an important part in many streamed class activities but, like theme work, I find it well suited to mixed ability groups, particularly because many of the activities I prepare require cooperation and shared research. Discussion about the material and methods of work is an important part of most of these activities. Children are also called upon to use other skills: to become editors, secretaries, or group organizers. It will, therefore, be the kind of work in which oral ability, practical and organizing skills, and personality play as important a part as the abilities more traditionally associated with English.

Let me now describe the working of some of the topics I've used with mixed ability classes, namely, town planning, television viewing, newspaper writing, the development of language.

Town planning was a third-year topic, but other teachers in the department have used the same idea and similar approaches with fourth years. I hoped to make the class aware of the problems of town planners, to see the effects of new development on people and to apply their understanding to the particular problems of their town, Hull. They would be required to use language for argument, both in discussion and in writing, and for presenting research and observation.

In the first lesson I drew on the blackboard a map of a mythical village in the East Riding and indicated the site of a new commercial airport, proposed as part of the plan to make Humberside 'The Gateway to Europe'. Also on the map I marked the properties belonging to people in the village who would be particularly affected by the airport, its approach roads and low-flying aircraft. The class provided a name for the village and its people, and were soon able to suggest additions to the villagers I'd already created. These were some of the affected inhabitants:

The Vicar – in charge of an ancient church with a very high steeple and delicate medieval stained-glass windows.
A local market gardener – owner of a very large expanse of greenhouses.
A prosperous farmer – the airport would take some of his fields and the approach road would separate the farm buildings from most of his land. He is also Master of the local hunt.
A retired businessman – living in a manor house which has been bought for its quietness and beauty. He is also a keen fisherman and ornithologist.
The postmistress – has lived in the village for sixty years.
A publican and his wife – 'foreigners' from Leeds who have

modernized one of the local pubs and turned one of the High Street shops into a boutique.

Another publican and his wife – 'natives' in charge of the genuine local.

The headmistress – of the village primary school which would be divided by the proposed approach road from the small estate where most of the children live.

Mothers and teenagers – from the estate.

Each child in the class was now given the role of one of the listed inhabitants and two I knew to be fluent and confident speakers were made representatives from the Department of the Environment and the Air Ministry. (You will notice certain similarities here with Les Stringer's description later of how *Tenement* operates.) I explained that a public hearing was to be held next day for everyone to express their opinions about the airport. I gave out paper and asked each child to list either their reasons for supporting the plans or for attacking them with detailed reference to their own situation. I had tried, in introducing the characters and their situations, to give only information and not to suggest too clearly the stand each might take at the hearing. I had also made sure in handing out the roles that I made the less confident children part of a group of mothers or teenagers, so that they could support each other, both in preparing their evidence and in speaking to the rest. I asked the two government officials to prepare short talks explaining their concern over the plans and the villagers chose two of their number as leading speakers to prepare speeches against the plans. I circulated, helping with lists where necessary and also checking that enough inhabitants would defend the airport and make the hearing a success.

I chaired the hearing in the following double lesson so that I could encourage any timid speakers and also introduce new issues if this proved necessary. Fortunately, the landlord of the Green Man Inn spoke so ardently in support of the airport that a heated argument soon developed which involved most of the inhabitants. At the end the village voted a resounding 'No' to the plans.

In the next lesson I gave the class a piece of written

work as the outcome of the hearing. They chose from three assignments:

1 a local newspaper's report of the hearing;
2 a statement by the character assumed during the hearing;
3 a letter written by the character assumed during the hearing to a friend or relation about the plans for the airport and the hearing.

As the report and the letter were the more difficult assignments, I checked quickly that the weakest writers hadn't chosen something outside their abilities.

These three or four lessons served as an introduction to the problems and principles involved in developing areas where people live and work. Another equally successful way into the topic was used by another member of the department who read *Carrigan Street* by John Pick in the Macmillan *Dramascript* series. After reading this play about the demolition of slums and the rehousing of inhabitants, the class carried the parts they had read and acted through into a public hearing.

The next stage was to list on the blackboard the areas in Hull where development was planned or was taking place. Three main issues seemed most important:

1 the plans for Hull's Old Town, a fascinating, decaying area, much neglected by the council;
2 the rehousing of people from inner city slums;
3 the building of new estates like the vast Bransholme, to the north-east of the city.

I directed the children into six mixed groups of four to five and gave each group their assignment. Two groups each worked on options 1 and 2. These were the four options:

1 Study the maps of the Old Town. Read about the work that needs doing there and the plans for the future. Discuss the way you would develop the area, taking each section in turn. Once the group has

decided on an overall plan, take a section each and explain and draw your ideas clearly.

2　Hull is changing a lot and many people hold strong views about the new development. Make a list of adults you could interview about their views, particularly on the areas we've talked about. You'll need to spend some time wording your questions and making arrangements to talk to people. Then you'll need to write up your findings.

3　Using the old photographs, the reference books and maps, prepare a talk for the rest of the class about the way that landmarks or popular places in Hull have changed. Hull-born grandparents may be able to help you with this.

4　Find out as much as you can about the buildings, layout, facilities, atmosphere etc. on Bransholme estate and in an area where old houses are being demolished, e.g. near Hessle Road. When you are sure of your facts, make two of the group into people who are to be rehoused from Hessle Road to Bransholme, and two into officials from the housing department. Record a discussion in which the officials try to persuade the people to move.

The groups spent nearly a fortnight on this work. They used books and relevant newspaper cuttings from the school's library, a set of old maps and photographs of old and new Hull, and information from organizations like the Central Library, the Information Bureau and the Civic Society. Group two's interviews with staff and friends took place in lesson time, but most of their interviewing was done outside school, and lessons were used for writing up their findings. Similarly, group one did most of their field-work in the Old Town in their own time, although it would have been possible to spend lesson time taking the whole class round the area. At the end of the topic, written work was displayed, group three gave their talk, and group four played their tape to the rest of the class.

A study of television viewing was a topic I used both

with a second-year group in their final term and with a third-year group. Television is obviously a big element in most children's lives and I hoped through this work to enable the class to look more objectively at their own viewing and to see this in relation to the rest of the class.

In the first lesson I handed out duplicated copies of a questionnaire and asked each individual to fill it in. As all the children had television at home (several had more than one set) there was no problem about non-participants. This was the questionnaire.

---

1 What is the average time you spend watching TV during a week night?
2 What is the average time you spend watching TV during the weekend?
3 How are decisions made in your home about the choice of channels and programmes?
4 Which channel is watched most?
5 Do all your family watch the same amount of TV?
6 List your five favourite programmes in order of preference.
7 List your five worst programmes, worst first.
8 What kind of programme do you like best? Why?
9 What kind of programme do you like least? Why?
10 Are there enough of the kinds of programmes you like?
11 What is there too much of?
12 Are there enough programmes which cater for people of your age? Should there be more?
13 Do you consider you watch: (a) too much (b) the right amount (c) too little?
14 Do you think you could survive if TV were abolished? Give your reasons.

The class took a lesson to fill this in.

The next stage was for each child to tear up the sheet into sections of related questions, i.e. section 1: questions 1 and 2; section 2: questions 3, 4 and 5; section 3: questions 6 and 7; section 4: questions 8 and 9; section 5: questions 10, 11 and 12; section 6: questions 13 and 14. The torn-off slips were collected together in their sections and I organized the class into six working groups of four or five children and handed out a section of answers to each one. I gave these instructions to the class:

---

1 Find out all the information you can from the answers and note it down in some form in rough.
2 Discuss your findings. Try to explain the reasons for them and decide what's most interesting about your discoveries. Think of possible ways of presenting your findings and your comments on them.
3 After four or five lessons you should be ready to present your material in two ways:
   (a) to go up on the wall;
   (b) as an explanation to the rest of the class of what you've discovered.

Most groups coped efficiently with the first stage of extracting information and had little trouble with the 'mathematical' presentation of these facts. Sections 1; 2, 4 and 6 seemed to be best presented in block graphs. Section 3 needed a complicated votes system to discover the class's top and bottom five. Difficulties arose with the second stage when the statistics had to be interpreted, so my chief job was joining in discussions with each group and drawing their attention, where necessary, to the significance of what they'd discovered. They also needed help with finding the right language for writing and talking to the class. Some groups were dissatisfied with the amount of information they could find from the questionnaire and followed it up with interviews. So, for example, children working on sections 1 and 6 wanted to talk to the student who was also working with the third-year class and who, in her questionnaire, had declared a lack of interest in any television programmes but BBC 2 classic serials.

At the end of the second week of the topic, a wall display was put up and the groups reported back on their research. I found many of the results predictable, but to the children they were often new and surprising. The general level of class discussion after the talks was high, both because it was informed discussion and because the experiences were common to all.

Another media topic was **newspaper writing** – second-year work. The end product of the topic was to be several group newspapers, but I wanted these to be based on examination of the contents, style and layout of real newspapers. I wouldn't expect children of this age to do more than discover something about the arrangements of material; the purpose of headlines and photographs; and the different styles of reporting used by different kinds of journalists. Some of the able children would be able to recognize the difference in composition and style between the 'popular' and 'serious' newspapers.

In the first lesson I organized the class into groups of four to five children and gave each group one or two newspapers and a work sheet. I had already told the class what we would be doing and several children had brought papers with them, usually local evening papers. I tried to ensure that each group had at least one local and two national papers, one 'serious' and one 'popular'. The leader, or secretary, of the group was to fill in the work sheet with information given by the rest. These were the questions:

---

1   Make a list of the different 'ingredients' in your papers, e.g. sports news, crossword, editorial, etc.
2   How are the ingredients arranged on the different pages e.g. what kind of news is on the front page? in the middle?
3   Look at the front pages. How did the editor decide which stories should be at the top of the page? at the bottom? at the side?
4   With a ruler measure the space taken up on the front page by headlines and then by the actual reports themselves.
5   Now look at the wording of the headlines. What's the purpose of them? Could the papers do without them?
6   Read two or three news and sports reports from your papers. Make a list together of the things reporters do

to make their stories interesting to the reader, e.g. how
do they start their stories? what kinds of words do football reporters use to describe goals?

7   What do the photographs in your papers add? Could
papers do without them?

This work took most of a double lesson, and in the last
quarter of an hour I asked each group to report back to the
class on one question, and encouraged the rest to make
additions to lists read out, or to disagree with conclusions
made.

In the following lesson I talked to the whole class for ten
minutes about the production of newspapers. I'd drawn a
plan of the different stages and people involved on the
blackboard, to make it as clear as I could. I explained that
each group was going to produce its own newspaper during
the next fortnight.

To avoid confusion and a waste of time in the initial
stages I gave them a set of instructions. Each group was to
appoint an editor to be in charge of production and
chairman of the group. The list of ingredients on the work
sheet would form the contents of the newspaper and the
group were to divide the reporting jobs between them. They
had to make a decision about the kind of newspaper they
were going to produce. Was it to be:

(a)   a national newspaper with imagined news stories?
(b)   a local newspaper with a combination of imagined and
      real stories?
(c)   a school newspaper with real stories?

The page arrangements they had noted down on the work
sheet would form the plan of their newspaper. Preliminary
discussions and organization took up the rest of the period.

In the third lesson, production began. I had provided
several different sizes of paper, sugar paper and card, scis-
sors and glue. My first job was to get a progress report from
each group. This enabled me to check that children had
opted for the reporting and writing jobs they were capable
of and to make sure that no one was doing less than his or

her fair share. In the following lessons I spent a period of time with each group, reading work, making suggestions, providing books and ideas if they were necessary, and chivvying any lazy members of the group. Only one group chose to compile a school paper, and they made arrangements to interview staff and other children, and sometimes did this during lesson time. At the beginning of each lesson I reminded the class of the deadline date and asked each editor to report briefly on the progress of his group. The completed papers were collected in at the end of the fortnight.

Looking at **the development of language** as a topic was again different in aim and practice. It's a topic I've worked on with both third– and fourth-year groups and I hoped to give children some idea of the nature and growth of language, culminating in a study of their own.

The first stage was to lead the children into situations in which they would question the nature of language, discover its importance and begin to wonder how it first began. I took the class into the hall for the first lesson and split them into pairs with the task of taking it in turns to communicate to each other some information or ask a question without using language. After five to ten minutes of animated gesticulation and expressive grunts, I brought the class together again to discuss what they'd discovered. Pairs then joined into groups of four and were asked to improvise a situation in which one of the four was a foreigner in England, trying to communicate information or a question to the other three English natives without speaking any English. The foreigner wasn't allowed to give up or hand on to one of the others until the communication had been successful. Again, findings from this situation were discussed. Finally, the same groups of four went away to discuss, and act out if they could, the 'birth' of language in a group of prehistoric men. After discussion of this I asked each child to do one of two pieces of research, as preparation for the following day's lesson. They either had to find out and copy down the words for different relations within the family (e.g. uncle, daughter, cousin) in four or five different languages, or copy down words from languages such as Greek, Chinese or Russian which use different alphabets from English.

Using the children's findings as a starting point, the next session was a whole-class lesson in which we looked at the words they'd collected, on the blackboard, and discovered similarities and differences between languages. I wanted to do little more than arouse interest in language itself and to give some idea of the 'families' of languages. The fourth-year group contained a Chinese boy who held the class spellbound with his talks about Chinese characters. This aroused so much interest that we continued talking in the following lesson, helped by further examples from the children's own experience.

The next stage was to focus on English, and in another whole-class lesson I built up, with the children's help, a picture of the different influences which have helped to form modern English. I duplicated a sheet of extracts to illustrate what we were finding out. These included sections in Anglo-Saxon from *Beowulf* and *The Seafarer*, and we also read them in modern English translations (i.e. in the Serraillier version of *Beowulf* in *The Windmill Book of Ballads*, Heinemann, and in *Voices I*, Penguin). There were also short extracts from Chaucer's *Canterbury Tales*, both in Middle English and a modern translation (i.e. parts of the descriptions of the Prioress and the Miller in the *Prologue*). All the children seemed to enjoy the detective work of sorting out meaning and tracing signs of modern English and French.

In the next session I gave each pair of children an etymological dictionary. Their work was to find and write down five words derived from each of the following languages: Anglo-Saxon, Latin, Greek, French and German. This took about twenty minutes and I then collected some of their words on the blackboard in order to show two things: firstly, the kinds of words which different languages had contributed, e.g. Anglo-Saxon words for tools and basic household implements, Greek for aspects of medicine and learning; secondly, how different languages have contributed to idiosyncratic English spelling – e.g. psychology, beautiful, science, etc.

Extended group assignments began in the following

lesson. I had booked the library for four lessons and asked the librarian to prepare the appropriate books. I gave each group one of the following subjects: first names and surnames, place names, food, sports, musical instruments, hobbies and arts, medicine, buildings. Their task was to explore the derivation and history of about twenty words connected with their subject and to prepare to give a talk about their findings to the rest of the class.

The work lasted for between two and three weeks, and with the third-year group I finished the topic at this point. Since the fourth-year group still seemed interested, I introduced a new piece of group work involving, this time, written work. I gave a dictionary to each child and asked them to look up a newly coined word, e.g. 'moon buggy' or 'monkey boots', which I knew they would be unable to find. We discussed the problem of keeping dictionaries up to date and then compiled a list on the blackboard of as many new words as the class could think of. Suggestions were made for the derivation of some of them and I chose one word from the list and asked pairs to work together on writing a definition. These definitions were compared and put alongside a dictionary definition so that I could introduce the different components of a definition and the idea of economic and precise description and explanation. I then gave each working group of four or five a subject from the following list: clothes, transport and roads, food and drink, pop music, space exploration, shops and amenities, weapons and war. Their assignment was to produce a modern dictionary of words associated with their subject. The editor or leader of the group was to be in charge of handing out and organizing the presentation of the work. This part of the topic lasted for about a week.

I'd like now to draw from these examples some general points about the preparation and organization of topic work. Several of the points have been made more fully in the first section on theme work.

In one sense, the preparation for a topic takes me less time and thought than that required for a theme, because the topics I've used last for a fortnight of lessons or, at the most, three weeks, whereas a theme which is working really successfully could be used for half a term. Most of my thought, though, goes into the structuring of the topic. I prepare the three or four opening lessons carefully, with the aim of giving the class information and of leading them to think closely about the issues which they'll later explore for themselves. This is unlike the opening lessons of a theme, in which I would aim to provide the kind of open-ended stimulus which would encourage the imagination and spark off related feelings and ideas. As most of the work is done in groups, I don't prepare graded work sheets and questionnaires as I know that groups will sort out any difficulties together. However, I do take care to try to word them as clearly as possible. The questionnaire I prepared for the television study was badly worded as there were several questions which proved confusing to all the children. I tend to hand out assignments to particular groups, rather than give a choice, as I would in theme work, and again I take care to word the instructions clearly and explicitly so that groups can start work without needing to consult me immediately.

The amount of materials needed for a topic will vary according to its nature. The town planning topic needed more preparation in this sense than the television study which tapped the children's own experience. Other kinds of arrangement often need to be made before a topic can begin. For example, one may be organizing visits out of school, arranging interviews with adults, or providing several working cassette recorders and/or cameras. The school library will probably play an important part in topic work. I'm fortunate enough to teach in a school with a permanent librarian who considers it part of her job to help provide relevant books and resource material and also to help children find books and use them. We can make arrangements to use the library in two different ways: either to take it over for the whole class for several lessons, or to send small numbers of children out of the classroom to do their own research by themselves or with the librarian's help.

The problems of organizing topic and theme work in the classroom for a mixed ability group are similar, so many of the points I'm about to make now are by way of reiteration, since they will have been considered in the earlier section on theme work.

The room itself needs to be suitably arranged and equipped. For the kind of topic work I arrange, the children need to have learnt how to work independently and in a self-disciplined way. Once the group work has begun, I lay out all the necessary material at the beginning of each lesson and I expect children to find what they need, arrange the group's seating, and start work straight away. I usually have a quick word with the class as a whole after they've settled and at the end of the lesson to remind them of the time left, of any particular problems connected with the topic and to answer any questions.

The initial arrangement of children into groups is an important part of the organization. The kinds of activities I set work best when the small groups are mixed in ability, unlike some other activities in English where the ability composition of the group is of less significance. The work usually requires a combination of skills such as writing, thinking, reading, discussing, illustrating, operating machines, organizing, leading, and story-telling. Such skills are best provided by a group which combines varied intelligences, interests, practical abilities, experiences and personalities. To ensure this, I arrange the groups myself, but I've often found that friendship groups are usually naturally unstreamed, since concerns outside the classroom bring them together, so there is often very little organizing to do. It's also true that, if mixed working groups are arranged at the beginning of the year, they will often work amicably and efficiently together for a lengthy period of time, although it's useful to ring the changes on group composition every now and again in order to provide a range of experience.

Once the second stage of the topic, i.e. group work, has begun, I spend each lesson moving from one group to another with several jobs to carry out. I check first that, if the assignment has required the allocation of different tasks to members of the group, this has been done sensibly. This would be particularly important, for instance, with the newspaper writing. During the course of the topic I discuss each individual's work and, where this is written work, I read it and make suggestions and corrections. I shall know already which children have difficulty with writing so, for instance, during the newspaper topic, I helped one boy who was writing a report about the loss of a trawler at sea by writing the stages of the story for him as he explained it to me, so that he could build up his report from my notes. Similarly, I would watch for the poor readers during work which required research and help them either by providing, if possible, a simpler book (e.g. one of the *Ladybird Leaders* series) or by asking them to retell a short section of what they'd read. Many children who write imaginative work of high quality without any help from the teacher find logical reasoning difficult so, for instance, during the preparation for the airport hearing, I spent time with several individuals to help them to deduce information from the facts given and to think out their point of view and their reasons.

My job with the good writers and able thinkers is not usually to correct them but, more often, to question them in order to extend their capabilities and to make sure that they are seeing all the possibilities in the work. For example, in the newspaper topic I discussed with them the possible ways of interpreting news and of suggesting bias in reporting style and attitude. One able girl had done so much interviewing of friends and relations during her work on the town planning topic that she needed help handling the voluminous material, with sorting out the important from the irrelevant, and with finding a way of summarizing her conclusions.

Most children need help with using reference books for their research. Too often, factual information is copied out from a relevant book and little understanding will have been gained from the exercise. The skills of note-taking and summarizing do not come naturally to most children and have to be learnt. I spend lessons on these skills with the whole class, timed, where possible, to come before work which will need them. For one exercise in summarizing, for instance, the children work in pairs. They both read the same short passage of information, perhaps from a textbook for another subject or extracts I've duplicated from newspapers and reference books. Then one hands over copy and repeats the main points of the passage from memory, while the neighbour checks the original. They then discuss the points which were left out and decide how important they were to the meaning of the passage. They follow this by reading a second short passage and, without consulting each other, make a list, in their own form of notes, of the points they consider important. Then they exchange lists and comment on each other's choice of points and note-taking style.

One important aspect of this kind of work for a mixed ability group is that children, through collaboration on a topic, learn from each other. When children are working by themselves they are working to their own time scheme and achieving, or failing to achieve, their own goals. When they are sharing in the production of a piece of group work they are working to the group's time scheme and towards the group's goals. I've found that this stimulates most children to their best work. When they have a double audience, consisting of the rest of the group and the teacher, or other interested readers, they need no urging to write clearly and correctly, to copy out work a second time, and to present their writing attractively.

The sense of shared effort also promotes the kind of atmosphere in which weak writers ask for, and receive, help from the competent writers. There is mutual help in other directions, too. The good leader or organizer is often not the most intelligent child in the group, nor is the tape recorder expert, nor the child who is gifted at displaying material. In discussion, for instance, of the newspaper work sheet or at the airport hearing, children who normally struggle painfully to express their thoughts on paper often talked articulately and fluently. They often expressed quick, intuitive insights which a more rational child could then take up and develop.

In one way, keeping a check on the class's progress during a topic is easier than during a theme, as they are working on a more closely defined area and often in quite similar ways. Watching individuals is sometimes more difficult, when each one's contribution is not necessarily a readable and markable piece of writing. Sometimes the written or spoken result of a fortnight's work will seem small. For example, editors of a group newspaper or collection of material might seem to me to have produced very little, unless I've watched them at work regularly and seen the way they have read others' contributions, organized the next stage, and suggested new ideas. Much topic work is difficult to mark in the traditional way when there is individual written work, e.g. that set after the airport hearing. I read it, write comments on it, and record an effort grade in my mark book. Group written work is usually displayed and read by me and the rest of the class. Talks are listened to, and tapes played back, and, at the end of the topic, I encourage the class to discuss critically their own work and that of others. Where relevant, I add to a child's record card any particular comments about strengths and weaknesses and contribution to group work during the topic.

Topic work is only one of the several English activities I use with mixed ability groups. During one year with a group I would probably cover one topic of the kind I've described each term.

APPENDIX

Possible themes and topics

The topics suggested for 14 to 16 year olds are generally not suitable earlier on in the school but, apart from this, many of the other subjects could, with a little thought and ingenuity, be adapted for almost any age. Thus, the indications given here are merely guides which will depend, above anything else, on the understanding, awareness and approach of the class and on the attitude, outlook and preferences of the teacher.

11–12 years
1 My neighbourhood
2 Taste/touch/smell/hearing/sight/sixth sense
3 People
4 Bonfire night/fireworks/fire
5 Travel and transport
6 Fair/circus/pantomime
7 The sea
8 The desert

9 Discoveries
10 Public servants
11 Words and word games
12 Animals/birds
13 Cowboys and indians
14 My family
15 Spring/summer/autumn/winter
16 Comics
17 Adventure
18 Games
19 Lost and found
20 Myths and legends

12–13 years
1 Friends, enemies, fans and gangs
2 Newspaper writing
3 Christmas
4 School/teachers
5 My village/town/city
6 Heroes and heroines
7 Visits
8 Predators
9 Night
10 Wanderers
11 Food
12 Strange creatures
13 Machines
14 Underground
15 Unusual hobbies
16 Contests
17 Shops and shopping
18 Tall stories
19 Folklore
20 The elements

13–14 years
1 Other worlds
2 Superstitions
3 Town planning
4 Television viewing
5 A day in the life of my street/village/town/city

6 Exploration
7 Dreams/fantasy
8 Growing up
9 Rooms/buildings
10 Parties/celebrations
11 Earthquake/volcano
12 Disasters/accidents
13 Festivals
14 Fish/fishing
15 My autobiography
16 Power and authority
17 Advertising
18 Magazines
19 People and animals
20 What's funny?

14–15 years
1 The development of language
2 Social class
3 Family and personal relationships
4 War and peace
5 Rebel/outsider
6 Births/weddings/funerals
7 Part-time jobs
8 Stories: ghost; detective; horror; humorous
9 Town and country
10 Farm and factory
11 Marriage
12 Fashions
13 Sports/athletes
14 Pop culture
15 Education/planning the perfect school
16 Old age and youth
17 Leisure
18 Communications and mass media
19 Men and women
20 The social services

15–16 years
1 Other cultures/Third World
2 Crime and punishment

3   New and old
4   People and science
5   Rituals
6   Moments of truth
7   People's beliefs/campaigns
8   The future
9   Disabled people
10 Meetings and farewells
11 Black/white/yellow/brown
12 Life and death
13 Poverty and wealth
14 World of work/unemployment
15 Censorship
16 An author or genre
17 Moral dilemmas
18 Films: the western; horror; comedy; war; musical etc
19 England and the English
20 The people, music, stories, sights of, for example, India, United States, Australia, Indonesia

3 Literature as Literature

SHIRLEY HOOLE

In the kind of English teaching discussed in this book children from their first year in secondary school will be dipping into literature in the way Judith Atkinson describes in her chapter. Since the 1960s there has been a continuing supply of excellent and beautifully produced source books, usually arranged thematically and using literature from the Sagas to Sylvia Plath.

Much of the work I do with mixed ability groups is on a thematic basis, and part of the enjoyment is 'to invade literature like a monarch' and take whatever one wants. Decide to explore with a fifth-year group the theme of parents and children and it's sheer self-indulgence to think of ideas: *Lear, Romeo and Juliet, Dombey and Son, Père Goriot, The Rainbow, The American Dream, A Taste of Honey, A Night Out*. A dozen other possibilities will spring to mind, and this is before even considering short stories, poetry, and film. There is likely to be time to read only one novel or play in full, and generally extracts will be used. But all the children will at least have heard or read *something* of Shakespeare, Dickens, Balzac, Albee, Delaney, Pinter. For abler or interested readers one can have copies of the books and others on the same theme, or by the same authors, available in form and school libraries, or use the teacher's own copies. With such a system, less able readers will come into contact with literature they could not tackle on their own and which, because of the assumptions we make about such children, they would be unlikely to meet outside a mixed ability group.

The great drawback to using literature in thematic work is, of course, that it is a Procrustean process, literature cut or stretched to fit the theme. It seems perfectly valid to consider the tragic course of Lear and his children in exploring the love, conflicts, and roles within the family. Yet I am aware of the absurdity of cutting down Lear to this size. It is the *reductio ad absurdum* of thematic work to debate whether to slot *King Lear* into outsiders, old age, or parents and children. It could be argued, too, that in using extracts we are butchering literature, that whether it's a Shakespearean play or a children's novel, a work of literature is a work of art, and is meant to be seen as a whole.

Of course, the radical reappraisal of the aims, content and methods of English teaching in the last twenty years has brought about a long overdue reaction against a literature-dominated curriculum. New ideas about the scope and range of activities in English have meant that in many classrooms the emphasis has been on direct experience, imaginative writing, thematic work, individual and group assignments. Many teachers have arranged their work to include opportunities for different kinds of talking and listening, especially exploratory talk in group discussion. This sort of teaching obviously involves changes in classroom organization, and, especially in mixed ability classrooms, frequently a 'workshop' situation with a range and choice of activities going on simultaneously, with an emphasis on individual and small-group work.

In all this multiplicity of activities, it is easy to lose sight of literature for its own sake. My concern is that it should still play a vital part, involving individual, group and class reading.

Organization

What is needed, for literature as for other activities, is a flexible approach to work and organization. Sometimes a child will be with the whole class listening to a story or reporting back from discussion groups; another time she will be recording a play with a small group; another time reading on her own. In the hectic school day, I think children need the occasional quiet time when everyone is reading or working quietly alone. For some children the concentration-span will be short, but it's possible to make sure that everyone reads for, say, a quarter of an hour, then those who want to can continue to do so, while others get on with some quiet work. It's vital with mixed ability groups always to have work in progress; an assignment on a theme or a book, set over several weeks so that everyone doesn't have to do everything at the same time or, more important, at the same pace. There is always work to get on with, so that abler children don't have to waste time and less able children can work at their own speed, changing activities when they need to.

It's essential, too, to have a variety and choice of books available in class libraries to cater for a wide range of interests and reading abilities. At the same time, the shared experience of reading a book together as a class can have an enjoyment and a value of its own. I'm not advocating a return to the old class readers, often read a paragraph at a time round the class, slogged through word for word at a uniform pace. But what was wrong was not the idea of sharing a novel together – it was the approach, the method, and often the choice of book. A traditional method has been to issue each class with one novel or play, one poetry anthology, and one course book to be used concurrently for a term or even a year. (A colleague remembers, for instance, having *The Merchant of Venice* for a whole year.) It is not a system I would ever use, and it's unthinkable for mixed ability teaching. In my own department we have, firstly, a very large and varied stock of source books, anthologies, thematic materials, and audio-visual aids of different kinds, freely available from stock-rooms and meant to be constantly in circulation.

Secondly, we buy as wide a choice as we can afford of full sets of novels, short stories and plays allocated to each year. Each of us chooses what we will read and when, reserving sets of books in advance with the colleague who organizes stock. People are asked to keep them, with rare exceptions, for not more than half a term, to allow maximum choice to everyone. Except for Heinemann Windmill, all the books I have bought have been paperbacks: Penguin (including Puffin), OUP, Fontana, Longman, Macmillan Topliners and so on. They last quite well when covered with mercury film.

Thirdly, every term each English group has a new form library with at least fifty different titles (from one to six copies of each). Details of the content and organization of class libraries are given in the last section of this chapter.

Having the books is, of course, only the first step and it's of little use unless children really want to read them. Before going on to suggest what books might be read, and ways of tackling them, a look at some of the things which could get children 'hooked on books', might be helpful.

Ways of stimulating interest

I have found that children of all ages have enjoyed visits to book bonanzas, to central and local libraries and to bookshops. One of our main booksellers is very pleased to have small groups of children from schools browsing around his shelves. In school, bookclub schemes, talks and readings in the school library, visits by children's writers and by librarians all help. There is a new generation of children's librarians in public libraries, who are enthusiastic, informed and very ready to meet and talk to children and to give staff advice on books for children of different abilities. A school bookshop is ideal. Children can order their own copies of books, besides having the opportunity to browse at leisure in familiar school surroundings, whereas they might find a visit to a city bookshop somewhat daunting on their own. There is the benefit, too, to the children involved in running the bookshop.

The school library can, of course, play a vital part in encouraging reading in school, and block loans of books from public libraries are always available to augment stocks. Often, I think, these are arranged for topic work and are mainly non-fiction; we should also take advantage of their supplies of fiction, and use their expertise when buying books for less able children.

We need school librarians who are knowledgeable about children's as well as adult literature, and who are available to give guidance or advice. As English teachers, we need to know the library, and to know what there is for children of differing reading capabilities. I prefer this to the system of coding books (by coloured labels for example) according to reading difficulty. It is very important to make sure in any comprehensive school that there are reference books, and a large number of non-fiction books in general, which are easily readable. Often subject teachers set children topic work involving the use of reference books and it is not unusual to see children who have severe reading problems trying to cope with the *Junior Oxford* or even the *Encyclopaedia Britannica.*

When a children's book is serialized on television I often buy a copy to read to the class, or a few copies for the form library (using a lost-books fund for petty cash). Then, as soon as money is available, I buy more copies or a full set. I have done this with Penguin copies of *The Diddakoi, On the Run, Carrie's War, Marianne Dreams, A Pair of Jesus Boots, Pollyanna, Grange Hill, The Machine Gunners, Maggie,* and others. There have been some brilliant television adaptations of children's novels and I find that children, including many weak readers, become very much involved and keen to read the book. The same applies to older pupils and adult novels.

Schools broadcasts offer a great deal. Television's *English* (for ages 14 to 17) has shown *Zigger Zagger, A Taste of Honey, Hail Caesar, The Government Inspector, The Plough and the Stars* and *The Long and the Short and the Tall. Scene* (14 to 16), though not a literary series, has included programmes on W. H. Davies and Morrison's *Child of the Jago, A Collier's Friday Night* and London's *The Law of Life.* I have found these series very successful with mixed ability groups.

Television's *Scan* and radio's *Adventure* (ages 13 to 16) and *Inside Pages* (ages 10 to 12) include contemporary children's literature. Radio's *Books, Plays, Poems,* (ages 14 to 16) has included *A Man for All Seasons, A Place to Live* (how Scots and Welsh poets see their rural and urban land-scape) and *Coast to Coast* across the USA in poetry (a radiovision programme). Other radio series, for instance *Living Language* (ages 9 to 11), and *Listening and Writing* (ages 11 to 14), include some radiovision broadcasts.

Listening and Reading (ages 11 to 13) for slow and reluc-tant readers, records readings at a deliberate pace which children can follow in the text. These can be taped and used by individuals or groups of children during a workshop period. The headteacher of one of our local primary schools taped himself reading stories which his children enjoyed hearing and following – a much more interesting and personal approach than the commercial listening labs they also used. The same man held spellbound an audience of mixed ages and abilities when, in the secondary school, he read Dylan Thomas's *Memories of Christmas*.

Given time, we can read and record stories, poems, and plays ourselves. The many advantages of doing this include recording one's own choice of literature, saving on commer-cially produced materials, providing a variety of source materials, and being in several places at once – if only as a recorded voice. One of the criticisms of mixed ability teaching is that the teacher has not time to get around to see all the children who need help. By recording like this, we can be with different groups at the same time. Just as important one can avoid 'death by work card' or children reading literature 'cold'. The teacher's voice will read a poem or tell a story, provoke discussion, and so on, for an individual or group. Cassettes and cassette recorders are very reasonably priced and capable of being operated by people even as mechanically hopeless as I am. Children often have their own recorders and I have found that they are quite ready to bring them into school.

Most schools have video recorders, and recordings of radio and television programmes, and local authorities' libraries of other commercially produced recordings are a useful source of supply. Some of the slide/film strip with tape/cassette background material I find very helpful with older groups. Of course it's possible to produce this oneself, particularly for fairly local writers, given time, some money, a camera and a recorder. It is a good opportunity to work with the children and to cooperate with history, art, and music departments. All this is obviously good practice with any sort of teaching group; we often assume a background knowledge which children don't have.

There are, of course, some excellent (and some appalling) films of novels and plays. The Education Department of the British Film Institute has a checklist of British and American literature on film/video.

Unlike film, television and radio, the theatre is not part of children's everyday experience. Yet it is the most dramatic way (if the pun may be excused) of bringing literature to life, and theatre visits have been a regular activity in the English departments I have worked in. My experience is that in a streamed school it is generally A stream children who join in, whereas with mixed ability groups a cross-section of the children become involved. Unfortunately there are few plays produced which are suitable for younger children, so that theatre-going, unlike other activities, cannot be built regularly into the programme, and there is often an initial reluctance to join in such a foreign activity. I have found several things help to break this down: being involved in drama themselves; seeing 'theatre' in familiar surroundings when youth groups or theatre-in-education groups have come to the school to perform; visits to the local drama centre and to studio productions which are less formal than those in the main theatre; and playdays when actors, in a relaxed atmosphere, talk to the children about the play before giving a performance.

The simulation games which Les Stringer discusses in his chapter can usefully be applied to literature. For instance, if we 'set up' a parallel situation to one which arises in the book they are about to read, or are reading, children can discover for themselves the analogy and better understand the concepts underlying the book – and perhaps their wider relevance.

Children are involved from their first year in school in reading, acting, improvising their own plays, writing their own poetry, short stories, novels, and their own drama scripts. Adapting part of a novel, or short story for stage or television is another activity which makes them aware of the different techniques and forms of literature. Longman's collections of television scripts include examples of camera scripts. All these activities make children aware that literature is something which is going on here and now – that it's alive and kicking. Particularly important, I think, is to make them aware of themselves as writers, not shutting away their stories, plays, poems in old exercise books but displaying them, publishing them in broadsheets and magazines and making annual collections and binding them to put on the library shelves with other writers' work.

All these approaches are, I believe, good practice in teaching any English group. The vast majority of the children we teach live in a non-literary, even anti-literary, world and need to be convinced that books are for pleasure. It seems to me particularly foolish not to accept and use whenever possible the powerful oral and visual media which are a central part of all our lives, when in so doing we have the opportunity to break down barriers between different cultures, school and home, 'us and them'.

Suitable material

What can one read with a mixed ability group? In my belief, almost anything one would judge worth studying with a streamed group. The powers which are needed in responding to literature – such as sensitivity, perceptiveness, imaginative insight, the ability to realize implicit as well as explicit meanings – these do not necessarily correlate with technical proficiency in reading. It would be interesting to consider how many of the 'semi-literate' children we describe as 'good orally but . . .' do in fact have these gifts. Their oral contributions to lessons frequently show considerable insight. One of the most interesting lessons I have observed was a reading and discussion of Lawrence's *Snake* with a third-year mixed ability group in a large comprehensive school. I recorded and analysed the lesson, and so it is not just from fleeting impression that I remember that some of the most perceptive comments were made by two boys who had most of their other lessons in their stream in the remedial department. Their measured reading ages were about ten. Of course, other very literate children showed insight, but my point is that children who, it is usually assumed, cannot read literature do in fact show understanding and can enlighten others who are apparently more able.

There may well be remedial teachers who have read *Snake* with their groups, but my experience is that children in such classes are usually given poor quality material produced by some of the publishers and writers who cater for this section of the market.

When I've had the opportunity to meet a remedial group of younger children in a school, I have often used the time to tell them stories of Beowolf, Sir Gawain, Troy, and I have never met a group who had been told any myths or legends before. Because the teachers of remedial groups are rarely English specialists, and because of the assumptions we make about 'lower streams', such children are likely to be starved of good literature and of good films, television and radio.

The Newsom Report (1963), quoted again in Bullock, claimed that all children, including those of very limited attainments, need the 'civilizing influence of contact with great literature, and can respond to its universality'. We might quibble today with the Leavisite 'civilizing' but otherwise I would only make it even stronger and say that all children have the *right* to come into contact with such literature. Not the least of the many arguments in favour of mixed ability teaching in English is that it can make certain that they will do so.

In such groups there will of course be children who find difficulty in reading at all. But this should no more prevent their hearing and discussing literature than the fact that a child is physically handicapped and unable to climb a mountain should prevent his being helped up so that he too can see the view. The most important consideration in reading a book together is not that every child should be able to read it in the technical sense, though of course it is desirable. That problem can be overcome when a book is serialized, read aloud in the classroom, heard on tape and so on. The less able readers, like the abler ones, will be engaged in close reading of their own form library books at the same time, so reading will not be neglected, and the next book shared by the whole class may be easier. The really important factors, in my view, are that children should enjoy the book, that our enthusiasm should arouse their interest, and that its content is emotionally and intellectually appropriate.

Many schools have been using contemporary children's literature with young classes for some time, and 'literature' is a word not lightly used here. Reference books such as the Penguin *Good Book* guide, Margery Fisher's *Intent upon Reading* (Brockhampton) and John Rowe Townsend's *Written for Children* (Penguin) are very helpful, as are the journals *Children's Literature in Education* (APS Publications) and *Growing Point* (published by Margery Fisher and available from her at Ashton Manor, Northampton NN7 2JL).

Lists of suggested books for different years appear later. I should like to mention here some which have had success when read with the whole class in mixed ability and in banded groups in first and second years. For instance,

Historical fiction
Barbara Leonie Picard *One is One*, OUP.
Rosemary Sutcliff *Brother Dusty Feet*, OUP.
Geoffrey Trease *Cue for Treason*, Penguin.
Henry Treece *Horned Helmet* and his Viking trilogy, Penguin.

Myth/fantasy/adventure
Lloyd Alexander *Book of Three; The Black Cauldron*, Fontana.
Crossley-Holland *Beowulf*, OUP.
C.S. Lewis *The Magician's Nephew*, Penguin; *The Lion, the Witch and the Wardrobe*, Penguin.
Ian Serraillier *The Silver Sword*, Puffin.
Dodie Smith *The Hundred And One Dalmations*, Heinemann.
R.L. Stevenson *Treasure Island*, Penguin.
J.R.R. Tolkien *The Hobbit*, Allen & Unwin.
Rex Warner *Men and Gods; Greeks and Trojans*, Heinemann.

In a realistic setting
Nina Bawden *Carrie's War*, Heinemann.
Betsy Byars *Pinballs*, Puffin.
Gene Kemp *Gowie Corbie Plays Chicken*, Puffin.
Jan Needle *A Game Of Soldiers; My Mate Shofiq*, Fontana.
Robert Westall *The Machine Gunners*, Puffin.

Bette Green's *Philip Hall likes me, I reckon maybe* and Louise Fitzhugh's *Nobody's Family is Going to Change* are both about black American families and have a strong central girl character. It is good to see girls, and black families, in a central, positive role.

Some of the better-known books may well have been read in the earlier stages of schooling but there is so much excellent contemporary children's literature in English. The ones listed here are enjoyable stories in their different ways but all have depths which can be explored. Some have the classic situation in which children, with parents/responsible adults well out of the way, face challenges and adventures and come through, with their characters strengthened in the process. In others, children are alone in a different way, a way experienced by many of the children we teach. They face problems which they overcome in the face of adult foolishness/weakness/prejudice/rejection/cruelty. There is always in these books the wise, caring, adult figure too, but the children find their own salvation.

To explore a book in some depth I find it valuable sometimes to set a carefully structured assignment closely based on the book and I have produced at least one example for each year which members of the department can then employ, adapt, dip into and use if they wish as a loose model for their own schemes on other books.

The example for a first year assignment given on *Horned Helmet* starts with notes for the teacher and goes on to provide work suggestions for the children. Here it is.

First Year (11–12 years):
An assignment on *Horned Helmet*

The assignment includes opportunities for talking, listening, writing and reading in a variety of ways. For instance, there is *talk* in pairs, in small groups, and to the whole class; imaginative reconstruction of the story; improvised drama; logical argument and factual reporting of research. *Writing* includes poetry; imaginative and factual prose; a play script; and a written report on research. Again, some work is done alone, some in pairs, some in small groups. *Reading* involves the novel itself; poetry; reference books; reading for imaginative understanding; for the implicit as well as the explicit; and for factual information. The children are encouraged to think and to use language on a variety of levels. They are, for instance, selecting and ordering relevant information, making analogies, exploring their own as well as literary experience, making evaluative judgements, all, I hope, on appropriate levels.

There are opportunities for collaborating with the history, geography and art departments. The children may have learnt/be learning about the Vikings in history, and the department is most helpful.

Drama possibilities include starting with individuals wielding, in slow motion, 'Brainbiter', the great two-handed axe, building to pair work and to group fights; the villagers creeping stealthily up to surround the Vikings at the Howe (in a darkened drama hall with pool of light on the Howe) and the voice coming out of the darkness as the Vikings are about to leave – it's a dramatic scene! Among other things, the children are learning about movement, control, contrasts, timing. There are opportunities, of course, to invent their own situations or to use their own experience (a raid on an apple orchard, fights, bullying, etc.).

All good children's literature will involve people, problems, situations which have a wider relevance, and which we should bring into the children's own lives and experience. Of course, children need fantasy, adventure, escape and the stories we read with them are enjoyable simply as stories. After working on an assignment such as the one suggested here for *Horned Helmet*, we might like to use the next book we read together just as a cliff-hanging serial.

The last but one suggestion in the list of assignment possibilities is finding out about gods and heroes. This could be developed as a whole new area of work. There is much to be done on Norse and Teutonic mythology. Great opportunities for drama, illustration, model-making, writing alliterative poetry or prose.

I would always include an element of choice, making clear which questions were compulsory and which were to be left until we had read/discussed them together.

---

1   When we've read about Beorn being chased by Glam, write about a time when you were being chased, or were afraid, or were being bullied. Remember who was there, what happened, how you felt. How did it end?

2   When you've read up to chapter 4, write a *factual* description of Reindeer.

3   Draw her. If you'd like to – make a model.

4   Later (page 81) Beorn lies on deck stroking the planks as if stroking a horse, saying 'Oh Reindeer my sweeting'. Read the poem on page 58 again. Notice the alliteration as we saw it used in Beowulf; notice the names the Vikings give things (e.g. Swan's Path, Whales's Way for the sea). Now try to use this sort of language to make up a poem about Reindeer as Beorn might have done.

5   When you've read what Gauk says about Starkad as a baresark, write a poem or a vivid description – Baresark.

6   Draw one, or decorate your work.

7   As you read the book, collect in your preparation book all you discover about the Viking way of life; beliefs; how they behave and talk, etc. When you've finished the book, write all you know about them, giving examples from the book. Then say what you admire and what you don't like about them, and why. See also in class libraries *Viking's Dawn, The Road to Miklagard, Viking's Sunset*, by Treece.

112

(This could be used for group discussion, or for two sides collecting and arguing the good and bad points.)

8   What brings Starkad and Beorn close, and leads Starkad to give Beorn the stag?

9   Have you ever been given or do you own something very special? It may not be worth much money, but it may mean a lot to you. Write about it, saying how you got it and why it means so much to you. (Some people might like to bring in their 'treasure' and talk to the group about it. For others, of course, it may be very personal and private.)

10 When we've read chapter 8, 'Dead Man's Howe' – divide into pairs. One be a villager and tell the other all about what happened. Include how these strangers behaved in the face of death, and your opinion of them.

11 Drama: in pairs, in groups, or the whole class. For example, act out Beorn's escape from Glam (improvise another chase/escape adventure)
    – the raid on the Howe and the rescue
    – the raid on Starkad and Katla's home
    – Beorn's return.

12 When you've read to the end of chapter 13, 'Blind Beacon', think: have you ever felt fierce jealousy as Beorn does? Perhaps hurt someone's feelings as he does? Write about it (as a poem if you like).

13 Collect examples of the Viking way of speaking, for example, when they're in a tight corner or when things are going really well. What do you notice about them? How do they compare with us in the sort of things we say when things are going really badly, or very well?

14 You are Beorn. Write about your return to Starkad and Katla (story or poem). Look back on your adventures, your decision; include your feelings when you arrive home.

15 When we've read together part of *The Seafarer* and Kipling's *Harp Song of the Danish Women*, and heard about the first Viking raid on Lindisfarne, in groups devise scenes for a television film about a Viking raid.

16 Research on the Vikings. Ask history teachers, use libraries. On your own, or with a partner, choose an aspect of Viking life: clothes and jewellery; weapons

and fighting; homes and way of life; journeys and explorations; ships; Vikings in Britain and what they've left us. Write up and illustrate your findings, and prepare to report back to the class.

17   *The Gods and Heroes.* Find out all you can about: Odin; Thor; Loki; the Valkyrie; Freyja; Tiw; Asgaard (treasure of); Beowulf; Siegfried. What connections are there between our days of the week, some place names, and the Gods?
Use the library – ask the librarian for help.
Use: *Brewer's Dictionary of Phrase and Fable;* Encyclopedias: history section.

18   Design a new dust cover for *Horned Helmet* and/or illustrate any scene from the book.

It is difficult to find books of myths and legends for this age-group which keep something of the heroic spirit yet don't confuse less able readers. Old faithfuls such as Warner's *Men and Gods* (Heinemann) and *Greeks and Trojans* (Heinemann) are tough going for them, as are Greene's retellings of Greek, Norse and Arthurian legends. Simpler versions usually reduce the stories to comic-strip level, or to the cosiness of *Tanglewood Tales*. The obvious way around this is to learn from the best primary school practice and to develop skills as story-tellers ourselves – something I believe we should do throughout the school.

The Beowulf story is beautifully told by Rosemary Sutcliff in *Dragon Slayer* (Penguin) and Serraillier's version in the *Windmill Book of Ballads* (Heinemann) keeps the spirit and form of the original, including the long alliterative lines. I have sometimes told the story including extracts from both; at others I have used the full versions with mixed ability classes, and they have enjoyed it and the ensuing drama, art work, writing of their own versions, and experimenting with alliteration.

I find that well-liked children's books such as *The Secret Garden* F.H. Burnett (Penguin) or *Treasure Island* R.L. Stevenson (Penguin) are still enjoyed by younger children. Of course, the language, particularly Stevenson's, is difficult for less able readers. With such an author I prepare the material as if I was reading to them, rather than with them; cutting, serializing, inserting link-passages, on page-markers so that the book bristles with slips of paper. By using this method it's possible to give less able children some experience of the book, while abler readers can read it all. I've used *Treasure Island* in this way and found that second years enjoyed it, including work which arose from it:

Second year (12–13 years): An assignment on *Treasure Island*

1 (a)When we've read about Billy Bones and the visit of Black Dog, imagine you are either Jim or Billy Bones. Work with a partner. Tell him/her about what happened.

(b) Act the scene of their meeting and the fight.

(c) Write as a play script. You might like to discuss television scripts with your teacher. Watch some scenes on television *carefully* and see how cameras use different shots etc. A third year book, *Conflicting Generations*, explains the words television people use, and shows you a camera script. You might look at them, then try your own for the scene from *Treasure Island*.

2 When you've read about the death of Blind Pew talk and write about it in different ways:

(a) Work in groups. One be a newspaper reporter, interview Jim and Mrs Hawkins and perhaps one of the Excise men. Tape what they say then play it back. Work together to prepare a radio news report, or work out a television news item with interviews included. We'll discuss this first.

(b) You are Jim. Think about Blind Pew and how you feel about him. Write (as a poem?): Blind Pew. Make people's blood curdle.

3 The Black Spot! Make one, with a warning message on it. See who you can plant it on. (One boy slipped one into the deputy head's hand during school dinners. It

said: 'You will not live beyond midnight'. Did he think there'd be poison in the rice pud?)

4   Make your own treasure map. It may be the actual *Treasure Island* one, or one you invent. Notice the symbols, and the decorations on old maps. Ask history department staff. A piece of strong paper or thin card can be soaked in milk then scorched over heat. Take care – have parents handy. One girl set her map on fire – dropped it into the freezer, which was badly scorched. Try using a quill pen (goose quills are available). Learn how to prepare and sharpen them. You may use red ink for blood – we don't expect the real thing!

5   Long John Silver. Collect notes about him as you read the book, and when you finish it write a pen portrait of him. Despite everything, Jim has a soft spot for him. What do you think about him?

6   Do you know a real 'character' like this – someone who's a rogue but you can't help liking in some ways? Write about him/her.

7   The apple barrel. Have you ever overheard something, maybe about yourself? Or hidden away, and seen or heard something frightening? Use your own experience, or make up a situation where this happens and write the adventures which follow. Before you start, look carefully at the way speech is set out and punctuated in *Treasure Island*. Try to make sure you do the same.

8   When you've read about Ben Gunn – imagine you're marooned on a desert island. Look in an atlas and choose a possible island. Write a note to put in a bottle (bring in a bottle!) as an SOS, trying briefly to give some information about where you are.

9   Alone on a desert island. Discuss in your group how you would cope. Consider shelter, food, drink, clothes, keeping yourself from going mad. For ideas read extracts from Robinson Crusoe and extracts from *Lord of the Flies* (ask for a copy). Write an account of how you'd cope.

10   What and who would you miss most? Think about people, places, things you enjoy doing, food and drink.

Would you ask for cheese, like Ben Gunn . . . if you were ever found?

11 In groups or pairs, choose your favourite episode and either improvise a play to act for the others, or make a script and tape it – or both. Remember sound effects. Ideas include Blind Pew's visit and his death, the apple barrel, the battle of the stockade, Jim and Israel Hands in the 'Hispaniola', the march to find the treasure . . .

12 When you've finished the book, imagine you are Jim. You're back in Bristol and you send your mother a letter telling her you'll be home, saying something about your marvellous adventures and the surprise you have for her. Again you might try a quill pen. No envelopes in those days – letters were folded over and the address written on the outside. They were then sealed with sealing wax and seals. (We have both available.)

Everyone wanted to make the Black Spot and the treasure map, of course, and enjoyed writing Jim's letter, and sealing it. I asked everyone to do the pen portrait of Silver, and to choose at least one from 1, 2 and 11, so that everyone was involved in some discussion and drama work. It is important to allow for choice, but equally one must make sure that no one can spend all the time drawing treasure maps or doing improvised drama. I agree with Judith Atkinson that a lengthy assignment can be daunting, and it's necessary to allow plenty of time as well as choice. My own method is to set outside time limits, within which children can work on different things at different speeds. Sometimes everyone is doing the same thing – for instance the children write about Blind Pew immediately after reading or acting the episode. Some people will have difficulty in reading the assignment and understanding it, and of course it's necessary to sit down with individuals or a small group to help them. In the cooperative situation one tries to build, children also help each other. There is absolutely nothing wrong in giving the same work to everyone in a mixed group, as long as we do not expect the same quantity and quality.

I think it's all too easy in English, without realizing it, to have an unbalanced programme of work. At least in the old days the system made sure that everyone did poetry on Tuesday and grammar on Monday and Friday. Devising assignments, like the knowledge that one is to be hanged the next morning, concentrates the mind wonderfully. A variety of groupings and a cross-section of activities in English are consciously included. We can again use the best primary school practice in keeping records of the different types of work each child has covered in a term, noting strengths, weaknesses and progress in each aspect of English. This seems to me much more useful than recording strings of grades. For reading I keep notes under headings: measured reading age (only useful if it's regularly measured over the years to show progress); amount read; comprehension; written work arising from books; reading aloud.

There is so much one wants to do in English that I would work on novels in the depth suggested for *Horned Helmet* and *Treasure Island* no more than twice or three times a year. There are plenty of other novels which can be read just to enjoy as a story, perhaps as a serial, and there are, of course, some collections of short stories for this age group.

The shorter concentration-span needed may be useful for less able readers but I find that children often have difficulty in seeing the point of a short story. It is of course a mistake to suppose that short means easy; difficulty is often in inverse ratio to length, in prose as in poetry. Short stories can be good starting points for discussion and writing and since we often ask children to *write* short stories we ought to give them the opportunity to read some.

Drama

Some English teachers feel strongly that with younger children improvisation should replace scripted plays, and doubtless they would claim this especially for mixed ability classes. I find that children very much enjoy reading plays – as a completely different type of experience from drama lessons. Bolt's *The Thwarting of Baron Bolligrew*, Ayckbourn's *Ernie's Incredible Illucinations* and the old favourite, A.A. Milne's *Toad of Toad Hall*, are all plays I've used in first and second years, either with the class as a whole, or in small groups. *Ernie* especially lends itself to tape recording as a radio play – or at least to the lavish use of sound effects. There are plays by Aidan Chambers aimed at less able children in this age-group which some teachers (and certainly some children) like, such as: *Johnny Salter, The Car, The Chicken Run* (HEB paperbacks).

The scripted plays included in Adland's *Group Approach to Drama* series have evolved from improvisations, and groups can do this themselves, particularly since the shy or inhibited who do not shine in active drama can write down scripts or help with sound effects and recording.

Reading and acting plays with the younger ones is, I think, entirely for enjoyment – it's certainly preferable not to explore the anti-populist elitism of *Toad of Toad Hall!* But children enjoy drawing or modelling stage sets or characters, writing pen portraits or their own scenes for the play, and going on to write their own plays. In discussing Toad, Ratty, Bolligrew or Oblong they are beginning character evaluation.

In reading a play or novel aloud with a group there are obviously problems. I always keep one part myself to hold the thing together and to set the pace. There are always the extroverts who volunteer to read, the shy ones who can read well when gently pressed, the poor readers who *will* volunteer, and those who find difficulty in reading at all. It is vital to build an atmosphere of tolerance and cooperation. This is not easy, especially when the school itself is streamed though the English department isn't. In any sort of group I have found that children become impatient with poor readers. It's possible to avoid discouraging them and tactfully to allot small parts to such children. The reluctant readers present a different problem. They may, however, be more ready to read in a small group and we need to provide opportunities for such group work, using stockrooms, corridors, colleagues' rooms.

I feel very strongly that the dramatic presentation of literature should not be merged with practice in reading, as in the old 'reading round the class' system which, unfortunately, is still with us. With a little initial help most

children can understand the idea of a dramatized reading
of a novel with a narrator, and actors reading the different
characters' dialogue.

Poetry

As with novels and plays in these early years, there is
nothing I'd use with a streamed group which I wouldn't use
with a mixed ability group. Most children of this age enjoy
choral verse, ballads, haiku, concrete poetry, limericks, free
verse, nonsense poems and riddles. It's chiefly poetry for
sheer pleasure at this stage, but I find that children of all
abilities can appreciate, and begin to use in their own
poetry, imagery, sound and shape, rhythm, alliteration.

It's a good idea to include poetry books in form libraries
and to have an assortment freely available in the form
room, including funny ones like Spike Milligan's *Silly Verse
for Kids* and *Milliganimals* (both Penguin), books of riddles,
puns and limericks. We tend to use full sets of poetry
anthologies, but it's useful to have these small sets of a
variety of books for the children to read for pleasure, to find
a poem on a theme, or to copy out and illustrate a poem.
Children's own poems can be 'bound' in hard covers and
used in the classrooms in this way.

Lists of suggested anthologies are given in a later chapter
but I should like to mention especially for the younger
children Maybury's *Thoughtshapes* and *Wordscapes*
(Oxford), Williams' *Tapestry* and *Dragonsteeth* (Arnold), the
Bentons' *Touchstones* (EUP) series, Summerfield's *Voices*
and *Junior Voices* (Penguin). All are beautifully presented
and illustrated. *The Windmill Book of Ballads* (Heinemann)
has delightful woodcuts and an excellent version of
Beowulf.

Third year

The third year is an in-between stage whatever the organization of teaching groups. For the first two years, there is
the whole of children's literature; for older pupils there is

much adult literature to choose from. But it isn't easy to find novels and plays for study with third years. Hines' *Kes* (Penguin) and Waterhouse's *There is a Happy Land* (Longman) I have found successful. Both are good for encouraging children to explore their own experience, and write autobiographies. *Kes* especially has a wide appeal, as does Steinbeck's *The Pearl* (Heinemann) in a very different way. Schaefer's *Shane*, Faulkner's *Moonfleet* and London's *White Fang* can go well, with plenty of scope for drama as well as character study. Zindel's *The Pigman* (Macmillan) and Lingard's *The Twelfth Day of July* (Penguin) both explore relationships, loyalties and betrayals. The first between young teenagers and an old man, the second between Catholic and Protestant youngsters in Northern Ireland. *The Great Gilly Hopkins* by Katherine Paterson won the Children's National Book Award in the United States. It starts with Gilly sticking chewing gum into her hair as she's taken to yet another foster home. She is a tremendous character who comes to reassess the idealized mother who rejected her, Mr. Randolph the blind black neighbour, and Trotter the rough and ready foster mother. There is humour and compassion but no sentimentality.

Among plays I have found useful with groups of this age are the Longman television series, for instance Marland's *Scene Scripts* and *Conflicting Generations*, and one-acters in collections such as Mansfield's *Play-makers* (Schofield and Sims). I have also used shortened versions of plays which would be too difficult as a whole, for instance Shakespeare's *Macbeth* and *Romeo and Juliet*, and Shaw's *Androcles and the Lion*. A cooperative venture is for the group to write and produce its own play – a melodrama often works well. There are activities for people with very different abilities and, at the same time, they are learning about a special form of drama.

Jack Rosenthal's *Bar Mitzvah Boy* and *The Evacuees* have Jewish youngsters as central characters. The Barmitzvah boy, Eliot, (who has a great line in schoolboy wit and humour) looks with the penetrating eyes of adolescence at the adults in his family as he approaches his own initiation into manhood. There is some telling irony, plenty of humour, and keen observation of the human condition. The play can be a springboard for a host of activities: group drama (family conflicts etc.), research into initiation ceremonies in a variety of cultures, discussion of humour (racial jokes/stereotypes/sick jokes/black comedy), and especially investigation into the Jewish way of life (links with Religious Education, talks by Jewish pupils or teachers or visitors/trying Jewish food/visits to the synagogue). It's an opportunity to widen the scope of multicultural education and there is much literature to suggest for private reading, such as Banks' *One More River, The Diary of Anne Frank*, Green's *Summer of my German Soldier*, Minco's *Bitter Herbs*, Richter's *Friedrich* and *I Was There*, Trease's *Red Towers of Grenada*. It is a context in which one can discuss the holocaust. The Board of Deputies of British Jews produces a range of literature, including some on the holocaust, from Education Officer, Woburn House, Upper Woburn Place, London WC1H 0EP.

In this year I think one can begin to look more closely at literature, including poetry. I would stress that, as with all teaching, it is important to be well organized but flexible, to have a firm but friendly and encouraging classroom atmosphere in which one has developed attitudes of mutual tolerance and respect, and cooperation. The lesson on Lawrence's *Snake* which I recorded is an example of what can be done in this sort of classroom. The lesson began with a friendly interchange of people's feelings about snakes, including some factual information by one of the less able boys who kept a pet snake, and conflicting views of Alice Cooper! Next the teacher introduced and read Lawrence's poem, the children had copies in front of them. After a pause, she asked if anyone had found anything difficult to understand, and several children asked about words – 'fissure', 'perversity', 'paltry' . . . 'Hens and things', one boy offered, and such was the atmosphere that teacher and children laughed together with the boy about it. Some teachers might prefer to explain some difficult words and phrases before reading a poem but then it is the teacher's selection of words of course. Next, the children, who were sitting in groups, were asked to discuss some questions written on the board, with one member of the group acting as scribe. They were told that they would have about twenty minutes, then come back together as a class, and the teacher explained that some questions would need a close look at the poem. The questions included:

Find out all you can from the poem about the place and the weather.
What words and phrases make the snake seem attractive, and show that the poet likes it?
What do you notice about:

'He sipped with his straight mouth.
Softly drank through his straight gums, into his slack long body.
Silently.'

Why is 'Silently' on a line by itself do you think?
What do you think 'the voice of his education' is?

The questions went on to discuss the end of the poem and Lawrence's feelings about what he had done.

While the groups were working the teacher went round from table to table. When the class came together again and contributed their findings it was a boy who was in the remedial department for his other lessons who heard the sibilants in 'He sipped with his straight mouth . . .' and called out 'that hissing, that hissing, it *sounds* like a snake'. Another, after much class discussion, crystallized the difference between the voice of education and instincts.

The children had confidence to venture their ideas because of the relationships between teacher and group and within the group itself. Although this is what one hopes for in all teaching situations, it is vital in mixed ability teaching, and it isn't easy to build when teachers and children are products of competitive schools and classrooms.

Some of the boys in the *Snake* lesson would not have been able to write down their ideas in clearly readable English. A second-year girl has just written for me a very perceptive account of an episode in *Carrie's War* (N. Bawden, Penguin), but I had to guess a number of the words. Such children must have extra help to try to overcome such basic problems. How do we give it? One way is for children to help

123

each other within groups which have developed a cooperative and understanding attitude. Sixth-formers can come into the lessons or take children out for extra attention and their involvement builds more than the children's basic skills. English and remedial teachers may be timetabled to give help.

Fourth and fifth years

Perhaps many teachers would be ready to teach mixed ability classes in the first three years of the secondary school, but not in the fourth and fifth when examination courses begin. Various sixteen-plus schemes including GCSE make the idea viable and certainly some schools are teaching mixed groups in such schemes. With our 14 to 16 year olds we use the option of literature by course work, and the prose and drama we have studied together include the following:

Novels
Baldwin *Go Tell It On The Mountain*, Corgi.
Bates *The Triple Echo*, Penguin.
Bradbury *Golden Apples of the Sun*, Corgi.
Braithwaite *To Sir With Love*, Heinemann.
Golding *Lord of the Flies*, Faber.
Gorky *My Childhood*, Penguin.
Huxley *Brave New World*, Penguin.
Harper Lee *To Kill a Mockingbird*, Penguin.
Laurie Lee *Cider with Rosie*, Penguin
Orwell *Animal Farm* and *1984*, Penguin.
Remarque *All Quiet on the Western Front*, Heinemann.
Sillitoe *Loneliness of the Long Distance Runner*, Longman.
Steinbeck *Of Mice and Men*, Heinemann.
Waterhouse *Billy Liar*, Penguin.
Wyndham *The Chrysalids*, Penguin.

Short Stories
Barstow *The Human Element*, Longman.
Bennet et al *Spectrum*, Books One and Two, Longman.

Jackson and Pepper *Penguin Story*, Two and Three.
Maugham *The Kite*, Heinemann.
Naughton *Late Night on Watling Street*, Longman.
Sillitoe *A Sillitoe Selection*, Longman.

Drama
Behan *The Quare Fellow*, Methuen.
Bolt *A Man for All Seasons*, Heinemann.
Brecht *The Caucasian Chalk Circle* and *Mother Courage*, Penguin.
Brighouse *Hobson's Choice*, Heinemann.
Cooper *Unman Wittering and Zigo*, Macmillan.
Delaney *A Taste of Honey*, Methuen.
Hall *The Long and the Short and the Tall*, Penguin.
Lawrence *Three Plays*, Penguin.
Ed Marland *Z Cars* and *Conflicting Generations*, Longman
Miller *The Pressures of Life, A View from the Bridge, Death of a Salesman, All My Sons* and *The Crucible*, Penguin.
Nichols *A Day in the Death of Joe Egg*, Faber.
Pinter *The Caretaker*, Methuen.
Sheriff *Journey's End*, Heinemann.
Terson *Zigger Zagger*, Penguin.
Thomas *Under Milk Wood*, Dent.
Wesker *The Wesker Trilogy*, Penguin.
Wilder *Our Town*, Penguin.

A much closer and more detailed study of the text is needed at this level, of course, and I set essays which are much more structured. This in fact gives guidance to the less able people, and at the same time gives abler ones the opportunity to work at a more academic level. It is possible still to give a choice of work, but there are the constraints of the exam board's requirements and one's self-set standards in a course which is designed and marked internally, though moderated externally.

My own fifth-year group in a term and a half worked around the theme of Loners or Outsiders. We read together and they wrote about: Steinbeck's *Of Mice and Men*, the Richard and Elizabeth extracts from Baldwin's *Go Tell it on the Mountain*, Dorothy Johnson's *A Man Called Horse*, and two other short stories, *Flight* and *The Witness* by Doris Lessing. Poetry included Frost's *Death of a Hired Man*, Larkin's *Mr Bleaney*, Betjeman's *Death in Leamington*, Thomas's *Evans*, Sansom's *Almshouses*, and we read Miller's play *A View from the Bridge*.

I had previously read the play with an older group but had never tried it at this level. I had asked the group to watch *On the Waterfront* on television, and decided to use it as a launching-ground for *A View from the Bridge* – the Brando-figure and Eddie Carbone share the same world and face the same dilemmas of loyalty and betrayal in family and community.

We read the play together, acted parts of it on stage, and discussed many of the issues, and the group wrote four pieces of work:

Show how in Act I Miller reveals to us Eddie's obsession with Catherine, and how he builds the tension to the confrontation between Marco and Eddie at the end of the Act.

Three views of Rodolpho: look at him through the eyes (and in the words) of Eddie; Catherine; Marco.

Watch the ending of the play again. Think yourself into the skin of Eddie and write a poem – his thoughts and feelings as he goes out to face Marco. Do the same for Marco.

Write an extra scene for the play as Miller might have written it.

Consider the relationships of Beatrice and Catherine with Eddie and Rodolpho. Why do they feel and act as they do? What do you think about their attitudes as wife, niece, girlfriend?

Some of these were very good, some poor, but the level of achievement did not always correlate with the students' ability as assumed in the school's streaming system. Examination work, of course, must be graded, and on a comparative basis, which is particularly invidious in a mixed ability group. It's possible at times to give an additional grade for effort, but most important is the comment written by the teacher. I do not give grades except in examination course work since the only meaningful grading is against a child's own standard, and a full and constructive comment seems to me to be much more valuable.

Besides literature we study together, I always make available books which the children read on their own, although there isn't the time at fifth-year level for the amount of form library reading one expects from younger children. The library which linked with our theme included several copies of each of the following:

Wright *Native Son* and *Black Boy*, Cape.
Baldwin *Go Tell it on the Mountain*, Corgi.
Laye *African Child*, Penguin.
Solzhenitsyn *One Day in the Life of Ivan Denisovich*, Penguin.
Sillitoe *The Loneliness of the Long Distance Runner*, Penguin.
Waterhouse *Billy Liar*, Penguin.
Fitzgerald *The Great Gatsby*, Penguin.
Salinger *The Catcher in the Rye*, Penguin.

There is a range of books for all but the poorest reader. Three of the weakest girls chose to read *Native Son* and worked valiantly, writing conscientiously and at length about it, but with very little insight. Two of the abler boys chose the Solzhenitsyn possibly because it was the shortest book. They produced very thin essays which were not accepted and they repeated the work. The essays from the two girls and the two boys were given the same grades, but for very different reasons, as the comments made clear.

Several problems arise when the children are asked to read on their own. How much freedom of choice do we give? How much guidance? How much do we discuss, direct, structure the written work? What demands do we make? My own method is first to talk to the whole group about each book, being honest about the level of difficulty. If some people choose books which will be tough going for them, I have a quiet word with them and tell them so. But if one offers a choice of books, it would be quite wrong to prevent people from reading books they are keen to read. When everyone has chosen, I go round and talk for a while with an individual or a group who have chosen the same book, saying something about its background, and asking them to consider certain points in writing about it. If someone seems to have chosen an unsuitable book I adapt the suggested approach. Work can be made as individualized as one likes; the choice can be widened by using one's own books and library books, and it is always possible to produce a book and simply say, 'I think you'd like this one. Try it.' As with any teaching, but especially with mixed ability groups, we need to know our pupils in that way and to know their capabilities and potential and to accept nothing less than their best.

Class libraries

Although I've stressed the value of studying books together, children will not always be doing so, and much of their reading will be their individual choice from class libraries. One method of organizing such a library is to have, say, half a dozen copies of each of several books linked to a theme or to a book which the group is reading together. The advantages include opportunites for small groups to cooperate and share appreciation of a book, and the wider exploration of a theme in literature. Disadvantages include the restricted choice of books, and the difficulty of catering for a wide range of abilities. In my own department we have adopted this method only for fifth-year groups, partly because at this stage, when students often use the books as part of their examination work, I prefer to keep to a few books which I know to be of quality. So that part of the library linked to the Future theme includes several copies of: Huxley's *Brave New World*, Orwell's *1984*, Wells' *War of the Worlds*, Bradbury's *Fahrenheit 451*, Pohl's *The Space Merchants*, Asimov's *I Robot*, and three anthologies of short stories: *The Stars and Under*, edited by Doherty, and *World*

Zero Minus and *In Time To Come*, both edited by Chambers. The Asimov stories of robotics are not easy, but the last three collections, all by science-fiction writers of quality, are read and enjoyed across the ability range. Members of the department add their own books to augment any of the libraries and we have other libraries grouped around the themes of War, Crime and Punishment, Growing Up, and the Outsider theme already mentioned.

With the younger children we have developed miscellaneous libraries offering a wide choice, although of course some of the books link with the themes and with books which the whole class may share, for instance, myths and legends, animals, the past, and autobiography. There will be between one and three copies of each book – occasionally more – and each library includes at least fifty different titles at the moment. The range has to be very wide, of course. My current fourth-year library ranges from Dickens' *Great Expectations* to Joan Tate's *The Tree*, a Heinemann easy reader. The libraries circulate, each group having a new one every term, and although some of the books are duplicated, most are not.

In choosing books for the libraries I have included much children's (and adult) literature of quality, as well as books to tempt the reluctant reader – and, of course, books for less able readers. I do not belong to that school which says that it doesn't matter what they're reading as long as they're reading something. If they want to read *Dr No, Jaws* or *Son of Frankenstein*, they can, and will do so in their own time. I see it as part of the English teacher's job to put before children books they might otherwise not discover. If few become keen readers, and many later reject reading altogether, at least the opportunities have been there.

Books for less able readers can be a problem. Often the subject-matter is unsuitable for the age-group at which the books are aimed; discos, motor-bikes, and girl- or boy-friends predominate – a limited diet at fourteen, but sadly so at eleven. Illustrations and format are often poor by contrast to the usually well-produced paperbacks for abler readers, but there are notable exceptions.

Many public libraries issue lists of *Books for the Slow*

Reader. The important thing is not to offend a child with unsuitable content or oversimple language and format, and it is necessary to get to know the books, and the children and their needs.

In any mixed ability group there will be a range not only of 'reading ages', but of reading levels and reading interests – three separate considerations. A child in my second-year group, for instance, has a measured reading age which indicates that she is capable of reading *Tom Sawyer*, but the level at which she is reading means that she is unable to understand its subtleties, and her reading interests mean that she is unwilling to tackle anything other than books about horses. The library she has to choose from includes:

Alcott *Little Women*, Puffin.
Ashley *Terry on the Fence*, Puffin.
Bawden *On the Run*, Penguin.
Blume *Otherwise Known as Sheila the Great*, Piccolo; *Are you there God, it's me, Margaret*, Piccolo; and *It's not the end of the world*, Piccolo.
Byars *TV Kid*, Puffin; *The Cartoonist*, Puffin; and *The Eighteenth Emergency*, Puffin.
Chitty and Parry *The Puffin Book of Horses*.
Church *The Cave*, Heinemann.
Cooper *The Dark is Rising*, Puffin.
Dahl *Danny, Champion of the World*, Puffin.
Darke *A Question of Courage*, Fontana.
Glanville *The Puffin Book of Football* and *Goalkeepers are Different*, Penguin.
Green *Tales of Ancient Egypt*, Puffin.
Guillot *Kpo the Leopard*, OUP.
Kastner *Lottie and Lisa*, Puffin.
Kemp *The Turbulent Term of Tyke Tyler*, Puffin.
Leeson *Third Class Genie*, Fontana, and *Grange Hill Rules OK?*, Fontana.
Le Guin *The Wizard of Earthsea*, Puffin.
L'Engle *A Wrinkle in Time*, Puffin.
Mark *Thunder and Lightnings*, Kestrel/Puffin.
Milligan *A Book of Milliganimals*, Puffin, and *Silly Verse for Kids*, Puffin.
O'Brien *The Silver Crown*, Fontana.

Patchett *The Brumby*, Puffin.
Pearce *Tom's Midnight Garden*, Puffin, and *A Dog So Small*, Penguin.
Rodgers *Freaky Friday*, Hamish Hamilton.
Sewell *Black Beauty*, Puffin.
Smith *The Hundred and One Dalmatians*, Heinemann.
Storr *Marianne Dreams*, Faber.
Sutcliff *Brother Dusty Feet*, OUP, and *Knight's Fee*, OUP.
Treece *The Dream Time*, Heinemann.
Twain *Tom Sawyer*, Penguin.
Verne *Twenty Thousand Leagues Under the Sea*, Collins.

It also includes easier reading from the lists of Macmillan Club 75s, Cassell Solos, Abelard Grasshoppers, and Evans Checkers, among others:

Baudouy *Mick and the Motorbike*.
Chambers *Don't forget Charlie*.
Chilton *Contact from out There*.
Cleary *Ramona the Pest*.
Foster *My Friend Cheryl*.
Kings *Meet Linda Kings; Leather Jacket Boys*; and *Tests and Things*.
Martin *The Wild Woods of Wyoming*.
McKinnon *Sea Otters come Home* and *Spinning in Space*.
Morpurgo *It Never Rained*.
Owen *Free Style Champ*.
Plater *Trouble with Abracadabra*.
Ramsey *Ron Takes Over*.
Rogers *The Playing Field Horses* and *The Magnolia Tree*.
Rowe *Lone Wolf*.
Slater *Hamburgers House of Horrors*.
Smith *The New House*.
Sutcliff *The Chief's Daughter*.

In my second year class I would expect Angela, who is hooked on horsey books, to read *The Brumby* and *Black*

Beauty if she hasn't already read them, and *The Puffin Book of Horses*. Then I would hope to edge her over to the other animal books, such as *The Hundred and One Dalmatians*, then perhaps to *Brother Dusty Feet*, where the boy first runs away because his aunt is going to put his dog to death. It is, of course, an historical novel and might launch Angela onto a different type of fiction, and it involves some human problems which might encourage reading in a little more depth. I think, too, she might enjoy *Freaky Friday* in which a girl and her mother find themselves inhabiting each other's bodies and lives, and she may well become a Judy Blume addict, as many girls do. Set in an American context, the Blume books portray the adolescent world with humour and compassion.

Michael has a measured reading age of 9.2 and might be happier starting with Cassell books and working up to the Macmillan Club 75 and perhaps to the Byars books.

Kirsten, who loves reading and is something of a feminist, will enjoy *A Question of Courage*, which is about a Birmingham girl who goes to London and joins the suffragette movement, and she'll enjoy the joke of *Tyke Tyler*, which reveals all our assumptions about sex-roles. She'll go rapidly through the library and has already brought in for me a couple of books I hadn't read, which she'll lend to the library. I've brought in for her (and for anyone who'd like to read them) other Susan Cooper books. This sharing of enthusiasm and books is part of the pleasure of form libraries. For all the children one hopes that this will be a jumping-off ground and that they will go on to discover more books and authors they like in school, in public libraries, in bookshops, and from each other.

Paul Zindel's *Confessions of a Teenage Baboon*; *Pardon me, you're stepping on my eyeball*; *I never loved your mind* are deservedly popular (*My darling my Hamburger* perhaps more so with girls) dealing, as they do, with the pleasure and pains of adolescence with honesty and humour. I have some reservations about Cormier's *The Chocolate War*, but it is a powerful tale of individual courage against frightening gang cruelty in a boys' school. Zindel and Cormier are American, of course, and it's a far cry from their picture of adolescence to the Scotland of Cole's *Gregory's Girl*, based on Forsyth's film which appeals to boys and girls. There are plenty of war books and science fiction for older readers and some will be ready to read a wider range of more adult books. We have copies of *Plague Dogs* (Adams) and *Roots* (Haley), for instance, and a selection of classic novels, as well as the contemporary 'adolescent' literature. Macmillan Topliners and Nelson Getaways are aimed at reluctant as well as less able readers and this is another source of books to tempt the boys as well as the girls.

The American books in the libraries were not chosen from a multicultural point of view but, of course, they do reflect different cultures. Macmillan Orbits (for less able 13 to 15 year olds) are set in Australia. Johnson's *Cassandra*, Edwards' *4SS*, Stewart's *Six Days*, Dhondy's *East End at my Feet* and *Come to Mecca* are set among Asian and West Indian communities in England. *Sounder* (Armstrong) and *A Patch of Blue* (Kata) deal in different ways with racial prejudice in the United States. (Some teenagers at this stage, of course, could be reading Wright and Baldwin.) Lingard's *Across the Barricades* and *Into Exile* are set in the Catholic/Protestant conflict of Ireland. In Green's *Summer of my German Soldier* an unhappy Jewish American girl befriends a German prisoner of war. Michael Anthony writes of growing up in Trinidad in *Green Days by the River*, and Yevtushenko's *Precocious Autobiography* would give teenagers a rare chance to read about a teenager in the USSR. It isn't possible to discuss here all the books which one could recommend but there are lists of suggestions later in the book from all contributors.

If you use form libraries you have to give time to them. For instance, a couple of lessons to launch the new library, to say a little about each book, for the children to note down the ones they like the sound of, and to come and choose their first book. During the term there is time while other work is going on to chat to people about what they are reading, to make suggestions, and to check on the amount and type of reading each person is doing. It is essential to have a reliable record scheme, and we use a system of cards on which children record the titles of books read, and the dates when they have taken and returned them. Class librarians can help to organize the library and to check

133

the condition of the books, mending them when necessary. Mercury-film covering and requesting that books be carried around in polythene bags help to prolong the life of paperbacks.

We have one member of the department in charge of form libraries. She organizes the whole system, sending out libraries with card-mounted lists of titles, to which she adds new ones as they come in. The cards have rows of columns for checking in each book with a tick at the end of term, and recording absent and missing books. It then goes on with the library to the next class. Organizing the libraries is a big job and includes covering the books with mercury film, numbering them, and sticking labels inside for borrowers to record their names. There are always willing children to help with this and it is worth it, I think, in prolonging the life of the books when we are spending so much money on them.

We have bought large plastic crates for transporting the libraries and for storing them over the holidays (they stack). We have been lucky in having some English rooms with built-in shelves and all with bookcases. I do believe that English rooms should be bulging with books but I know that there can be daunting problems: having one's room used at break by crowds of large 14 year olds who perch on the shelves and may damage or 'borrow' books; not having book cases supplied; or, of course, not having one's own room. It is worth losing a few books, I think (and we have lost very few, considering our huge stock). One can often find unused bookcases about the school, but without a room one has to give in and lug crates of books about the school.

When one provides a wide range of reading for a group, there are bound to be people who choose books which are too easy or too difficult for them. To a certain extent this is acceptable; we all enjoy reading below our ability range at times, and we can also enjoy something which is not entirely within our grasp. What is important is to make sure that, generally, children are reading books which they enjoy, and which may stretch but not daunt them.

The problem arises of making sure that the children are actually reading the books. I do not believe in just providing the books and leaving it to trust. Some teachers of mixed ability classes are unhappy about the idea of reading a novel together with the whole class, and prefer not to do so, in which case the books which the children take from the form library will be the only ones they read in English. It seems to me particularly important to keep a close watch on the quantity and quality of the reading which each individual is doing. Some children undoubtedly try to pull the wool over their teachers' eyes, and there are also those children who can read a book in the technical sense, but are unable to understand what it is all about. In each case, firm or tactful intervention is called for.

The best recommendation to read a book is likely to be that of a friend or classmate, and 'book-chats' in small groups or in the whole class are useful, as are written reviews which can be 'bound' in some way and kept for the class to refer to. Another idea is a 'radio programme' on cassette, including book reviews, which can also be played to other groups. It's necessary to give some guidelines for the talks and written accounts if they're to be of value. Especially if the children are otherwise doing little or no reading of complete books in English lessons, they should sometimes write in more depth about a class library book. Character studies, writing an extra chapter for the book, adapting an episode for the stage or for a television play are some suggestions which I have found successful.

The Bullock Report pointed out that when people enrolling for the government's adult literacy scheme were asked why they thought they had not learned to read at school, the answer most often given was that reading had never been shown to be something one did for pleasure. The underlying aim of all that has been said in this chapter is that children should leave school as literate young people, who have had every opportunity to see reading as a source of interest and enjoyment.

4 Drama, Games and Simulations

LESLIE STRINGER

I

Opinions still vary concerning the place of drama in the school timetable. Certainly the case for the teaching of drama as a specialist subject has been convincingly stated. On the other hand, I imagine there are few teachers of English or drama who do not agree that it has a part to play not only in English but also in other subject areas. I have some sympathy with a good many of the arguments on both sides, but I believe that a more basic concern should be to see that every child in the secondary school receives experience of drama, and that all teachers, whatever their subject, are made aware of the value of dramatic activity, for its own sake, for the part that it can be made to play in the learning process, and for its role in the personal development of the individual.

A Language for Life defined drama in the school context as a 'fundamental human activity which may include such elements as play, ritual, simulations and role playing ...' (10.31). I would readily accept this definition, as I would the distinctions made between 'theatre' and 'drama'. It is claimed that whereas 'theatre' implies a performance to an audience, generally based on some form of script, 'drama' covers an extremely wide range of activities, verbal and non-verbal, whose common feature is that they depend largely on improvisation of various sorts.

The situation is not now as serious as it once was, but, even so, there still exists a tendency for these two kinds of practice to be in sharp opposition to one another – regrettable, I believe, since both approaches have their place. The ideal situation is where the two forms of activity are complementary, but both have their strengths, so why not draw from them? My opinions here derive from my experience of teaching in a large comprehensive school, which had no separate drama department, nor even a drama specialist, as such, but which offered children a considerable range of activities. A list of some of them might indicate this range.

1   Drama, taught in mixed ability groups, was a timetabled subject for all first- and second-year pupils.
2   Each of the twelve second-year forms, under the guidance of its English teacher, performed a play in a second-year drama festival at the end of the year. These were almost invariably unscripted plays developed through improvised drama and arising from work done in English lessons.
3   Drama was used extensively for a variety of purposes in other English lessons, at all levels.
4   The annual School Play – *Noah, The Good Woman of Setzuan, Sergeant Musgrave's Dance, The Crucible* – each one directed by a different member of staff, involved children from throughout the school.
5   An active staff drama group performed plays to the public – *The Caretaker, Waiting for Godot, Black Comedy.*
6   Pupils regularly visited the theatre – the professional theatre and amateur groups, including youth groups.
7   Where opportunity arose, touring groups were brought into school.
8   The English department assisted the history department in the production of historical documentaries on Education and the Navy, which involved the use of film, live drama, music and tape recorded material; the music department in the production of works by Gilbert and

Sullivan; and the modern languages department in Christmas entertainments in Spanish and French.

9 The English department possessed its own camera and made films; used commercially produced films extensively in teaching; and ran a well-supported film society out of school hours.

The specific benefits of drama have also been too fully dealt with elsewhere for me to need to repeat them in this context. We are, perhaps, only too familiar with the claims made for child drama as a 'creative' activity, providing, as with all creative activities, a medium through which the individual can express ideas. Drama, it is said, enables children to come to terms with the world outside their own private worlds, and extends and deepens their understanding of themselves.

My concern, however, is to consider drama from just one viewpoint, and to comment on a few of the claims made for it that seem relevant to the teaching of English in mixed ability groups, drawing attention to one area – the field of games and simulations – where, I feel that English teachers could find a valuable, and largely untapped, source of material, and from which they could derive interesting methods of approach.

Drama and group work

For English to be taught really successfully in mixed ability groups, there are certain prerequisites: the teacher must want the system to work and there must be an atmosphere within the group that fosters a spirit of cooperation amongst the children. In many instances, in the ways indicated throughout this book, children will be called upon to work together in groups of varying sizes, so that some degree of cooperation is essential if this type of work is to stand a chance of success. There are few activities better than drama for providing opportunites for cooperation in group work and for promoting an attitude of tolerance towards the ideas of others.

Drama and the less able

One of the real problems of mixed ability teaching is catering for the needs of the weaker members of the group. Another simple but important point is that drama helps to do just this.

There is a problem of measuring 'ability' with reference to drama, for the criteria of competence are not easily defined, but, clearly, creative or improvised drama does not require the sort of academic abilities demanded by many subjects in the curriculum. Thus, the carefully handled use of drama in an English lesson can provide a valuable boost to those who would generally be classified among the less able members of the group. The fact is hardly surprising when you consider the demands of drama in relation to the problems which must face these children for most of the time. Drama provides an activity which is relatively short-term and self-contained, with the result that a specific goal can be quite easily achieved; there is no written work, no homework, no examination to worry about; more often than not there is no teacher-intervention. In short, these children can participate on equal terms with everyone else; they can achieve success in the lesson and, in consequence, enjoy it.

I am not suggesting that all our weaker pupils are good at drama, nor that our abler ones are not successful – far from it. But, in my experience, many pupils of low academic ability have approached drama work with genuine interest, and have responded in lively, imaginative and sensitive ways. Their uninhibited enthusiasm and delight have testified to the effect that drama has had on the development of their self-confidence.

Furthermore, when the status of the activity is raised, so that pupils can see the importance which the teacher attaches to it, there is a consequent increase in its effect. I am not sure whether the question I have more than once been asked by pupils: 'Are we going to work today, or do drama?' is a mark of success or failure, but it is a reminder that, as teachers, we should be clear about our reasons for using drama, even if our pupils do not always see them.

As a rider to this point about status, I must add that participation by less able pupils in full scale dramatic productions – the school play, for example – seems to have a whole range of beneficial effects. I do not wish to give the impression here that young Masher Snarlup – who used to be an illiterate tearaway until he played Ophelia in the school play – is now at Cambridge reading Botany. But it is a fact that many 'unlikely' pupils have responded very well to the rigorous demands of public performance. Perhaps for the first time in their school careers they have been asked to shoulder genuine responsibilities, and they have proved to be an essential member of the team? Perhaps it is merely pride at achieving something worthwhile? The experience is certainly something that remains in the memory. The fact that many English teachers can look back at their own school careers and see drama as a highlight is evidence of the terrific hold it has on the memory.

Drama and language development

With reference to drama and English teaching, comments made in *A Language for Life* concerning the importance of improvisation in language development remain relevant. The Report makes the point that there is an important distinction between children's language in improvised drama and that of most of their written work in school. 'The one is open-ended, volatile and incremental in structure, the other is relatively closed and formalistic.' (10.35) Whereas writing tends to be merely a patterning of words into which thoughts and feelings are made to fit, in drama 'an element of invention lies round every corner, and dialogue has a way of surprising itself so that nothing is predictable'. The report continues, to make these points:

> An important aspect of the creativity of speech as distinct from writing is the inexhaustible fund of grammatical forms and idioms available to children from a very early age. If, as Chomsky argues, the 'normal use of language is innovative', it becomes a vital principle that the teacher should create opportunites most likely to produce innovation and general 'natural' language in all its forms. An increasing number of teachers of

drama . . . do in fact see their work as productive of such language. They would add that it helps to establish confidence in social intercourse, as well as familiarity with a variety of speech forms. They devise what might be described as a concentric series of situations. These vary from the known and readily observed, such as family situations, to a wider range of less familiar situations, in which the pupils are led to resort to unfamiliar language patterns to suit the roles they are playing. Drama thus has the capacity for sensitizing the ear for appropriate registers and responses. It encourages linguistic adaptability, often accustoming children to unfamiliar modes of language. (10.36)

An account of one of my own lessons, with a socially, temperamentally, academically, racially mixed group of third year pupils, in which I began with a 'known' situation and moved outwards from it to increasingly less familiar situations – might illustrate some of these points.

By way of background information I should mention that when I used the lesson I had only recently taken over the teaching of the group, and that they had come to me with something of a reputation for being badly behaved. So, one of my initial general aims was to get the class working productively in small groups, ideally to try to encourage a little self-discipline. My object in this particular lesson was to get the pupils to consider – and, where possible, explore through improvised drama – some attitudes towards stealing.

It was obvious from the outset that the class needed to be handled quite firmly. With this in mind I used to begin with a common drama exercise which I call 'statues'. The object of this is to get the children to move around the working area – in my case the school hall – and then on a word of command or a signal such as a bang on a tambourine or anything else handy, for each child to 'freeze' on the spot. The game may be elaborated by asking the children to freeze into a certain shape – an athlete in action for example. The point is that they do not move a muscle until instructed to do so – enabling any information to be given quickly and without fuss.

I have used the technique often as a means of getting attention quickly, and have found in practice that most children realize that to stand still immediately on a word of command, listen to an instruction and then get on with the lesson is more enjoyable – or at least less boring – than waiting for a whole class to come to attention in its own time.

Having used this as a warm-up exercise I began the lesson proper. Some type of initial stimulus is always necessary in drama, and for this reason I chose a poem. A photograph, a film, a slide or set of slides, a physical object, a piece of music, not to mention a well-told anecdote from a teacher or pupil can be just as useful. However, in this instance, I used Raymond Souster's poem *The Man who finds that his Son has become a Thief.* This twenty line poem shows the various mental stages which a father goes through, from the time he first hears the accusation against his boy of shop-lifting, to the point at which he comes to believe it is true.

I read the poem to the whole class, twice, and after the briefest of discussions, to ascertain that all the pupils had at least understood the narrative of the poem, I asked them to stand up and walk around the hall, imagining they were walking round a store such as the one referred to. Here I emphasized that everyone was working on his/her own, and insisted that they were all to ignore what the others were doing. This is an injunction I often use – partly in the hope that it will help to persuade the more self-conscious members of the group that their classmates are not simply watching *them.*

I allowed a few moments for them to get used to this idea of walking round the store, and then introduced a basic mime exercise by asking the children to pause at a particular counter and have a closer look at one item they were interested in, suggesting they should pick it up and examine it, hinting that they should consider its weight, the size and shape, the texture and colour. While they were doing this I walked round the hall and asked individuals to describe to me in some detail the object they were looking at. (For the girls: rings, bracelets, various items of make-up and a football scarf. For the boys: a pocket radio, a wristwatch, football badges and scarves, a model-kit and in one case a set of pens and pencils.)

Apart from this discrete questioning, the first stage can be carried out in complete silence – so that as well as setting the scene for the rest of the lesson it can be used as a means of concentrating the attention of the individual on the task in hand. The children having explored the store, I then asked them to become detectives following someone they suspected of shoplifting. Again this exercise was done with the pupils working entirely on their own.

A number of ways of developing the lesson from this point suggest themselves. If you are interested primarily in movement, and it is perhaps unfortunate that many English teachers see this as an area outside their concern, you could concentrate on this area alone, breaking off at this point to discuss with the pupils the way someone walks when wandering aimlessly round the store; the way they move when they have stolen something; or the way detectives follow someone. The introduction of music might help there. With pupils used to this sort of work you could perhaps build up a polished dance drama, involving a chase and arrest.

My own interest, however, lay in exploring the poem in terms of the attitudes and motives of the three characters – the father, the son and the store manager.

Thus, beginning with a situation familiar to all my pupils – that of walking round a large store – I moved on to one which, in fact, *some* had experienced and others might envisage without stretching their imaginations too far – that of stealing. (Although I must add that I took great care to feign naivety by not revealing that I knew that some of my pupils had been in trouble with the police for similar offences.) I asked them, again working individually, to act out the stealing of an object from the store, including the walk to the exit.

My next step was to divide the class into groups of three – the composition of the groups being determined by the pupils themselves. My reason for asking for groups of three was primarily because of the three principal characters in the poem, but these small 'friendship' groups have always seemed to me to work successfully, in at least one respect.

This is a purely subjective assessment, but it appears to me that restricting the size of the group to three tends to minimize (I don't say eliminate) one of the more serious problems of this type of activity. The problem to which I refer is that of the quiet or timid or inarticulate child being squeezed out of group drama work by the brighter, more articulate ones, who not only tend to take the 'best', the largest and most enjoyable parts in 'performance', but also tend to dominate discussions and planning sessions by their more original and/or forcefully expressed ideas. A disturbing feature for teachers is that they are unable to protect the 'weaker' children by direct intervention.

With the class in groups of three I allocated each of them to a specific area of work, and asked them to discuss, to plan and to act out in sequence four separate scenes.

1 The boy/girl bringing home the news of the accusation to his/her parents and convincing them of his/her innocence.
2 The parent, believing the child's story, angrily confronting the store manager.
3 The manager in calmer mood slowly convincing the parent of the child's guilt.
4 The scene between parents and child *after* returning from the interview with the manager.

I allowed about five minutes for a general planning session where I insisted that the groups sat down to pool their ideas and decide upon roles, and then five minutes or so for them to act out each scene. Every five minutes I indicated to the whole class which scene they should be moving on to next, so that after twenty minutes they had all been through the full sequence once.

Thus, I had moved from situations very close to the experience of the children to those which were completely unfamiliar. The idea of the manager's controlled and reasoned argument finally overcoming the parent's indignation and instinctive loyalty to the child was difficult for many pupils to grasp – although some managed it well – and here I felt it worthwhile to interrupt a number of groups to ask them to think about this scene very carefully.

What I found most interesting, however, was the pathos of the final scene from several groups, as pupils came to realize that a parent's reaction is not always to 'rant and rave' and 'go mad' as they had first suggested, and that the deeply injured, disillusioned tone of one girl, playing a mother, who asked, 'How could you do this?' was in itself as effective as any punishment.

Drama and literature

The importance of the relationship between improvisation and work on literature should not be underestimated, particularly as both these areas can be related to the personal experience of the pupils. Shirley Hoole indicates something of the nature of the relationship by including in her assignments some suggestions for drama work. (See for example the work on *Horned Helmet* in her chapter.)

On the simplest level, improvisation can be initiated by the use of literature as a stimulus. The account of my own lesson illustrates this – the reading of a poem forming the basis for the rest of the work. I know from talking with a group of sixth-form students that Serraillier's account of the story of Beowulf remained in the memory of many of them – as it has remained with me – as a result of a series of improvisations they worked on in a first-year mixed group.

Conversely, improvised drama can provide a physical context for the printed word to come to life. Thus, we have a relationship between literature and improvisation. Literature initiates improvisation; improvisation illuminates literature.

But, consider at the same time the place of the child's personal experience, and the way that it would be used in practice in an English lesson. Surely, this third aspect – the child's own first-hand experience – constantly intrudes into these two secondary forms. Personal experience could be used to illuminate literature which might then be used to initiate drama. (The child's own experience of lying awake at night and hearing a strange noise might be discussed first to help appreciate the feelings of Beowulf and his warriors as they lay waiting for the arrival of

Grendel, and this in turn could be used to promote a piece of improvisation.)

Literature could equally well illuminate a child's own experience, which in its turn might initiate drama. (A first-year child, reading of Tom Sawyer's attempts to avoid school by feigning illness, may come to realize that his own attempts to do the same have a precedent, and if he can then be persuaded to relate these experiences to a friend or friends we have already the basis of an improvisation.)

The astute teacher will perceive the inter-relationship of drama, literature and the child's first-hand experience and will make full use of it.

II

Games, simulations and simulation-games

Although the use of games and simulations in teaching appears to be increasing, I feel that as a teaching method it is in danger of being overlooked by English teachers, as it tends to be seen as the province of the teacher of history, geography or social science. My purpose here is to examine the effectiveness of games and simulations as educational tools, and this I hope to do by illustrating their possible uses.

As a working definition, 'games' might be distinguished from 'simulations' in terms of the presence or absence of two factors: competition and realism. It has been said that a 'game' is any contest between adversaries, operating under the constraint of rules and having an objective; a 'simulation', on the other hand, has been described as a simplified slice of life – 'an operating representation of the central features of reality'. A 'simulation-game', therefore, is something which contains elements of both of these. It combines the features of a game (competition, rules, players) with those of a simulation (the incorporation of critical features of reality).

Games, simulations and simulation-games may take several forms. They may be based on a conflict situation. In this case, various groups, some or all with opposing interests, would be engaged in conflict of some kind. Another common type is the 'in-tray' simulation, where individuals are presented with problems to solve, with case histories to help them. A variant of this is the committee simulation where a group rather than an individual is given a problem. There may be conflict in this, but it is usually contributed by the character of the participants rather than the nature of the game itself. Finally, there are those which involve role-playing and cooperation rather than competition. In all of these it is possible, and in most cases it is desirable, to have a post-play discussion. It could be said that these feedback sessions are the most valuable part of the exercise.

There may be many reasons for using games and simulations and not all of them will be applicable to the English teacher. It is claimed, for example, that a situation or concept may be illuminated or clarified by the use of a game. The use of a game might provide an insight into quite a complex problem – hence the number of business and commercial games. In games and simulations, patterns of interpersonal behaviour may be discerned and used to compare with real life – hence their use in the training of teachers and youth leaders.

The game *Starpower* provides an excellent example of this, although I would earnestly urge the greatest caution in using it. I have heard of two accounts of the game, one from a theatre director who claims he had been hit by someone while playing, and one from a College lecturer, who had played the game with his colleagues and whose telling comment was that 'the RE chap sat on the sidelines and refused to have anything to do with it!' I have used the game with a group of secondary school teachers and with two groups of fourth-year pupils. On each of the three occasions the game seems to have had such an unerring and frightening facility for engendering enmity and bringing out the very worst in people that I would be reluctant to use it again.

Despite my objection to *Starpower*, the players' emotional involvement illustrates what I believe is the greatest strength of games and simulations. Of the commonly held reasons for their use, perhaps the most readily apparent is that they stimulate interest. The promise that games and simulations offer of transforming the classroom from a collection of passive spectators into a workshop of active participants in the learning process is probably their greatest attraction. Moreover, the breadth of application, the scope which games and simulations offer for adaptation to a variety of purposes make them valuable to an English teacher with a mixed ability class. If we accept the rather loose definition of a simulation as being essentially a simplified slice of reality, then for most simulations there is an obvious advantage in having participants with a broad spread of interests, abilities and background.

As an illustration of the way that simulation could be used I refer to three separate simulations; *The Parkhurst Simulation, Tenement* and one called *Forum* devised by a colleague.

The Parkhurst Simulation

My own involvement with games and simulations as a teaching method was first stimulated by the centre page spread of the magazine *Teaching London Kids* (No. 3). Against the rather dramatic black background of the double page was arranged a collection of twelve documents: letters, notes – formal and informal, memoranda, and a newspaper headline. The common theme of this collection was the attempt by some pupils at 'The Parkhurst School' to organize a 'walk-out' by pupils in support of a teachers' strike, and the reaction of teachers and senior staff when this attempt was discovered.

On very realistic looking headed notepaper was a letter to parents from the headmaster, describing the effect on Parkhurst of the proposed teachers' strike:

> ... I am pleased to be able to tell you that, since only eight teachers from this school are joining the strike, we are not closing on Thursday ...
> ... It has come to my notice that certain subversive groups have taken advantage of the situation to urge some of our pupils to stage a 'walk-out' ... any unexplained absence ... will be treated with the utmost severity.

Less formally a note from the headmaster to his deputy read:

> I'm at a Rotary lunch and will be back later this after-
> noon – but we must do something about this . . .

There were notes from pupil to pupil:

> Steve – tell the others the meeting will be Lloyd's room
> at dinner time but go in quietly because Grope is on
> the look-out. JR

Notes between members of staff:

> Mike – can you please come over and take my 1st years?
> Gross scotched John Rhodes' plan to have a meeting in
> my room at dinner time . . .

There was the newspaper headline:

> *THREE 'WALK-OUT' KIDS EXPELLED*
> Parkhurst's strong line headmaster . . .

By way of explanation there was one short paragraph:

> This collection of documents was duplicated on A4
> sheets and used as the basis for discussion for simulated
> scenes with fourth and fifth-year pupils. All the names
> and incidents are fictitious. One approach was to divide
> the class into four groups. One group was to become
> the production team of a television current affairs
> programme whose job was to decide how to cover the
> incident in a ten minute slot. The three other groups
> were to represent the striking pupils, the teachers and
> the senior members of staff; each of these had to work
> out what line they would take on the programme.

I tried out a simulation along almost exactly the same
line. I chose a mixed ability fifth-year drama group to test
reactions, and was surprised by their reception of it,

surprised by their initial interest and willingness to participate, and surprised by the intensity of their involvement.

Here was, in fact, something directly relevant to the
pupils' own experiences, yet sufficiently out of the ordinary
to be interesting. Since it was for use in a drama lesson
that I had originally used the idea, my first interest in the
simulation was in the obvious possibilities it presented for
role play. However, I was impressed too by the flexibility
of the material. Leaving aside the value of the role play,
the preliminary discussions I had with the pupils would
have justified its use to me as a teacher of English.

To begin with, it was obvious that the stimulus of this
material gave rise to a level of discussion far higher than
that which I had come to expect with this particular group.
Such discussion began with a genuine interest in the hierarchical nature of a school staff – clearly evident from the
documents. Two letters, one from the headmaster and one
from an obviously 'junior' member of staff, to the fourth-
year teacher caused some surprise, and featured later in
the role play. From this point the group went on to consider
the effects on the staff of the involvement of the press and
television, and the influence of parents, not only in this
incident, but as a whole.

After a while, however, discussion centred on the need to
examine the characters and deduce the motives of the
various authors of the documents, and, above all, the need
to appreciate the tone of the writing. Two points which I
would have been anxious to communicate in English
lessons had arisen naturally and directly out of the
demands of the simulation, out of the need to adopt a role.

To my regret I took the simulation very little further.
When I later considered the opportunites I had missed in
not following up the work, particularly in terms of written
assignments which I indicate later, I realized just how
superficial my start had been. It had, however, made me
aware of a number of possibilities, and it was this that
prompted me to look into the use of other games and simulations in the classroom, and to try them as part of my
teaching method.

My first really successful use of simulation came with
Tenement, and it is to this that I propose to refer in detail.

Tenement

There are several reasons for recommending *Tenement*. It was designed specifically for schools by the education section of Shelter, is inexpensive, easily obtainable and, having been widely used, has the advantage of having been tried and tested.

Before describing it in any detail it might be interesting to look briefly at a description by Mr Pat Tansey of the manner in which it originated. In the booklet edited by Chris Longley (1972), Tansey describes his involvement with the earliest stages of the development of *Tenement:*

> The first thing to do before designing a simulation is to decide on its educational objectives, and the more precise these are the better.
>
> The Shelter workers were concerned to expose to students some of the problems and frustrations of the homeless. They wanted to organize a situation in which students could explore some of the attitudes commonly held about the homeless and the poorly housed. This is an 'attitude changing' simulation – designed, not to inculcate the 'right' attitudes but rather to encourage participants to examine their own and other people's prejudices in the light of their simulation experience.

Two points here, I feel, have general application: the need for predetermined educational objectives, and the nature of the simulation.

In its published form the aims of *Tenement* are stated quite simply:

> *Tenement* is a simulation concerned with the problems of a family living in a multi-occupied house in a large city. The idea of the simulation is to make people aware of some of the difficulties and frustrations of living in such a situation and to point to ways in which some of those difficulties could be solved by the introduction of agencies concerned with such problems.

From the point of view of an English teacher the rationale for the use of *Tenement* will almost certainly involve a number of other objectives. I list a number of purposes for which the simulation could be used.

1 To stimulate the use of role play – either to put pupils into someone else's shoes, allowing them to develop an understanding of other people's feelings, or to enable them to explore their own reactions in a previously unknown or only half-known situation.
2 To promote interesting, relevant and purposeful discussion in small groups which are not directly supervised by a teacher – offering, thereby, opportunities for peer-group and cooperative learning.
3 To offer a rich source of factual information and background material for future discussions, either in small groups or with a full class.
4 To provide a stimulus for a number of different types of writing.
5 To provide a source of written material which pupils will want to read and comprehend.
6 To provide an activity which can genuinely be shared by every member of the group and which every member of the group can succeed in and enjoy.

Obviously an individual teacher could have one specific aim in mind, and aims differ according to circumstances. Opinions of the importance of Shelter's stated objectives will differ. What I hope to indicate, however, is that the methods adopted to achieve those ends are relevant to an English teacher in other respects.

To be more explicit about the simulation, the kit contains a number of A4 size sheets of information.

One sheet, headed 'The landlord' has a brief description of the owner of the property.

You own the multi-occupied house, a drawing of which is on this sheet. You bought the house shortly after the war at a low price and finished paying for it ten years ago.

It describes the condition of the house.

The house is not in a very good condition. It has not been properly converted into flats to enable a large number of people to live comfortably in it ...

There is also a description of the tenants; a brief description of each family unit, including details of how long they have lived in the house, the amount of rent each pays, the conditions of the rooms and other salient background information.

The next set of sheets describes the families in more detail – one sheet per family. There are seven families. There are, for example, the Campbells, a West Indian couple with three young children, living in four basement rooms, two of which are uninhabitable due to dampness and dangerous electrical wiring:

... You live and cook in one room and sleep in the other. All the children have to sleep together in one bed as the room is very small. You have separated the bedroom with a curtain. The dampness puts up your heating bills. The rooms have very poor ventilation.

There are details of the family's income and basic expenses and a paragraph of other information which hints at the effects on the members of the family of living in these conditions.

There is a similarly detailed account of each of the other families – including Mr White, a sixty-eight year old pensioner, and Emily Brown, an unmarried mother with a nine-month-old daughter.

The next set of sheets has information about six local and government agencies from whom the families can obtain help. Full details of the services these agencies can offer, including council or housing association property available, are described on the appropriate sheet. The agencies are: Citizens' Advice Bureau, Local Authority Housing Department, Voluntary Housing Aid Centre, Rent Tribunal, Department of Health and Social Security and the Department of Employment.

There is a series of 'chance-cards', which may be used at the discretion of the controller (usually the teacher). These contain such pieces of information as: 'Your ceiling has just fallen in', or 'You have been made redundant'.

Finally, there are notes for the controller which introduce the simulation, explain the parts, describe the methods of playing and give suggestions for post-play discussion.

Materials and preliminary organization

In addition to the actual *Tenement* kit, very little else is needed by way of materials. I find it helpful to have large notices to identify the various agencies. I usually pin these to the walls at intervals around the room – although they would serve the same purpose standing on tables. It is useful, though again not essential, to have badges to identify the families. These are not supplied with the kit.

There are fourteen parts altogether, so that you really need at least fourteen pupils to play the simulation. However between twenty and thirty players are preferable, as more than one person can 'man' an agency, and families can be played by more than one person, depending on the size of the family and the age of the children.

I would say that the material is best suited to fourth- and fifth-year pupils, although it has been used very successfully with children in the third year.

The simulation is best carried out in a large area, such as the school hall, although it is possible to use a classroom. An often much neglected area in schools is the canteen, or dining-room – especially if it is permanently set out with tables and chairs, making it useless for more traditional 'drama'. This type of area is ideal for *Tenement*, not only because of its size, but because the furniture can be so easily rearranged to form offices and waiting rooms, adding that extra little touch of verisimilitude.

Operating

The first task is for the controller to allocate the parts, to issue the information sheets and make sure that each participant has details of the role. A word of warning here: it is advisable for the controller to know the pupils and the information on the sheets fairly well, for it is useful to some extent to fit the players' interests and abilities to the requirements of the parts. For instance, the Department of

Health and Social Security requires someone who is reasonably adept at arithmetic. I would say, too, that the landlord, who will probably have to withstand much criticism, needs to be played by someone who is reasonably extrovert and uninhibited, with a fairly resilient and forceful personality – although to typecast him as a sort of villain of Victorian melodrama is not necessarily helpful or accurate.

When you are allocating the families, it is better if you can persuade pupils to pair off into 'mums and dads', although I am aware that this is not always an easy task with pupils of this age. I have found it useful to emphasize constantly from the start of the exercise that pupils should try to identify with the role they are playing. The success of the simulation depends largely on how well the controller manages to do this.

Having assigned the roles and given out the information sheets – and I also give the pupils a sheet of paper to record useful information – I send them either to their places of employment (in the case of the agencies) or to sit in family groups, to read and digest the information on their sheets. Obviously, then, at this stage pupils could be working on their own, in pairs or in groups of three or four.

If you were looking for a justification for using *Tenement* in an English lesson you might offer the fact that at this point in the simulation the pupils are provided with an excellent test of comprehension – with a built-in motivation. Unless participants comprehend the information on the sheet they are unable to progress. It also has the added advantage, in a mixed ability group, that it provides an excellent means for more able pupils to help the poorer readers, in a natural way, that causes no embarrassment. It has been my experience that pupils scarcely able to read at all for themselves, once they have had the sheet explained to them by a classmate, are quite able to adopt their role – and have often been very good indeed at the actual role-playing.

I usually allow ten to fifteen minutes for this stage, where I insist that each pupil sits down and reads and takes in the information. At the end of this time I remind them again that they have adopted a role and that they should stay in character from this point onwards. My own method of actually starting play is to ask the families if they are satisfied with their living conditions. The inevitable chorus of 'no' in response is the cue to tell them to go and do something about it, and that from this point onwards they are on their own. My final request as a 'teacher', before allowing the simulation to follow its own course, is to ask the families to record details of where they go and what sort of response they get, and the agencies to make a note of the people who come to see them and what, if anything, they have been able to do for them, as an aid to the post-play discussion.

In classes not too used to this sort of activity there could well be a few moments of puzzled silence. But, normally, with very little further prompting the families will get up and go off to see the landlord to complain, to the Housing Authority to try to get a council house or the Citizens' Advice Bureau to ask what to do next. What happens in practice, initially, is that pupils will begin by working in friendship groups. Rarely is the adopted role strong enough to overcome the natural preferences of the pupil to work within the relatively safe framework of a group of friends. At first, anyway, a family with a problem will tend to seek advice from an agency staffed by friends – whatever the agency! This is not really a drawback, as it provides a not too disturbing beginning for those who may have difficulty relating to others and need the security of friends. Having made this 'easy' start such pupils are more ready to move on to another agency for reasons prompted by the simulation.

It is usually best if the controller stays out of things completely from this stage onwards, except maybe to give out a few 'chance' cards to families who look as if they might need a little added motivation, for with any luck the simulation will begin to snowball from this stage.

The notes to the controller supplied with the kit suggest:

Unless absolutely necessary, players should not be led by the controller to the agencies. In a real life situation a family in need of advice has to discover for itself where it can get the help or advice. *Tenement* is an attempt to simulate that situation.

This role of 'observer' may be a new one to some teachers, but in this instance – and I am sure many other similar instances arise teaching a mixed ability group – it is an essential one. It *is* difficult for a teacher simply to stand back and let children get on with things; you feel you are abrogating responsibility. But, to a large extent, the point of the simulation is destroyed if the teacher is too intrusive once it is under way.

Assuming that things are running smoothly, the pupils are all actively engaged in discussions, there is a general buzz of chatter and excitement in the room – when do you stop the simulation? A time limit can be imposed at the outset, but I have found that it is far better for the controller to make the decision to stop at discretion. It should be pointed out that in a real-life situation offices tend to close at a stipulated time each day, and if a family still has not sorted out its problems at that time they will have to wait until the following day. So, stopping the simulation before all families have solved their problems is a true-to-life situation.

Concerning time-limits, I have had a group of fifth-year pupils of very different abilities – ranging from those considered unable to take external examinations (and those merely waiting for their sixteenth birthday!) to good academic pupils – work on this simulation for over an hour with remarkable enthusiasm and enjoyment. That a group like this should be able to share the experience of working on such a project and enjoy the activity could be considered a recommendation in itself. Normally I find that about forty minutes is ample for the actual playing out of the situation, and at this stage I stop all activity and prepare the group for a discussion. The 'Notes for Controller' are useful in suggesting points that could be taken up and discussed, and as these are questions directed at each family and agency, it is possible for the pupils to stay in their roles. Addressing them by the names of the parts they take will help them to do this.

The whole exercise including the post-play discussion should take just over an hour, but I have found that pupils enjoy the activity sufficiently to make it worthwhile repeating the simulation in a subsequent lesson, changing roles, so that the families play the agencies and *vice versa*. This serves to give the pupils a more rounded picture of what is actually happening.

The value of the dramatic activity involved in the exercise I hope is self-evident; so too, I think is the social value of learning something of the Department of Employment or the Department of Health and Social Security. However, these are not my prime concerns, and I should like to consider the numerous 'spin-offs'. I have mentioned already the importance of the need for pupils to read and understand the written material contained in the information sheets. Consider, too, the possible writing tasks arising from this activity. To assist pupils to use the information given on a particular sheet, they could be asked to extract and note down the essential points; if they are to remember what has happened to them over a period of forty minutes, they could be asked to record the events they considered important or significant. What better way is there of introducing the notion or explaining the technique of 'summarizing'? Along similar lines pupils could be asked to assess the characters of the people with whom they came into contact.

As a follow-up activity, the writing of letters is an obvious example. Pupils who have played through the simulation could be asked at a later stage to write a letter they might have had to write in the role which they played. Writing letters would be a normal part of the daily duties of the staff of the various agencies and the participants readily recognize this fact. Tenants could easily be called upon to write to the landlord or one of the agencies; they might be moved to write a personal letter to a friend, commenting on their situation, describing their feelings of frustration, disappointment, helplessness or whatever. One only has to take note of the comments recently of examiners to realize that fifth-year pupils often experience difficulty finding adequate material for letter writing. *Tenement* not only supplies pupils with material and background information but, if it is successfully played, creates feelings and attitudes which they want to express.

A letter which a fourth-year pupil in the role of Albert White wrote to the landlord is not only an improvement on

158

anything else he had previously written, but it is a forceful and effective letter in its own right, despite its obvious technical weaknesses.

Dear Sir,

I am complianing about the condistion I live in this is my last warning before I go to the rent Turbulal (Tribunal) I have had enoff you have muck me about in the past. I am feed up the conditions are that the room is cold and damp and the window does not open. Plaster is falling of the wall and rain often comes through the ceiling and my bed is affected by damp I am so cold at night I want you to put New Slates on the roof and the ceiling fixed. I want the hole room fixed. I am old and can no longer fix it myself so if you do not fix it I will go to the rent tribunar and let them lower the rent as well. I have to share the kitchen with other people and it semells of bad food. And I have to share the Tolet with all the people in the house I can not keep food in the kitchen with out coming back and find it all gone. I am 68 years old and it is all bad for me so I want something to be don to it. the whole house is rotting away slowly so if you do not do something about if you shall be one tenant less than before.
Yours faithfully,
Albert White

An assignment sheet to be given to a fourth- or fifth-year group, involving a series of further writing tasks arising directly from the simulation could include the following choices:

---

1 Describe factually the condition of either the basement or one of the attic rooms.
2 Find out about and write an account of how you would deal with rising damp or dry rot.
3 Imagine you are the mother of three children living in the basement. Write an account of a typical day.
4 Choose any of the tenants you have played or come

into contact with, and write a diary of a week's events in his/her life.

5   What would be the thoughts of a mother having to bring up a family in this house? Write these in free verse if you wish.

6   Write a story called 'The day the ceiling fell in'.

7   Imagine you work at one of the agencies. Write an account of a typical working day.

8   As a member of the staff of one of the agencies write a detailed account of an interview with one of the families.

9   Write a short play, a scene from a play, or a story based on any of your experiences in the simulation.

10 Find out about and write an account of the work of Shelter.

11 Find out about and write an account of any of the agencies involved in the simulation.

12 Why do certain urban areas become so seriously over-populated? What do sociologists claim are the effects on the inhabitants of such areas?

A group of fourth-year girls tackled question 3 on the assignment sheet. I include here some extracts from their work to illustrate their understanding of the condition of the house and their sympathy with the occupants.

Jane went home and wrote a twelve-page account of the day in the life of a mother. When I asked her for permission to quote her work in this chapter, she chose these extracts from her writing to give a flavour of the whole:

A day in the life of Mrs Anne Ward

I woke up feeling very cold and tired. I pulled what few blankets I had up around my neck and turned over to lie on my back. As I lay there looking up at the ceiling, which had plaster hanging from it I remember thinking 'Oh God, not another day to face. I don't think I'll be able to face it, not living here, not in all this filth and dampness. I can't let my children grow up in a place like this . . .'

I've often thought of taking the kids and going to live in a hostel, but I don't like those places much ...

I hadn't been silly at all in thinking that Jean was dead. It could easily happen with all the dangerous loose electrical fittings around.

It takes me much longer than it does anybody else to do the washing. For a start I have to do it all by hand, and secondly there isn't any hot water. The house is a very old one and I have to heat the water on the cooker ...

I didn't like going into the shops. The assistants could tell that we didn't have much money and they used to watch us like hawks, even the children, just to make sure we didn't steal anything.

I used to watch their eyes light up as they pressed noses flat against the windows, longing for all the different toys. I'd have given anything to have walked into the shop and bought them something, but I knew I just couldn't afford it.

It's funny, but sometimes, living in those two rooms really got me down and made me depressed. That's why I was so jumpy and irritable and why I was always shouting at the kids. Other times it didn't seem so bad really. At least we did have somewhere to live. Somewhere private.

I wondered what mood I'd be in tomorrow, hoping I wouldn't feel depressed. That's bad for all of us.

Along the same lines Alison writes:

... We usually spend the afternoon at the group organized for mothers and their children. There are a lot of unmarried mothers in the same situation as me, and we are all sympathetic to each other. The other mothers are kind to us, and do not scorn us because we are poor. The children all mix and play together. I like going there because I get away from the depressing atmosphere of our house, and the scorning eyes of other people. I like to see the children laughing. The usually solemn faces crack and break into wide smiles, and the

usually old looking, dull eyes, spectacled by dark lines,
change into gleeful, dancing, children's eyes . . .

Alison had worked with Joanne on this exercise so I
imagine that it was not coincidental that Joanne too had
been struck by the idea of poverty being reflected in the
eyes of the children.
She writes:

I turned round to see three little white faces looking
up at me, their eyes hollow and circled by big black
lines. Their cheeks are sunken in, and their hair is
grubby and un-brushed . . .

The concern for the effects on the children of living in this
type of house was evident from much of the writing. Tracy
writes:

Every day is the same old routine, I get up out of my
springless bed at around 6.30 am. The children are
already up waiting patiently at the breakfast table,
hoping that this morning will be lucky for them. But
no it is Friday morning Tuesday's allowance has
already been swallowed up . . .
     The walls are black, the cooker has broken down, the
rooms are a disgrace, and the children get the worst
end of the stick . . . I really wanted to be out of here
before Christmas so the children could have a better
one for once. But there seems no chance of that now.

Lorraine is more explicit:

I got up at about 6.00 to get my husband John off to
work, I made him some breakfast and then he went.
After he had gone I sat down and had a drink and a
smoke. The children didn't get up till about 11.00 and
they did nothing but moan, I hit Jane the eldest, and
sent her to bed for the rest of the day, sometimes it is
the only way to keep her quiet. Susan the youngest
went with me to do a bit of shopping and I mean a bit.

When we got back home I made the children something to eat then Jane went back to bed.

When John came home he wasn't in a very good mood and when I told him Jane had been playing up he hit her very hard. After I had told Susan to go to bed I started to do some washing, while John went down the pub, he came back in a stinking mood and started to knock me about. The kids woke up and came to see what the matter was. He started belting the kids and there was a big row. I took the kids and walked out. We walked round for a while and when we come back John was in bed so I put the kids to bed and went myself.

It is my practice to ask children to read and comment on each other's work. An unsolicited and unsigned comment on one piece read: 'a very descriptive paragraph showing the *real* things she had to put up with'.

If you work on a thematic basis, along the lines that Judith Atkinson describes in her chapter, the simulation could well provide an excellent starting point for a theme called *Homes and Families*. The possibilities of follow-up work based on literature for this age group are extensive. The effects of environment (even specifically this type of urban home background) on the individual are amply illustrated:

Hines *Kes*, Penguin.
Braithwaite *To Sir with Love*, Heinemann.
Barstow *Joby*, Heinemann.
Barstow *A Kind of Loving*, Penguin.
Sherry *A Pair of Jesus Boots*, Heinemann.
Causley *Timothy Winters*.
Spender *My Parents kept me from Children who were Rough*.
Delaney *A Taste of Honey*, Methuen.
Terson *Zigger Zagger*, Penguin.
Hopkins *A Game-like-only a Game*, Longman.
Brecht *The Good Woman of Setzuan*, Penguin.

To conclude, may I offer a few pieces of advice to an English teacher using *Tenement* for the first time.

1   Make sure you are aware of the contents of the information sheets, so that you can advise on the choice of roles.
2   A good way of finding out about the problems involved is to try the material out on your colleagues before using it with your pupils.
3   Don't spend too much time at the beginning of the session explaining principles and objectives. Let the pupils participate.
4   Don't push unwilling participants too hard at first. *Tenement* allows you to cater for this type of child very well. As an additional member of staff at one of the agencies or as a son/daughter of one of the families a reluctant pupil can coast along, being part of the exercise without being overburdened with responsibility, until he/she discovers that it is not too difficult to participate, and that involvement is actually enjoyable.
5   Be prepared for the simulation to begin slowly. Don't get too anxious if nothing happens at first.
6   Be prepared for a noisy session once it does get under way.

Forum

The logical progression from using commercially produced material is to develop your own for a specific purpose.

Forum was named after the Youth and Community Centre at the school at which I teach and was first developed for use with a Drama Club, run after school hours for first- and second-year pupils. The prime educational objective in this instance was to involve a group in an activity they would find enjoyable and which, since attendance was purely voluntary, would sustain interest for a number of sessions. Previously the group had tended to concentrate on activities which lasted only for a single session.

The simulation is set in a youth club with some space 'outside'. It is helpful if music is provided and one corner is set aside for a coffee bar. No elaborate props are needed but the coffee bar, disco unit, entrance and 'outside' area must be clearly defined and recognizable to the participants.

The children are then separated into three groups. At this point it may be useful to consider the methods which could be used to group the participants in a simulation, since nearly all simulations need some group work.

Basically there are two different approaches: child-determined grouping and teacher-determined grouping. Where grouping is determined by the children, groups build up almost invariably on the basis of friendship sets. Where much teaching depends on small group work, this is often, of course, a familiar and easy method for the children to cope with. Groups like this have the obvious advantage that the children know each other and mix together socially. There are, however, several disadvantages. One group, for instance, may be particularly disruptive, or withdrawn, or talented. Children may miss some of the broad social experience that simulations provide. Ideas may stagnate.

In the area of teacher-determined grouping two chief possibilities are open. Firstly, the teacher may be able to eliminate some of the disadvantages mentioned above by carefully deciding in advance who will work with whom. The alternative is to group children using some method of random selection. The unique advantages of this method are that over a period of time, each child will probably work with everyone else in the class, and that the grouping process itself can be made to be 'dramatic'. For example, where a teacher wishes to divide a class of thirty-two into eight groups of four, each child could be given a number between one and eight and the class could then be told to break up into their own groups without speaking or using their fingers to indicate a number. The thoughts and processes involved in solving the problem nearly always succeed in stretching the imagination and providing a useful 'warm-up' before the simulation proper begins.

To return to *Forum*, the three groups required are:

1 The 'good' members (Group A) – These people are members of the youth club and they are the ones who

are always prepared to help at the coffee bar, sweep up afterwards etc.

2   The 'bad' members (Group B) – Although members of the youth club these people are not really prepared to help in its running. They are rowdy, uncooperative etc.

3   The 'outsiders' (Group C) – These are not members of the club, don't want to be, and spend club evenings trying to spoil the enjoyment of the members. The club leader (the teacher) refuses admittance to this group.

The simulation begins at the beginning of an ordinary evening at the club. The members arrive and take part in whatever activity suits the role they have been given. The outsiders, of course, remain outside. After a somewhat truncated club evening, the club leader steps in to announce that, owing to complaints from local residents about rowdyism and damage after meetings at the club, the Council has decided that the club will have to close.

What happens from this point onwards depends on the group, but the club leader should attempt to stay out of the way after closing up the club. Some possibilities that have been observed are:

1   Group A turns on groups B and C
2   Groups A and B turn on group C
3   Various courses of action are suggested: petitions, marches, starting another club
4   Mayhem

Whatever happens it is unlikely that anything will finally be resolved in the first session, so that a second session can be begun at a later date with the participants having had time to think about the problems that face them.

The second part of the simulation begins at school the next day at breaktime. The closure of the youth club is the main topic of conversation, at least amongst the members of groups A and B. Again several different reactions are possible. One of the advantages of the new situation is that if chaos threatens or if the problems quickly come to seem insoluble, the teacher, in the guise of the teacher on playground duty, can intervene and if necessary offer suggestions and advice.

From now onwards there are numerous possibilities for further development, not only in dramatic activities but also in other fields. A post-play discussion could be the next step where pupils, no longer in role, could view the simulation objectively, offer comments on it, and compare it with reality.

In an English lesson an assignment sheet, similar to that suggested for *Tenement*, for example, offering a choice of writing tasks could be provided to follow the practical sessions. These tasks would obviously bear in mind the age of the participants, but they might include, say, the writing of letters to the Council asking for a reprieve; to the youth leader asking for advice; or to a local newspaper commenting on the situation, perhaps hoping to change local opinion. They would include writing expressing personal reactions or narrative writing relating to the final outcome envisaged. They would also include such tasks as the wording of petitions, the design and making of banners and posters of protest, or even composing the words of a song or chant to be used on a 'demonstration' march.

'Creative' drama can be made to play a most valuable part in the social education of all children, particularly when they are taught in mixed ability groups. The very nature of drama is such that it enables children to respond to its demands on their own level. It has, too, a vital part to play in the language development of the child. Its uses with regard to literature are many and varied. But, in all this, a flexible approach is essential if the full benefits are to be derived.

With the more specialized form of dramatic activity involved in games and simulations, I have tried to offer several reasons why their use might be contemplated. Of these perhaps the most important is that a game or simulation can offer the child insight, interest and involvement – a chance to participate in the learning process. It is a tool which can offer the teacher the opportunity to invigorate and revitalize an approach to many of the more traditional aspects of the work. Use of simulation is one strategy which I have found useful and which English teachers may wish

to try. As Tansey pointed out: 'A tool which motivates and
involves children, persuades them towards cooperative
effort and shapes attitudes in such a way that they are
their own attitudes, reached by them and not forced on
them, must be a powerful tool'.

APPENDIX

Useful games and simulations – materials and sources

A guide to most of the games and simulations available in
this country may be obtained from the Secretary, Society
for Academic Gaming and Simulation in Education and
Training, 5, Errington, Moreton-in-the-Marsh, Glos.

Two valuable sources of information about games and
simulations are: Youth Service Information Centre, 37,
Belvoir Street, Leicester, LE1 6SC and National Youth
Bureau, 17–23 Albion Street, Leicester, LE1 6GD.

There are many games available from the United States.
Some of them could be useful – if only as a source of ideas
– but since not all of them travel well I have deliberately
omitted mentioning them.

In addition to *Tenement* which I have described in detail,
available in revised form from Shelter Youth Education
Programme, 157 Waterloo Road, London SE1 8XF, the
following are easily obtainable:

Man in his environment
Widely used in schools and colleges, the kit consists of
a magnetized board which simulates a geographical area
containing forests, farms, rivers and a small urban development. The kit also contains ten 'projects' such as an Airport,
a Motorway and a Shopping Centre – each with its own
merits and drawbacks. The class is divided into teams
representing the various interests, including non-human,
and through argument and debate decides whether or not
to accept each project. The wisdom or otherwise of the
decisions is decided as the game progresses.

The Coca Cola Export Corporation, Atlantic House, Rockley Road, London W14 0DH.

The Spring Green motorway
A role-playing game for up to thirty. A simulation exercise on the advantages and disadvantages of building a motorway.

South Street hostel storm
A role-playing game for up to twenty-four. Some of the members of South Street Residents' Association feel very strongly about the Social Services Department's plan to locate a hostel for the mentally handicapped in South Street.

Greenham District Council
A role-playing game for eight to fifteen players. A simulation of a council meeting which aims to make the players more aware of how councils work and how decisions are made. The players take on the roles of councillors and discuss the seven items on the agenda, all concerned with the development of Greenham, and ranging from the shopping facilities to the provision of a site for Gypsies.

Spring Green motorway, South Street hostel storm and *Greenham District Council* are all available from The Advisory Centre, Community Service Volunteers, 237 Pentonville Road, London N1 9NJ (Tel. 01 278 6601).

In addition to these the CSV Publications List 1986 gives details of four other games and simulations.

Growing up
One of twelve units in the Schools Council General Studies Project, this contains a simulation with four case studies called *Control in school*.
The Publishing Manager, Longman Group Ltd., Resources Unit, 35 Tanner Row, York.

There is a considerable range of material published by the Longman Group, including history games, geography games, science games. Some of the material could be adapted for use in an English classroom.

169

Streets ahead
A game designed to help children face and understand the problems of city life.
Priority, Harrison Jones School, West Derby Street, Liverpool 7.

The poverty game
A game for eight to thirty players from thirteen years old upwards. A game demonstrating the vulnerability of people who are poor and who live in a difficult climate. Participants play the roles of subsistence farmers in the savannah region of Africa. Dice, chance and disease cards to a great extent control their fate.
Oxfam Education Department, 274 Banbury Road, Oxford OX2 7DZ

The aid committee game
A game for players of fourteen years old and upwards. Participants study one developing country and its problems and decide what projects they would help if they had the money. Oxfam.

The trade game
A game for players of fourteen years old and upwards. People play the parts of consumers, traders and retailers of a commodity such as bananas, sugar and coffee. Oxfam.

Nine graded simulations
This series, published by ILEA Media Resources Centre, aims to develop communication skills of all kinds; discussion, argument, reporting, interviewing and presenting a case, among others. The nine individual packs contain documentary information, controller's notes and notes for the participants.
The Media Resources Centre, ILEA, Highbury Station Road, Islington, London N1 1SB.

Passport
Originally designed for sixth-formers but used very successfully with twelve year olds. Designed by Keith Bradford, Community Relations Officer in Coventry, to give partici-

pants some sort of personal experience of the realities of racial discrimination . . . 'a kind of giant Monopoly set, with the dice loaded against the black players'.
Passport Production, C.R.C., 14 Spon Street, Coventry.

The Careers Research and Advisory Centre, besides marketing the Esso games – *The star river project, The Esso students' business game* and *The Esso service station game* – advertise *Work experience projects* – six units containing material for a classroom simulation on a variety of real work situations, and *Speedcop*, a careers simulation using techniques common to most family board games. It can be played by groups of all abilities and ages.
Hobsons Press (Cambridge) Ltd, Bateman Street, Cambridge CB2 1LZ.

BIBLIOGRAPHY

Drama and simulations

Adams, R. *Teaching Shakespeare*, Robert Royce, 1985.
Allen, J. *Drama in Schools*, Heinemann, 1981.
Bolton, G. *Drama as Education*, Longman, 1984.
Evans, T. *Drama in English Teaching*, Croom Helm, 1984.
Hayes, S. K. *Drama as a Second Language*, NEC, 1984.
Heathcote, D. *Drama as Context*, NATE, 1980.
Jones, K. *Simulations. A Handbook for Teachers*, Kogan Page, 1980.
Longley, C. (ed.) *Games and Simulations*, BBC, 1972.
McGregor, L. et al *Learning Through Drama*, Heinemann, 1977.
O'Brien, V. *Teaching Shakespeare*, Edward Arnold, 1982.
O'Neill, C. *Drama Guidelines*, Heinemann, 1981.
Pemberton-Billing, R.N. & Clegg, J.D. *Teaching Drama*, ULP, 1965.
Robinson, K. *Exploring Theatre and Education*, Heinemann, 1979.
Scher, A. & Verrall, C. *100+ Ideas for Drama*, Heinemann, 1975.
Stabler, T. *Drama in Primary Schools*, Macmillan, 1979.
Tansey, P. & Unwin, D. *Simulation and Gaming in Education*, Methuen, 1969.

Walford, R.A. *Simulation and Gaming in the Classroom*, Penguin, 1971.

5 Visual Stimuli

GORDON TAYLOR

The use of visual materials in English teaching has developed rapidly in recent years, because teachers have seen in them new and exciting ways of working. It's my belief that such developments have a valuable part to play in streamed, setted and mixed ability teaching.

The last situation makes exacting demands on us. We can no longer rely solely on conventional teaching methods and materials. Mixed ability emphasizes the needs of the individual, and in order to fulfil these needs we must have as wide a range of teaching strategies as possible; we need a diversity of approach, a wide range of activities, and flexible classroom organization. The use of visual materials helps us to achieve this. They extend the range of resources and activities available, and these activities lend themselves to a variety of ways of working: individual, group and class-based work are all possible.

Before considering the benefits of visual materials in more specific terms, I would like to make clear what material I'm referring to and what activities I have in mind. For the sake of clarity I've divided them into materials that the teacher brings into the classroom, and the practical activities that the students can undertake and which centre on the production of visual materials themselves.

First, then, the materials. Among these I include:

1 A variety of evocative objects that can be brought into the classroom, i.e. bones, seashore debris, food, masks, etc.

2 Still photographs, colour slides, postcards, reproductions of paintings covering a wide variety of subjects, i.e. people, scenes, shapes, animals etc.

3 16 mm film and video tapes including shorts, extracts, and full length feature films.

Secondly, the activities. Apart from the central activities of writing and discussion these include:

(a) Drama, painting, collage etc.

(b) Producing sequences of photographs or colour slides accompanied by cassette recordings or writing.

(c) Making 8 mm movie films or video tapes.

What part, then, can such materials and activities play in the mixed ability situation, and what specific benefits are there in terms of our students' English? They provide extremely powerful stimuli for a variety of tasks in the classroom. Their impact is immediate and creates a high motivation for learning. Above all, though, they are accessible to the whole range of ability.

An object brought into the classroom, for instance, is not an abstract system like the written word with rules and perhaps associations which may create problems for the less able. It can be touched, felt, smelt, tasted and closely examined, and such immediate sense responses generate a flow of language and anecdotes in students of all abilities. If these objects are a focus of a class or group discussion, this talk will form the basis for valuable processes and activities: students will be developing their language resources; they will be re-examining the familiar and the unfamiliar; they will be developing accuracy of observation. They can also be led to look at the language they use and see how it works as a tool to express their understanding, and as an object in itself with qualities such as sound, rhythm and 'feel'. They are, therefore, encouraged to make a deeper imaginative response to the world and have a new interest in the vitality of language that leads to accurate, fresh writing, drama, role play and story telling.

What I have outlined above about real objects is equally true of photographs, 16 mm film, and video. They offer us an immediate, concrete experience that is a familiar aspect of life and, as such, one that is readily acceptable to our students. Good photographs and films, like some poetry, crystallize moments of experience and offer us insights into our lives and the lives of others. They therefore give students the scope for deep and rewarding study. Groups of students can talk about them, argue about them, discover more and more about them, until they perhaps reach some conclusions, and ultimately learn something new from the experience they capture. Photographs present themselves as a whole to the imagination and don't have to be built up detail by detail, painstakingly in some cases, as in reading. That is not to say that reading isn't important but we have to build up confidence in some students by getting them to work with a more accessible medium. By doing so, we can encourage them to enter willingly into the processes of talking, writing and reading and stimulate them into producing something of value on which they can build. In short, visual materials such as these provide a bridge to the verbal and, for the less able, an essential bridge.

Photographs and films, of course, have an advantage over real objects in that they considerably widen the range of appropriate material. They can present people in a variety of situations and places, from cities to deserts. They offer us an opportunity to examine the relationships between people, and the way language is governed by such relationships. Much interesting work on story and dialogue is possible, therefore, both in writing and improvised drama. Students' responses are not, of course, limited to imaginative work. Photographs, films and paintings can sometimes present aspects of modern life more graphically than through other media. I'm thinking of scenes of pollution and the suffering of human beings which have powerfully stimulated discussion and discursive writing.

Photographs, films and paintings are art forms and as such have their own perspective on experience and their own way of expressing it. They have structure and tone which is peculiar to themselves in some respects but in others is comparable to some aspects of writing. I'm thinking here, for example, of the way the visual can focus on detail, of the relationship between various elements in a photograph, between the central figure and its background or other figures, and the force of juxtaposition and contrast; equally, the idea of sequence in a film, the building up to a particular climax. Exploring these with students, I've found, has helped them to become aware of techniques they can use to add power to their writing and to understand the writing process more consciously. On one level, this has simply consisted in exploring the amount of detail that goes to make up a scene, a person and an incident. On another level, the medium's power of suggesting meaning without actually stating anything has allowed us to explore how detail can be selected to express character, or create a particular mood, and from there to move on to the qualities of language which heighten the effect. Similarly, we've explored the way the relationship between people can be suggested through their physical position and mannerisms, the way mood can be suggested by background and the enormous power that comes from simply placing one picture next to another and, by extension, one idea next to another. The narrative sequence of film has enabled us to explore what makes an effective sequence, why one scene is better next to another, and the idea of speed in building up to a climax. Even a form such as the ballad can be powerfully illuminated by seeing the film *Ballad of Crowfoot*. This may sound a little beyond the range of some students in a mixed ability group, and if we were dealing with such techniques without the use of photographs and film, it could be. However, given suitable concrete examples in visual materials, such discussions become not only possible, but fruitful.

Consideration of technique in film is, of course, valuable in itself. Film is a powerful medium and the discussion of its techniques provides a basis for discrimination. Moreover, I've found comments on the effectiveness or otherwise of particular techniques have been spontaneously offered by students of all levels of ability which has led me to believe that we shouldn't underestimate their ability to understand what appear to us to be sophisticated ideas.

I've made some comment above on the way photographs and films are related to writing. It doesn't end with the students' own writing, however. Through the visual we can introduce a particular area of experience, and provide a framework of discussion and writing that will enable students to understand more clearly what professional writers are saying. For instance, I have used the film *Dream of Wild Horses* to precede a reading of Ted Hughes' enigmatic poem *A Dream of Horses*. Not that seeing the film is the only way of dealing with such a poem, but seeing the film and discussing it allows us to feel that the introduction of such a poem would not be out of place in a wide ability situation. Even the weak reader will find such difficult material more accessible. Following literature with film or photographs on a similar theme is equally valid.

Practical activities, such as making films and slide sequences, are also of great benefit. On the one hand students are learning the purely technical processes involved in taking a photograph, from the need to focus, to the complexities of continuity and editing. All this again provides some basis for reasoned discrimination. More important, these activities are a stimulating framework within which talking, writing and drama can take place.

The idea of making a film or taking photographs is usually sufficient to arouse interest in the most apathetic student. It provides an alternative to the pen as a means of responding and perhaps a more congenial one; not so flexible, perhaps, but at least one that isn't associated with failure. Students write stories and convert them into scripts. This, in itself, provides valuable opportunities for structured group work in which all can participate. Students will need to use language to cooperate and organize themselves, whether it be simply ordering a sequence of events, writing a story, or converting it into a script. They will be forming concepts of structure in this process as the need arises to decide which event comes where, how much emphasis needs to be put on a particular event, which dwelt on, etc.

I've talked here in terms of making films from scratch,

but this isn't the only way of working. Literature can provide the starting point for such activities, though these activities in themselves are a means of re-examining that literature and expressing a response to it. This applies as much to the simpler process of making a collage or drawing, as to the more complex processes of making animated cartoons, slide/tape sequences, or films using actors. Students involved in this have to consider the meaning of the original. This means understanding the text and its implications. For instance, anyone working on the opening scene from *Of Mice and Men* would first of all have to examine the text to find out what happened and where it happened. Then, since it is an opening, they would need to consider how to establish the sense of place and the character in visual terms. This means a return to the text to examine its mood, to come to some understanding of the characters of Lennie and George and their relationship. Then they will have to make an attempt to translate these into visual terms through camera position, angle, movement and so on. The ending of the novel presents similar problems; you cannot make an attempt to translate it into visual terms without fully understanding its meaning and implications and that means a close examination of the text.

These, then, are the reasons why I feel visual materials can play an important part in mixed ability teaching. I would like, at this point, to emphasize that this is only a part of English teaching and one that must take its place alongside others of equal importance. Visual materials have their place, and provided they are used with specific objectives in mind, rather than a means of occupying time or providing entertainment, can be of real benefit to English teachers and students.

Objects

The range of objects I've found useful in teaching at all ages is very wide. Some I've used because, in themselves, they are worthy of close examination; some because they relate directly to students' experience; others because they are particularly evocative. Ideally, they should combine all three aspects.

Occasionally I've used objects to stimulate accurate and fresh descriptive writing. For instance, I ask students to bring in, or I provide them with, oranges, apples, or some seasonal fruit, and explore their shape and texture and find words that describe their feel, taste, smell, etc. We make a collection of these words and discuss their merits in terms of appropriateness and accuracy. In this situation, I concentrate the initial reaction on a personal response and collection of words and phrases by individuals or pairs of students. But some items, when a variety of objects is under scrutiny (autumn debris, for instance), can be dealt with in groups of five or six students, exchanging words or phrases amongst themselves and compiling a group list. The discussion that follows the initial reaction often includes comparisons which arise spontaneously and their merit as a means of self expression has formed the basis of further class or group discussion, as have sound or other word qualities. One of the responses to this initial work is personal writing in either free verse or prose, though it need not necessarily be confined to these. Students with severe writing difficulties may feel more at ease and be more encouraged to produce a fluent response using a tape recorder, and perhaps later making a transcript of the tape, or having it made for them by another student or the teacher in the way that Richard Mills illustrates in chapter one. Alternatively, some students could make a display of the objects, if this is appropriate, with written information. This work needn't be confined to what can be brought into the classroom. Visits either simply to the school grounds or the local park, museum or other places of interest can provide a great deal of accurate observation to work on.

In some instances, objects stimulate an exploration of personal experience. This can be deliberate as when students and I have brought in objects of personal value and have in turn explained what value they have for us and why. This offers an insight into each other and mutual understanding in the group can be built up. The discussion can move out to a consideration of other personal possessions, people's rooms, and what a person's individual possessions and the way they live tell us about them. This in turn can lead to writing about personal possessions and rooms, and later to groups of students examining writing which deals with this aspect of experience such as extracts from Muriel Spark's *You Should Have Seen the Mess* and Philip Larkin's *Mr Bleaney*. Other groups have written autobiographies, and others have seen short films such as *The Visit* or *Paul Tomkowicz*. They consider the lives of these people and answer such questions as: 'What do we learn about these people from the way they live?' and 'What do they value?'

In other circumstances, objects spontaneously generate discussion of personal experience as an off-shoot of other activities. Apples, for instance, apart from being useful in descriptive writing as outlined above, have sparked off talk of 'scrumping', and through anecdotes to related areas of experience such as fear, daring and heroes. Following this, groups have discussed the section in Stan Barstow's *Joby* where Joby is caught shoplifting (a passage that seems popular with Judith Atkinson, I notice). Questions like: 'Why does Joby steal?' and 'Could either Gus, Joby or the shopkeeper be described as heroes?' have provided small group discussion with some direction. Similarly an examination of bones and skulls has led to a discussion of dead animals that students have found, and pets they have lost, and later to an examination of Ted Hughes' *View of a Pig* and Seamus Heaney's *The Early Purges*.

Alternatively, I have found concentration on the shape, texture and colour of objects has been a powerful stimulus to the imagination of students. Bones or driftwood are useful for this, as are bottled biological 'horrors'. The latter have proved particularly powerful in stimulating work on fear or monsters. The initial reaction can be a class sharing their personal fears if the right atmosphere making mutual confidences possible exists. Or the class can work in groups and individually on a variety of tasks: drawing pictures of monsters and writing descriptions of them; reading poems like *Beowulf* or short stories like Ray Bradbury's *One Who Waits* and tape recording them with suitable sound effects; or writing similar stories and plays of their own and tape recording them; making lists of reasons for and against a belief in the existence of life on other planets and presenting the evidence with conclusions to the rest of the class, and perhaps writing essays on the subject. Any one or all of these options could be suitable follow-up work to the original stimulus.

I have listed below objects that I've found useful which can be treated in the ways I've suggested:

Driftwood
Spring buds and leaves
Pets
Live laboratory animals
Items of personal value to
  students
Fossils
Masks
African or Eastern curios
Skulls and bones
Autumn leaves and twigs
Bottled biological
  specimens
Seasonal fruit
Scientific or medical
  instruments

Rocks and coloured stones
Ornaments
Flowers
Insects
Stuffed animals
Shells
Old farm implements e.g.
  scythes
Hunting traps
Brass rubbings
Old books e.g. family Bibles
Ships in bottles
Oddly shaped coloured
  bottles
Sweets

Photographs and colour slides

Photographs on a wide variety of subjects are now a common feature of many anthologies of prose and poetry. Such photographs often include reproductions of paintings which are equally useful to the English teacher. Some publishers are also producing colour slides to accompany their printed materials though these are still comparatively rare. You can, of course, produce slides yourself without too much difficulty, and then you're able to include features of local life and the local environment, as well as particular subjects and treatments of subjects which may not otherwise be available.

Photographs and colour slides can be used as a stimulus in a way similar to objects. They can generate exploration and experience, stimulate the imagination, as well as provide discussion of language itself. For instance, good still photographs or reproductions of paintings, or scenes such as building sites, city centres, and children, and tramps provide an excellent stimulus for discussion, and personal and descriptive writing. If you are dealing with the theme of childhood, for instance, one group could examine some of the excellent photographs of children that are available. A series of questions can direct their attention to the essential qualities of childhood that are revealed in the photograph. After the discussion, various tasks can be attempted in groups or as individuals: imaginative writing based on the picture, lists of children's games with rules, childhood memories, autobiographies, descriptions of younger brothers or sisters, the examination of Dylan Thomas's short stories and poems, writing children's short stories etc. The photographs need not always be provided by the teacher. I have had many successful discussions on people and places based on photographs of students' relatives and places they have visited.

Colour slides provide an interesting variation on stills. A series of slides on a particular theme backed by appropriate music and readings can create a powerful impact. A series of slides of coastal scenery backed by Debussy's *La Mer*, for instance, can open up this whole area in an original way. As a starter to a theme it's surprising how effective slides taken with a simple camera can be. A department interested in this work will, of course, build up its own collection of slides, together with the appropriate tapes. Photographs can be used to focus on techniques of writing and explore some of the ways we can make language work for us. I have indicated some of the possibilities here in the opening section, and I shall now elaborate on these, and provide some specific examples.

Accurate observation

Students' writing can lack detail because they have not been able to visualize clearly what they are describing. Concentration on individual photographs or slides can increase their powers of observation so that they eventually develop an 'inner eye' and can imagine more fully when no visual stimuli are present.

To this end, small groups of students closely examine photographs of people or places, picking out all the details and as a group build up a word picture of them. Faces are particularly good for this, being followed by word portraits or, if appropriate, wanted posters.

You can go on to look at the way *selecting* details can create a particular effect, for instance the way a person's character and way of life can be suggested through concentrating on details of appearance. Again, concentration on photographs of people is valuable here. Imagine a group has a picture of an old man rummaging through a dustbin in an alley of a large city. He's untidy, unshaven and wears old clothes. The group could be asked:

1   What do you learn about this man and his way of life from the picture?
2   Pick out particular details that support your ideas.

Each group then reports back to the class and selected detail is discussed. Students can go on to speculate on the lives of people in various pictures, where they live, their jobs, and build up case histories, stories, diaries, or monologues.

Similarly, work can be done on examining the mood of a particular photograph. Pictures of bleak landscapes or bright Spring mornings can be studied with the object of choosing detail that establishes their mood or atmosphere. Much interesting work can be done on Haiku here, with groups examining the way Haiku poets choose detail to create a word picture or establish a mood. The students can then go on to write their own from appropriate photographs.

None of this, of course, is inseparable from the language used to express this detail, and I've found examining this can be valuable. Students consider the way we express our attitudes towards people or things not only by the *detail* we choose to describe, but by the language we use. For example, they could consider the implications of words like:

fat, well-built, tubby, greasy, sallow, pale, florid etc. as they examine specific photographs of people.

Likewise, students can examine the mood of advertising photographs and how the advertisement language itself describes the mood or reinforces it. This work can serve as an introduction to the language of persuasion.

As I suggested in the opening section, people reveal their relationships by their physical positions and mannerisms. Individual photographs can generate discussion of this, but so too can film shorts and extracts. For instance, there is an extract from *A Kind of Loving* which shows Victor and Ingrid in a cafe. Victor is obviously not interested in Ingrid and what she is saying; this is not only suggested by the fact that he doesn't speak or listen to her, but also by his slouched position and his turning away from her, to examine other couples in the cafe. Ingrid, on the other hand, is bent towards him, eager to attract his attention and tell him her news. A great deal can be got out of simply examining this aspect of the visual image, and seeing that we can add details like this to descriptive writing.

Sequence

Series of photographs that can be put together to form stories can offer work on narrative and sequence. These consist of between six and ten photographs, which can be made with cut-outs from magazines, or photographs you have taken yourself, or packs of such series which can be purchased. Students can build up narrative sequences by simply putting the photographs into an order and writing the story they tell. The better series will allow for a variety of arrangements within a specific sequence by the judicious choice of photographs. Students who have produced different stories from the same sequence can compare each other's work and discuss why they chose their particular sequence.

Similar work is possible with film. Students can consider the effectiveness of the sequencing of a film. Take for example *Incident at Owl Creek* which is about a man who is hanged in the American Civil War. We see him escaping but it is not until the end of the film that we realize this was imaginary – his last living thoughts. The question that can be discussed is how effective is this sequence of shots. *The Boy Next Door* is a film about two boys exploring an empty house. It builds up to a climax with the caretaker frightening them away. Again, the class can explore how effective the film is in building up to this climax. Following discussions like these, classes can write their own stories with a twist or a climax, or perhaps examine other stories with these qualities.

The force of juxtaposition and contrast can be illustrated by putting two still photographs together; for instance, a new car next to a scrap heap. A film that uses this technique particularly effectively is *Very Nice, Very Nice*, made entirely of stills which juxtapose many images of modern society. Literature which explores contrasts, like Ted Hughes' *Pike* or *To Paint a Water Lily* can be usefully discussed here.

Photographs and abstract paintings which do not depict real scenes or people can be used to evoke personal imaginative writing without the help of guidance from the teacher, apart from: 'Let the shape work on your imagination and write freely from your thoughts'. The subject need not necessarily be abstract, but might simply explore the symmetry and beauty of the shapes of natural objects. In this case they can provide the basis for work on concrete poems, or shape poems which explore the relationship between shape and word.

Apart from leading to writing, photographs, or films for that matter, can also be the stimuli for role play and work on dialogue. Here I've chosen photographs that simply show interesting places, such as an old house, a cave, or one depicting a mysterious or interesting object, or photographs that show a particular relationship between people, or that highlight a dramatic situation. In the case of the places or objects, small groups of students dramatize an incident in the place or make up a play centred around the object. In the case of photographs of people, the possibilities are wider. Apart from enacting the scene that is suggested by the photograph, for example an argument, or a thief discovered, the group can examine how people in different social situations might talk. Does the boy in the photograph speaking to his teacher express himself in the same way when he's talking to his friends? Students can try out these differences in role play.

I have dealt in general here with photographs and slides that the teacher can provide for the students. However, a great deal of interesting work can be done with groups of students making their own photographs and slides. The following are some suggestions:

1 A group of students working on a theme can produce a series of slides on the theme and a tape recording of appropriate music and readings of poetry and prose that they have chosen (see the earlier suggestion on coastal scenery).

2 A story written by students or a suitable story or part of a story they have read can be illustrated by slides they have taken of themselves acting it out. The finished product is shown with the story as a tape recorded background. An alternative to this is to use a polaroid camera, which has the advantage of instant results. The photographs are mounted with the story either as a wall display or as a book. Poetry that students have written can also be illustrated by suitable photographs, thus producing their own poetry cards.

3 Visits that might be part of a theme in progress can be recorded either by slides or stills. Still photographs can be mounted with an account of what happened, and slides can be shown with a tape recorded commentary. Individual photographs can also be used as the stimulus for writing.

4 Students can make a documentary on a subject connected with a theme using slides and tape recordings of music, songs, poetry and interviews. Subjects such as the impact on an area of a motorway, or first-year impressions of school provide good material for these activities (See Appendix Three).

5 A series of slides as advertisements with a tape recording of music and advertising language, or photographs and written accounts, are also possible. I have had some success here with students advertising the school under

such headings as: 'Send your child to . . . school – the chance of a lifetime', or advertising the local area: 'Visit . . . , the world's most fascinating place!'

Film

The possibilities created by the use of film in English teaching are great, whether you are dealing with full length feature films or shorts and extracts. Their accessibility makes them a powerful tool for work with mixed ability classes and they are flexible enough to be used with one class or several classes together.

Anyone wishing to use films will soon realize that they create the need for careful planning. You will need a selection of distributors' catalogues from whom you can hire suitable films. Films need to be ordered one or two months in advance and, if you are working thematically, programmes of work have to be planned with this in mind and sometimes adjusted to fit in with their arrival. You also should be sure a room with blackout and screen is available, as well as a projector in working order. This may seem daunting, but once your department has established a routine the administrative details pose no real problem. I have included as an appendix a list of films that I have found useful.

This should be referred to for further details of films mentioned below. Having ordered and received the film there are many possible ways of using them. I offer here some of the more important of these.

1 Some films are particularly useful as a one-off experience as a stimulus for imaginative writing. You can show *A Dream of Wild Horses* or *Snow* to a mixed ability class and simply ask them to write an individual response to it in any form they wish. On the other hand, you can structure the work in a way similar to that outlined in the section on still photographs.

2 Having seen the film, the group (it could be a class or several classes) breaks up into small groups for

discussion of their initial response. These groups could operate alone, or with staff, or students in training. The discussions could be free or structured by questions intended to focus attention on important aspects of the film or related personal experience. Some of these discussions could be taped for further consideration later. Students could then pursue one of a variety of activities arising from the film: different types of writing – personal, stories, plays etc; role play; making collages or posters to advertise the film. This could follow immediately after the discussion or after a re-run of the film where this has been planned.

3   Much can be done by using poems and written extracts which are on the same theme as the film. The approach outlined in the previous section could be followed by examination of related literature in subsequent English lessons. Such literature can help to illuminate the key themes of the film from a different angle. Alternatively, the viewing of the film and the initial work can be used as a means of illuminating literature or related themes. For example, *I Think They Call Him John* could lead into a study of Philip Larkin's *Mr Bleaney* and other literature on the theme of people who are alone. In this way the whole subject of people can be set in motion. The film *Snow* can be followed by Auden's *Night Mail* and work on onomatopeia, rhythm and alliteration can be begun. *Morning on the Lièvre* could lead into Haiku or other writing expressing mood. A study of related literature could, of course, precede the film. Individual pieces can be studied and related to each other and their common theme. By this means the students' attention is directed to certain significant issues. They then watch the film approaching it via this background of initial discussion of written material. Their focus has been sharpened by the time they reach the film itself. The movement of a series of lessons may be:

students' real experience → film → support material

or any one of the other five permutations of this

formula, providing that the permutation chosen is appropriate for the film. For example, *Incident at Owl Creek* should be shown without preliminary discussion.

4   If the class is working on a particular theme or topic they will have read or studied various pieces of prose and poetry, discussed visual material, listened to tape recordings and records, perhaps made a visit or had a visiting speaker. They can now go through all the stages of planning to make a film and this activity either culminates in actually making this film or it stops just before the last stage. At this point a film on the same subject, which the teacher had already planned for, is hired and, after seeing it, students discuss the professional film in relation to the one they might have made. Each film may be measured against the other in terms of content, attitude and visual impact. With some projectors and many video recorders it is possible to stop the film in order to concentrate attention for a few moments on a particular frame.

5   Sometimes the sound track of the film can be tape recorded for later consideration, provided you have made the appropriate arrangements. This would be, perhaps, particularly relevant where the support material contains dialogue, or where work on the music and sound effects of the film might be relevant.

Making a film

Film making with students has all the glamour of the professional world, reinforced by the excitement of using the equipment. It is therefore taken up with much enthusiasm by the majority of students. It has, of course, its own problems. It demands reasonably good lighting conditions which limit you in general to outdoor subjects unless you can arrange sophisticated lighting. There is also a time lag between shooting the film and getting it developed. Most classes, however, are prepared to accept this as inevitable, and continue with other work while they are waiting. Some people may be put off by the apparent need for some kind of photographic expertise, but not a great deal is required as most cameras these days are fully automatic. Though we are obviously concerned with producing a film that is reasonably successful, what is important are the processes that have gone into the making of the film, rather than the end product. Film work, like other visual materials, can lend itself to small group work or whole-class involvement depending on the subject and its treatment. Whole-class work can present problems of involving everyone, unless the subject uses crowds of people for long periods of time. However, whether working with a small group or the whole class, I have found the following sequence a useful guide for organizing the work:

1 Each member of the group writes a story, one of which will be chosen by them as a basis for the film. Some of those chosen will sometimes be rather ambitious and you will need tactfully to suggest some alterations. Alternatively, literature can form the basis of the film.
2 The group then needs to consider the problems they are likely to encounter in making the film: the location, costume, camera positions, etc. I favour here the group producing a shooting script. This is a writing of the script with notes on matters such as length of shot, camera angle etc. Again one is not looking for a professional product, merely encouraging the group to consider the problems they will meet when they begin shooting.
3 The actual making of the film can now begin. Without doubt this is best done in one session, though this is not always possible and it is surprising how enthusiasm can be maintained. I favour students taking it in turns to operate the camera and a group responsibility for directing, though it is possible to delegate these jobs to individuals.

The actual subjects for the films are as varied as those outlined for use with photographs and slides: the documentary, students' original stories, plays, short stories and poems, visits and advertisements – all can be equally rewarding subjects for films. I've made films from students' ideas and from literature with whole classes. One based on students' ideas was with a group of third years and was about a delicate old man who was set upon by a gang of ruffians. The old man, however, had a wonder pill which, true to the tradition of such films, gave him immense strength and enabled him to rout the ruffians. The film ended with him walking into the setting sun surrounded by an admiring group of girls, the one-time girl friends of his attackers. The finished product was no technical masterpiece, but it brought this group together in a joint venture that had tremendous vitality.

Another film I made, this time based on literature, was with a second-year group. We used *The Weirdstone of Brisingamen* by Alan Garner. They first worked to adapt the story which involved closely examining the original and considerably abridging it for their own purposes. The film required exotic costumes and masks, some of which we got from the school costume cupboard, others the students made themselves. We used special effects to make objects appear and disappear and to allow the forces of evil to materialize. Again, the important feature of the venture was the renewed sense of purpose within the group, and the fact that talking and writing became a natural and necessary part of the work.

Animated cartoons

A very different approach to film making is that offered by animated cartoons. There are two basic approaches:

1   One method uses two dimensional cut-outs. These are placed on a flat surface and filmed from above. The figures and settings can be drawn and painted by the students or cut out from magazines. Figures can be articulated by joining the limbs to the body with pins, which saves the necessity of having to draw separate figures for each movement. Special effects are easily achieved with these: they can fly or sink, appear or disappear.

2   The other method uses three dimensional figures (made from plasticine, for example) or manufactured

toys. Again the figures and settings can be made by the students. Special effects are more difficult here as the figures are subject to the laws of gravity.

The basic principle of animation is the same in both cases. Each movement in the cartoon picture must be filmed separately. This is done with the camera on single exposure setting and allowing between four to eight shots per part of a movement, depending on the speed of the action. This is best illustrated for students by drawing a series of stick men on flexible cards so that when they are flicked the figure executes a movement. In order to reinforce this idea, students then make their own.

All this may sound rather complicated, but the techniques are easily mastered, and animations have certain advantages over conventional film making. Stories and scripts which are unsuitable for conventional films can be made into animations. Stories with exotic settings and characters requiring special effects, like costume and the ability to fly, are possible. You don't even have to be bound by conventional ideas of character and plot; films can explore movement of patterns. Animated cartoons also solve the problem of having to film outside, since they can be filmed indoors using an angle poised light. They don't require a great deal of space and acting ability, of course, is not a consideration.

I've found these cartoons work best with small groups, either as one activity amongst many, or when the whole class has divided into groups for a cartoon-making session. When I was working on the theme of monsters, the following ideas cropped up. Some people centred on monsters from outer space who landed on earth and ate the entire population of the world and then the earth itself, before they exploded; others created much nicer monsters, but they were destroyed by evil men; some based their film on the story of Frankenstein. On a more abstract plane, small yellow blobs escaped from mysterious packets and dropped into inkwells then climbed out, leaving a trail of footprints behind; balls of plasticine rolled around forming themselves into strange shapes and doing untold damage until they were trodden on by a boot which suddenly appeared from nowhere; mysterious houses had faces which appeared and disappeared at their windows until the houses collapsed in a heap, and so on.

Both animations and conventional films provide further work for students in the form of tape recorded speech, sound effects, and music to accompany them. Students can best work on this by using an editor. This is a simple machine with a small screen which allows you to inspect the film without the need for blackout and can easily find appropriate points for cutting and deciding where sound effects should be. This work can be slow and I've found it best completed as an out-of-class activity for a group of enthusiasts.

These, then, are some of the possibilities open to you when working with visual materials. In order to take full advantage of them a department needs to build up a large stock of objects, photographs, photo essays, series of slides, poem cards, useful films etc, and make them easily available to staff and students. They perhaps flourish best as part of a workshop approach, where students can move easily between the visual and the literary, benefiting from what each has to offer their developing language potential.

APPENDIX I

Addresses of film and video distributors

Audio & Video Ltd, 48 Charlotte Street, London W1P LX. Tel. 01 580 7161.

BBC Television Enterprises Film Hire Department, Woodston House, Oundle Road, Peterborough PE2 9PZ. Tel. 0733 52257.

BFI, 127 Charing Cross Road, London WC2 0EA. Tel. 01 437 4355.

BFI Film and Video Library, 9 Chapone Place, Dean Street, London W1V 6AA. Tel. 01 437 4355.

Canada High Commissioner's Office, Canada House, Trafalgar Square, London SW17 JBG. Tel. 01 930 9741.

Canadian Government Travel Film Library, 1 Grosvenor Square, London W1X 0AB. Tel. 01 629 9492.

Central Film Library, Government Building, Bromyard Avenue, Acton, London W3 7JB. Tel. 01 743 5555.

Columbia-EMI-Warner Distributors, 135 Wardour Street, London W1V 4AP. Tel. 01 434 1731.

Concord Films Council, 201 Felixstowe Road, Ipswich, Suffolk IP3 9BF. Tel. 0437 76012.

Connoisseur Films Ltd, 167 Oxford Street, London W1R 2DX. Tel. 01 734 6555.

Contemporary Films Ltd, 55 Greek Street, London W1V 6DB. Tel. 01 734 4901.

Darvill Associates Ltd, 290 Chartridge Lane, Chesham, Bucks. Tel. 0494 3643.

Educational & Television Films, 2 Doughty Street, London WC1N 2PJ. Tel. 01 405 0395.

Film Distributors Associated, Building 9, GEC Estate, East Lane, Wembley, Middlesex HA9 7QB. Tel. 01 908 2366.

Gateway Educational Media, Waverley Road, Yate, Bristol BS17 5RB. Tel. 0454 316774.

Guild Sound & Vision Ltd, 6 Royce Road, Peterborough PE1 5YB. Tel 0733 315315.

Harris Films Ltd, Glenbuck House, Glenbuck Road, Surbiton, Surrey RT6 6BT. Tel. 01 399 0022.

ITV Education Secretariat, Knighton House, 52–66 Mortimer Street, London W1N 8AN. Tel. 01 636 6866.

National Audio-Visual Aids Library, Paxton Place, Gipsy Road, London SE27 9SR. Tel. 01 670 4247.

National Film Board of Canada, 1 Grosvenor Square, London W1X 0AB. Tel. 01 629 9492.

Rank Film Library, PO Box 20, Great West Road, Brentford, Middlesex TW8 9HR. Tel. 01 568 9222.

Scottish Central Film Library, Dowanhill, 74 Victoria Crescent Road, Glasgow G12 9JN. Tel. 041 334 9314.

United International Pictures, Mortimer House, 37–41 Mortimer Street, London W1. Tel. 01 636 1655.

VCL Video Services, 58 Parker Street, London WC2. Tel. 01 405 3732.

Video Arts, 2nd Floor, Dumbarton House, 68 Oxford Street, London W1N 9LA. Tel. 01 637 7288.

Videospace Ltd, 32 Eveline Road, Mitcham, Surrey CR4 3LE. Tel. 01 648 2480.

Videoview London Ltd, 68/70 Wardour Street, London W1V 3HP. Tel. 01 437 1333.

Vintage Television Ltd, Video City, Dunkirk, Halifax, West Yorkshire. Tel. 0422 40147.

Viscom Ltd, Parkhall Road Trading Estate, London SE21 8EL. Tel. 01 761 3035.

Visual Programme Systems Ltd, 21 Great Titchfield Street, London W1. Tel. 01 573 2940.

APPENDIX II

Films and video clips

Video clips used to promote pop songs are well worth exploring with students. Here are some questions which might be asked.

a) What makes a video clip worth watching? Which have you seen recently and what was special about them?

b) What images are repeated in the clips? What is the purpose of using these images frequently? What effect do they have on you?

c) Do you think it is easier to match the music to the visuals or the visuals to the music?

d) What are some of the common themes and appeals in video clips?

e) What is the purpose of making such a clip? How much does it cost to make one? How do bands get their clips shown?

f) Which style of clip do you prefer – one that relates lyrics and images together or where lyrics and images are unrelated?

g) Some video clips have messages about society. What are some that do, and what are those messages? Do you prefer those with messages or without?

h) Do you want to explore further the relationship between a song and a set of visual images? If you do, select a song and a montage of images (using magazines, photographs, drawings, etc) which do *not* fit that song. Other students design a montage and select a song to suit it. When both montages are complete, discuss the selected images. In what ways are they appropriate/inappropriate? What messages come across from the montages? Is the composition pleasing and effective?

Films which may be confidently used include the following:

1 *The Boy Next Door* (Canada House), *The Summer We Moved to Elm Street* (Canada), *Friends for Life* (Contemporary).
   Themes: childhood, fear, adventure. 11–12 years

2 *Un Enfant Un Pays* (Canada); *The Dreamer* (Concord).
   Themes: fantasy, growing up. 11–12 years

3 *Johnny* (Contemporary).
   Themes: outsider, home and family, games.
   11–12 years

4 *Snow* (British Transport), *Snow* (BFI), *Night Mail* (Central).
   Themes: winter, travel. 11–13 years

5 *One Potato, Two Potato* (BFI), *Buckets and Spades and Hand Grenades* (Concord).
   Themes: children's games, growing up, play.
   11–16 years

6 *Sunday Lark* (Contemporary), *Sandcastles* (Contemporary), *The Key* (Contemporary), *Les Jojos* (Connoisseur).
   Themes: humour, childhood, machines.
   11–15 years

7 *Terminus* (British Transport), *Everyday Occurrence* (Contemporary), *Multiple Man* (Contemporary).
   Themes: people, loneliness, getting lost.
   11–16 years

8 *The Red Balloon* (Connoisseur), *Ballon Vole* (Connoisseur).
   Themes: childhood, allegory. 11–16 years

9 *Morning on the Lièvre* (Canada), *Errigal* (Contem-

porary), *One by One* (Contemporary), *November* (Canada).

Theme: autumn/winter/nature – but more appropriately used as a stimulus for descriptive writing.

12–13 years

10 *A Dream of Wild Horses* (Connoisseur), *Araby* (Contemporary), *The Wild Stallion* (Connoisseur).

Theme: power and savagery in nature.

13–15 years

11 *La Première Nuit* (Contemporary), *Les Mistons* (Visual Programme Systems).

Themes: outsider, loneliness, sexual attraction, growing up.   13–16 years

12 *The Visit* (Contemporary). *Bleak Moments* (Contemporary).

Themes: old age, personal relationships.

14–15 years

13 *I Think They Call Him John* (Contemporary), *The Golden Age* (Concord), *Legault's Place* (Concord), *Application* (Concord).

Themes: old age, loneliness.   14–16 years

14 *Have I told You Lately That I Love You?* (Contemporary), *The Commuter* (Contemporary), *Little Man, Big City* (Concord), *Modern Times* (Davrill Associates).

Themes: personal relationships (lack of), modern life, machines.   14–16 years

15 *Now* (Contemporary), *Sunday* (Contemporary), *Now is the Time* (Concord), *Ivanhoe Donaldson* (Concord).

Themes: racial conflict, law and order, outsider.

14–16 years

16 *Very Nice, Very Nice* (Concord), *Tilt* (Concord).

Themes: modern life, people, communication.

14–16 years

17 *Young Offenders* (BFI), *Men in Prison* (BFI), *Women in Prison* (BFI), *Women in Prison* (Concord), *Prison Officer* (Central), *A Good and Useful Life?* (Concord).

Themes: crime and punishment, the rebel and outsider.   14–16 years

18 *Incident at Owl Creek* (Connoisseur), *Falls the Shadow* (Contemporary).
Themes: death, war, capital punishment, time.
14–16 years

19 *Culloden* (BFI), *The War Game* (BFI), *Hotel des Invalides* (BFI).
Theme: war.   14–16 years

20 *Phoebe* (Concord), *Il Posto* (BFI), *Family* (BBC), *Who is Sylvia?* (Central), *Let's Have a Party* (Contemporary).
Themes: family/personal relationships, communication.   14–16 years

21 *Children of Hiroshima* (Contemporary), *Children of the Ashes* (Concord), *Hiroshima. Nagasaki: August 1945* (Concord).
Theme: war   15–16 years

22 *Paul Tomkowicz* (BFI), *The Gentle Corsican* (Contemporary), *Work* (BBC).
Themes: people, work.   15–16 years

APPENDIX III

Tape-slide sequence

[This appendix is the work of Malcolm Henderson, formerly of Moreton School, Wolverhampton].

English teaching concentrates on the explanation of relationships between people rather than on the relationship between people and their environments. There seems to be a need to look at the ways that environments affect people socially. Children need to ask questions: Who am I? Why am I like I am? Whom do I relate to? How am I affected by my environment?

One way of answering these questions is by producing a tape-slide sequence. In the particular sequence we used, two boys of low ability chose to illustrate an aspect of their environment. They live on an estate built during the 1930s where conditions are poor.

1 They wanted to depict life on an estate.

2   They focused on one aspect – vandalism (their choice).
3   They needed to identify sources of information and opinion on the problem.
4   They decided to talk to householders, community workers, local authority officers and the police.

The Task
1   Prepare a shooting script for slides.
2   Organize taped interviews.
3   Take photographs.
4   Link photographs with tape with commentary.
5   Be aware of audience.
6   Achieve desired effect.

Language
1   Talk to purpose, to define the task, specify details, plan strategies.
2   Experience in formal language situations – contacting people, reading material, research.
3   Formulate questions, how to ask them, how to respond.

Meaning
1   Learning relationship between verbal and non-verbal material.
2   Sorting and organizing the taped extracts and slides.
3   Context of speaking and writing.

Other Benefits of the Exercise
1   Development of social skills in dealing with a variety of people.
2   Precise thinking.
3   Recognition of the value of their work.
4   Awareness of the complexity of the community.

Some idea of the value of the work and the degree of involvement of the two boys can be gained by reading the transcript which now follows. This project, which was offered as a part of their exam assessment, helped the boys to achieve an overall Grade 5.

Vandalism on the Scotlands Estate

1, 2, 3   (Sound of crashing glass.)

4   Vandalism is a major problem in Britain. It cost the rate payers £100,000 to repair the damage. Vandalism can cost lives too.

5   The Scotlands Estate in Wolverhampton is already designated an area of social priority.

6   These photographs show you the area. It has many problems.

7   Vandalism is a serious one.

8   We asked several people in the community to tell us how they see the problem. Pauline Long at the Scotlands Advice Centre told us, 'Well we've got quite a lot of vandalism but it mainly happens where properties are left empty for a long time. The housing department seems to have some trouble letting the property around here.'

9   The houses are left vacant for long periods of time and then kids seem to get in and smash them up.

10   There's a lot of broken windows, a lot of vandalism to doors and so on.

11   A local resident, Tom Huntington, supported this view. Vandalism, he said, was a major problem.

12   'The main problem in the area at the moment is vandalism. We've got a lot of kids on the night who have got nothing, well, they say they've got nothing to do. They go round breaking into empty houses. That's the cause of the main problem.'

14   We felt that the causes of vandalism might have something to do with the fact that on the estate about 70 houses like these are empty.

15   So we went down to the local community architect pictured here, whose office is in the centre of the area to ask him about the houses.

What happens when the houses are left empty with nobody in them for a long while? As you probably know, they tend to get vandalized.

16   Generally windows get broken, not always, but most houses get their windows broken and sometimes more severe vandalism as well.

17 Pipe work and copper tanks and things ripped out and in some cases worse again.

18 How much will it cost to repair a vandalized house?

19 Obviously it depends on what damage is actually done. It can be anything from about a hundred pounds up to thousands of pounds which was the case at number 97 Emerson Road which was reported in the paper, badly vandalized twice after it had been repaired.

20 The houses are empty because they are being allowed to deteriorate.

21 Tom told us: 'We're trying to get people in the area to take a pride in the area.'

22 We live on the estate and there is little to take pride in. The houses as you can see here are old pre-war, detached or semi-detached houses with few facilities. Many houses have no bath and no inside toilets. The area has been due for modernization for years. There are plans but these have been recently postponed.

23 Mr. Holt the architect explained: 'There are in fact about 950 or so houses waiting to be modernized and we hope we can start on them next year. Numbers 97 and 99 Emerson Road are to be modernized as part of a pilot project and actually the work has just started. Obviously when we can start depends on how much money the Government makes available to the Borough Council for this work and the Council's decision on which scheme should go ahead.'

24 The neglect by the Council has resulted in broken down doors, trampled fences and gardens which look like rubbish heaps. It's hard to take a pride in an area like this.

26 Couldn't the local residents help to clean the place up? We heard about a clean up project centred in Keats Road and asked Pauline Long about it.

27 'Well, we're having a cleaning scheme next week starting 16th July, 16th June sorry, for a fortnight.

28 What we're going to do is have 5 skips which we've got from the Council. They're great big skips 16 feet long and we're going to put them on different streets so people who live there can put their rubbish there.'

Wouldn't that be an expensive undertaking?

'This is costing quite a lot of money. We've got a grant from the council but we estimate the cost for the two weeks will be about £600 because we have to pay for the hire of the skips and we have to pay every time the skips are emptied and we estimate 45 times they have to be emptied in two weeks and then we have to pay the men who come round for the rubbish, pay for skips each time they are emptied which comes to around £600.'

29 But we discovered the skips themselves were an invitation to vandals. 'But for the next three we've got skips on the area and the main problem we're going to find is kids.'

It's been in operation since Monday and last night Mr Hughes found that one of the skips on Ruskin Road was all pulled apart and he had to spend half an hour of his time after kids had messed it up.

30 Clearly there is no short-term answer to the problem: so long as there are empty houses there will be vandalism. So long as children have nothing to do this is how they'll get their fun.

31 Long-term plans are ready for recreational facilities for children. 'There is, as you know, plans to expand the play area already, on the area behind Carlisle Grove.

32 We hope to improve the play area already on Byron Road and also the little toddlers' play area at the top of Keats Road. (33) hopefully to improve the facilities on Bushbury Hill and there's every possibility of extra facilities being provided somewhere in the middle of the estate near the Tennison Road – top of Newman Road – somewhere around there. There is of course the Adventure Playground off Chesterton Road and in about two years time there should be a play building provided to help with the operation of the playground.'

35 But in the meantime children will have to make do with the few facilities made available by residents.

36 These photographs show existing play areas. Pauline Long explained: 'The adventure playground, well, as I mentioned, we're hoping to make a play area in Carlisle Grove. That was a piece of waste ground which used to be allotment space which had never really been

used. It's very overgrown with a lot of rubbish on it which we had cleared and the grass cut. We've got some goalposts up now. We raised the money from a sponsored walk with the people and kids on the estate and we hope to get some play equipment made from telegraph poles, and maybe a toddlers' play area.'

We're hoping to get that but there's not really any plans at the moment for any other play areas. As the community architect can get a move on with modernization we might get some more play equipment when they start development schemes.

37 Tom Huntington is right when he says people should look after the area better. After all they have to live there. When the short campaign is over and the estate is tidy people must remember that they have the responsibility of the condition of the area.

38 If the void houses are repaired and occupied the target for vandalism would be reduced.

39 The alternative is further deterioration of the Scotlands Estate: and WE DON'T WANT THAT.

6 Small Group Work

RICHARD MILLS

The stance which each contributor to this book has taken on the matter of pupil grouping within a mixed ability structure is pragmatic and flexible. The kind of grouping adopted is dependent on the nature of the task and the pupils, the objectives being pursued and the numbers you are dealing with. Sometimes pupils will work alone (and often in a class much of the activity is of an isolated kind), sometimes in pairs and small groups of four or five, sometimes as a class of thirty, occasionally in a group of a hundred. Variety, consistent with good organization and clear aims, is to be encouraged, so that all may benefit from the linguistic, social, and ritualistic demands and experiences of each different method of grouping. No single way of organizing children is the panacea for mixed ability teaching but, since we believe children should often be encouraged to operate in small groups, some justification for this view, and some analysis of appropriate tasks, may be helpful.

As a way into this discussion, let us first consider some of the characteristics of the traditional class teaching structure in order to highlight some of its virtues and some of its limitations. I've labelled this method the *Shooting Star Model*. Choose your own interpretation of that metaphor: teacher as attractive source of energy whose power burns brightly and momentarily as it lands on two or three areas

Shooting Star Model

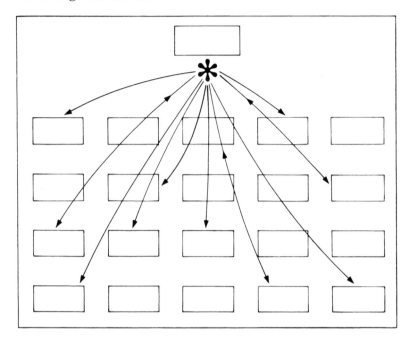

and is remembered briefly for its impact; or teacher as extra-terrestrial phenomenon, incomprehensible to earthlings who merely stare at the performance. Clearly both these are caricatures but they possess elements of truth.

The teaching situation represented by the diagram is unambiguous. The teacher is the focal point and can be seen more or less by everyone. The physical layout of the room testifies both to the status of knowledge and to some cf its apparent characteristics. The teacher possesses that knowledge and information to impart to recipients who are intended to be fairly passive overtly as they sit isolated from each other in their separate desks. They may be note-taking or merely listening, but they are not entering into discussion, although there may be two or three questions. The teacher teaches and the pupils learn. That is what the structure of the room is saying and there are many occasions when this is perfectly appropriate. I don't wish for a moment to decry a method of organization for learning which, in many circumstances, is quite acceptable and should be encouraged, particularly where there is factual information to be conveyed, or a process explained.

However, as I indicated in an earlier chapter, a so-called class discussion lesson held in this kind of setting may often become something of an interrogation, with the teacher asking the questions, giving or withholding approval, judging, guiding and controlling, selecting the speaker, and acting as mediator. The language required of the pupils is generally that of performance rather than exploration. As teachers, we've all held this kind of discussion many times and no doubt will continue to do so, since it is often a very satisfying activity for us. The fact that it serves to emphasize the corporateness of the class seems to be a positive gain and, provided we recognize its language constraints, and constantly make other additional arrangements to compensate for them, there is less of a problem. However, in this traditional class structure the pupils' language potential is so limited. They rarely ask searching questions of each other; rarely speculate or make hypotheses, using such phrases as: 'What if . . .', 'I wonder if . . .', 'Possibly . . .', 'It might be that . . .'; are rarely able to exercise initiative and control; can rarely respond genuinely to what other pupils say, since the attention is more often on the teacher as focal point than the item under consideration. In addition to all this, the teacher's own language, intonation and expectations will have their effects, and many pupils merely try to please by telling their teacher what they think he or she wants to hear. There may be barriers, too, thrown up by one's method of speaking. I sometimes wonder whether my own habit of asking a question, giving praise, then asking for further elaboration, doesn't in fact deter pupils. On the one hand, I'm trying to stretch them to articulate their thoughts in more detail; on the other, I'm aware of the danger of the predictability of supplementary questions, but some teaching habits are as tenacious as rust and keep breaking through despite efforts to eradicate them. What this adds up to is one of the major justifications for organizing children to work in small groups. Under such a system they have the opportunity to use different kinds of language and develop skills in questioning, speculation, exploration, initiation, and participation. As eleven year old Trevor says:

> When you're in er smaller groups you've got more chance to say what you want to, but when you, when there's a teacher out the front, you know, you have you have you have to wait and then er, the next thing you know the bell's gone and, you know, you have to wait until the next lesson. So it's better to work in groups so you can say what you like quicker.

This is supported by Andrew:

> When you're erm, oh yeah, when you're in a mixed, you don't you you talk louder usually, when you've got about four or five people all talking at once, but you don't start going all over the room to find someone to talk about what you're doing cos you're next to someone. You've got about four other people right there.

Incidentally, these two boys were in the same mixed ability class. One was a very weak reader, and the other a highly intelligent, very good reader. Perhaps you'd like to speculate on which is which.

With regard to the physical layout, small groups should be conveniently arranged, with chairs or desks close together, for virtual face-to-face discussion. By this means, no one is forced to talk to the back of someone else's head or respond to a disembodied voice. It's a structure as appropriate for eleven year olds as for older students. The following diagram may suggest other benefits too. I'll call this the *Measles Model* on the the grounds that it's what I imagined, probably erroneously, a measles germ would look like under a microscope. Further justification occurred to me later. Measles are contagious; people are affected by being in close proximity with others and catch something from them. The fact that it's an illness is unfortunate for the development of my metaphor but one might even, I suppose, make capital out of that, on the grounds that many

Measles Model

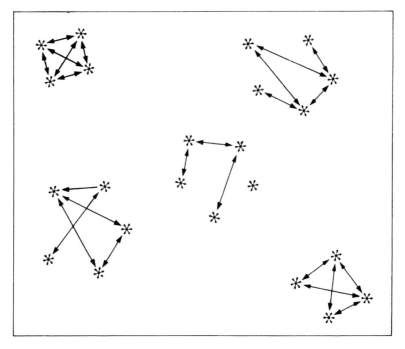

teachers are wary of small group work and endeavour to avoid it, as they would disease.

In this kind of structure, with which pupils are familiar from their primary school days, there is often greater involvement, even by the shy boys and girls who may feel less overawed. It should be a cooperative enterprise, with useful social skills encouraged, where pupils may learn from each other, with everyone, hopefully, able to contribute something, and the weak ones able to hear the language of the strong and perhaps in a better position to respond to it since the danger of being exposed is less. Pupils will get to know each other much better and the fact that some of them don't regard group activity as 'real work' may be a positive advantage. The teacher will learn a lot more about individuals and, perhaps, be better able to diagnose problems and weaknesses. Teachers unsure of themselves may even use small groups as a disciplinary aid, on the grounds of 'divide and rule'.

Above all, the structure is saying that pupils are, in themselves, learning resources, and have a contribution to make to each other; they can, at times, assume responsibility for their own learning and that of their peers and be trusted to operate independently. A sense of commitment, a reasonable level of motivation and a willingness to persevere in a task seem to me to be of more significance for the success of this kind of operation than above average intelligence or high reading age. Naturally, there will be difficulties. Nothing is ever all sweetness and light. There are organizational problems in constituting viable groups, often in small rooms with unhelpful furniture. A quick thinking pupil may be exasperated by a slow group member and the latter may hear language and ideas which are incomprehensible. There is, inevitably, a higher noise level and there is the teacher's professional fear that he/she may be presiding over a situation in which much irrelevant discussion may occur. There may also be the clash of incompatible personalities, as eleven year old Lynn observes:

> You know, if I was in Lesley, Lesley's form and erm, she was erm, in the group with I am and we was working in two's, she might, I'd just say to her something like this: 'Eh, Lesley, ooh, erm, what's this answer?' or something like that, 'What's this question?' or someat, but she'd say, 'Oh shurrup, I'm doing me own.' (*Lesley laughs.*)

What, then, is the teacher's role? Perhaps the phrase 'peripatetic adviser' best describes it. Once the structure has been determined and the tasks decided, the teacher should, I believe, move from group to group, in an *apparently* haphazard sequence, sometimes asking a searching and specific question in order to focus attention; sometimes giving a summary of points made and thereby indicating one of the functions of a chairperson, sometimes exercising a disciplinary function; sometimes giving information; often just remaining silent, listening and storing away all kinds of thoughts and impressions for later use.

When a teacher joins a small group he/she automatically becomes a focal point, a point of reference, and can, in a matter of seconds, dominate the group and deprive it of its independence, initiative and autonomy. We must be sensitive to this danger. There are occasions when a catalyst is needed but often a teacher may wish to be merely as a fly on the wall and a group will not easily permit that role. In any event, unlike a fly, the teacher's presence will, inevitably, modify the language used, at least initially.

Whether active or passive, teachers as overall coordinators are always present within the structure they have designed and the tasks being pursued. They are initially responsible for the way in which the groups are composed. This way may be random or intentional. If random, teachers may organize the groups according to previous classroom seating, or by arbitrary alphabetical selection or from a class list. If the grouping is intentional then teachers may organize according to the children – on the grounds of mixing abilities; giving variety of experience, of task; ensuring compatibility of personality, or deliberately engineering introverts to work with extroverts; or ringing the changes on previous groupings.

What of the tasks set? They seem, to me, to be of three kinds: exploration, production, analysis – and I'd like to spend the greater part of this chapter considering each of these in turn.

Exploration

Here the aim of the small group of four or five boys and girls is to open up or 'explore' some topic or area which it is felt is relevant to their needs and interests. These could include the following, although they are obviously not in watertight compartments:

first year:	bullying; adventures; being frightened; brothers and sisters
second year:	ideal school; cruelty to animals; neighbours; fashions
third year:	parents; superstitions; gangs; cruelty to children; cowardice and heroism
fourth year:	authority; pollution; war; outsiders, town and country; marriage

fifth year: minority groups; youth clubs; old people; work; crime and punishment.

Such an exploration is often the preliminary to some other activity – perhaps whole-class consideration or investigation of relevant prose or poetry text or film. Sometimes it may follow a whole-class stimulus of some kind. The intention is to involve the pupils and permit discussion to proceed in a fairly intimate setting so that all kinds of initial ideas may be agitated. Often this kind of exploration may have no clear objectives and no clear end, other than that signified by the bell or the teacher. It may only rarely stimulate real challenge and incisive debate, unless presented in some polarized form.

However, within these blanket themes or topics an issue may be presented in such a way as to force the small group participants to become decision-makers. Here the exploration may have more of a cutting edge to it and I've found that children often respond well to 'problem cards' such as the following:

Mary is a fourteen year old girl who has run away from school many times, threatened her mother with a carving knife, and has now taken to staying out all hours. Her mother, with two younger children to look after, can do nothing with her. A psychiatrist's report states that Mary is of above average intelligence, alert and interested, but has never really recovered from the death of her father ten months previously.
What advice would you give the mother?

Lennie, aged thirteen years, has come before the magistrate's court as being 'in need of care and protection'. He has five brothers and sisters and lives with them and his mother in a two-roomed flat. Father has gone off with another woman. Lennie has recently stolen some torch batteries and an alarm clock from Woolworth's.
What should be done?

Sometimes a quotation may help to initiate a discussion. In the example which follows I was working with some eighty mixed ability fifth-year pupils who considered in their groups certain questions set out on cards and then came together for a plenary session at which a spokesman for each group reported on points made. The activity lasted the whole afternoon, with a break of some twenty minutes.

Card one
Because I am all for everyone having the same chances of education, streaming would be necessary. But it should be arranged in such a way that each child would be in good streams for good subjects and bad streams for bad subjects, and not in a bad stream for every subject if they were not very academic.

Girl, 14

Which are the 'good' and 'bad' streams? Why?
Do you prefer streaming or mixed ability grouping? Why?

Card two
At present our entire secondary educational system is geared to examinations.

Boy, 13

Would you abolish exams? Why?
What do you think teachers feel about exams?

Card three
History and geography are dealt with adequately, but psychology and politics, drug-taking and smoking and love and death are not mentioned in the school syllabus at all.

Girl, 13

What subjects would you like to see excluded from your time-table? Why?
What subjects/topics should be covered which are omitted at present? Why?

Card four
One has to learn sometime that life is not all sweetness and light and school is the best place for discovering this. I would not abolish rules or strict teachers.

Girl, 14

Which are the sensible rules? Why? How would you enforce them?
Which are the silly rules? Why are they silly?
Should teachers observe the same rules as pupils? Why? Why not?

Card five
School should be a place where the literature teachers are poets, the history teachers political advisers, the geography teachers explorers . . . a place where literature is discussed in the geography class.   (Boy, 14)
Should the curriculum be divided up into separate subjects? Why? Why not?
What do you think of this boy's views?
What do you look for in a teacher?

Card six
My idea of a school I'd like would have understanding teachers (who are few and far between at present) who would try to understand the pupils' difficulties and not look upon pupils as illiterate sub-humans. The pupils would also be treated as individuals and not as a flock of sheep all with the same purpose in life . . . The teachers would work in unison and not think that the maths teacher was aloof from the PE teacher or too proud to mix with the laboratory assistants.

The pupils would be of all nationalities and creeds: boys and girls, Jews and Moslems. This would help them in later life to have no colour prejudice and to know that one nationality or creed is no better than another.

213

The school (and beyond) would be a one-class society; nobody rich, nobody poor . . .'

Boy, 13

What is your idea of the ideal school?

I've also worked with a similar group of ninety fifth-years for a similar period of time on the subject of education in a Design for Living course and this time gave a forty-minute illustrated talk on the aims of education and followed this with a question sheet from which each group selected a topic of interest. In this instance there was no plenary session; we'd had enough of education for one half-day. The sheet read as follows:

Design for Living course – aims of education

Choose any *one* of these topics for your group discussion:

1 If what I've said about education is correct, then a school aims to:
   (a) prepare its pupils for society outside school
   (b) prepare for job selection (via exams)
   (c) foster the full development of each individual person.
   How far has your own education met, or failed to meet, these demands?

2 Think of the nine children you saw on the slides and discuss what could be done in school to help any one of them over his/her problems.
   Should a school be so concerned about the personal problems and backgrounds of its pupils?

3 In some areas of the country the education service is divided into three parts:
   (a) infants (5–7 years)
   (b) juniors (8–10 years)
   (c) secondary (11–16/18 years).

Suppose we became so bankrupt that one of these parts had to be abolished. Which should it be?

4   Imagine you are dictator of a country. Your national budget has to be spent on:
(a) housing
(b) transport systems
(c) medical services
(d) education
(e) defence
(f) industrialization (i.e. developing factories and businesses).
Which, in your view, is the most important?
Which the least?
Where does education come in the list?

Production

With the second of the three kinds of small group task originally identified, I am thinking of the kind of group activity which leads to a recognizable end product of some sort. To begin with, the group meets to plan a subsequent way of working and to divide up the tasks. They are about to initiate work on a new project or theme and the group must first consider the options at its disposal. They are not concerned, as yet, with content, but with structure and *modus operandi*.

Their topic is, say, marriage. One individual undertakes to collect examples of marriage ceremonies from prayer books and individual wedding programmes from friends and relatives. Two others, working as a pair, decide to try two tape-recorded interviews, one with a newly married couple and one with an old couple married for many years; they discuss what questions they will ask. A fourth member of the group undertakes to do some research into the attitudes of one or two Eastern cultures and to find suitable illustrations. The last pair will find examples of descriptions of weddings in novels and plays and poems. The topic has been imposed by the teacher but the pupils are free to respond to it individually. They have planned their approach for the next few days and will meet together as a group when they have something to report and when the next stage of the project needs to be planned. They have adopted a loose structure for the present but this may need to be modified later. Discussion on marriage itself will, at least in the early stages, be incidental but they will, at some point, present their findings to others.

Such a way of working, to produce a collection of written and audio-visual material, is popular, provided it's not over-done, and it gives opportunity for children of varying abilities to make full use of such talents as they possess and to develop others. As with any other activity, the teacher must monitor what is happening so that, for example, the weak reader doesn't spend all the time illustrating other people's texts, or the average pupil all his/her energy with the tape recorder. Moreover, the teacher needs to be clear about the value of *group* interaction. Otherwise, each 'group' could merely be composed of isolated individuals going their own way. A useful analogy is that of the building site where each worker contributes a skill and must do so in concert with everyone else, and the end product is the result of team work. There is satisfaction for the pupils in being able to identify a clearly recognizable finish for their efforts – perhaps a display, or exhibition, a play or film, or happening of some sort.

Here are some more examples of group work leading to Production. Gordon Taylor suggests others in his chapter.

1 A miscellany of material on cassette, e.g. for a radio programme, i.e. music, sound effects, readings, interviews; slide-tape sequences on specific topics can be highly effective.
2 Production of a film or video, i.e. careful preliminary planning of plot, characters, movements, dress, location, dialogue, followed by actual shooting.
3 Writing of plays – highly popular even if time consuming; this could include the occasional scripting of an episode for a current radio or television series where characterization is so well developed that a

group could first make a transcript of part of an episode and consider the language habits of the characters involved before producing their own episode and then reading it to the rest of the class. Incidentally, not quite in the category of production, but well worth inclusion at this point is group reading of plays and short stories as a variation on silent reading. Certainly, the ability to read a character part well, in addition to merely being able to distinguish dialogue in type from stage directions in italics, (no mean feat for some pupils) is a sophisticated and praiseworthy attribute, as well as being very enjoyable to most children.

4 Putting in rank order photocopies of four anonymous essays written by other pupils in the school but younger than those in the group. It's a useful exercise in practical criticism and the fact that the pieces under consideration are examples of pupil's work should increase motivation within the small group.

5 Group observation of a process with a written report at the end. This could be a process within the school (e.g. the making of jewellery in metalwork; a curry in domestic science; a clay figure in pottery; a hydrogen balloon in science), or in the neighbourhood (e.g. demolition; motorway building; sheep shearing; unloading of fish; milking of cows). I recall seeing three ten-year-old boys recording, at different times over a period of three days, the movements of marked wood lice in a kind of home-built adventure playground for wood lice inside the classroom. It seemed to me excellent training in observational skills which underpins so much activity, not merely scientific. I'm sorry to report that all the wood lice died. Either the public scrutiny, or the gentle prodding with pencils to get them to perform, proved too much.

So much, then, for an indication of some kinds of group production. I've omitted drama and simulations since these activities are dealt with elsewhere and my colleagues give many other examples of how children may be encouraged successfully to operate in small groups with a clear end product in view.

Analysis

The third kind of small group activity which may be identified is that geared to analysis, by which I mean that the group has, as its focal point, a text of some kind. It may be a poem, a short story, an extract from a novel, a television programme, a film, or a tape. The task of the group is either to thrash out the answers to certain questions which have been set by the teacher – in other words, a kind of corporate comprehension exercise – or to use the text as the focal point of the discussion and to follow wherever that discussion might lead. As I stated in chapter one, I favour a firm structure early on (i.e. for several months initially and later at periodic intervals) with questions designed to take the participants into a text and help them to concentrate on specific words, phrases, ideas, characters, relationships, and often to be followed by a reporting back of some kind. Having had thorough training in how to approach the data in front of them, they should then be in a position later to be given texts without questions, for them to get to grips with the experience presented and be able to link their own world with that of the poem or story.

Here's an example (not a model) of a set of questions given to third year small groups after I had read aloud to them D. H. Lawrence's short story *Adolf*, about the effect on a family and on itself of a rabbit brought out of the wild into human civilization. Each boy and girl, in six groups of five in the dining hall, had copies of the story and each group a set of questions. The whole activity lasted sixty-five minutes and no group finished all the questions to its satisfaction. However, my own observations suggested that a good deal of learning of all kinds took place.

Adolf by D. H. Lawrence

1 Read the first three paragraphs again and think carefully about what sort of man the father is. Try to discover as much as you can about him. What appears to be the relationship between the children and their father?
What is your own attitude towards him?

2   Look carefully at how the mother reacts to the arrival of the rabbit. Look at the different ways in which she makes her comments. (One member of the group could read them out.) Do you think she has had any previous experience of this sort of thing?

3   Judging her on what she says and does, what sort of person does the mother appear to be?
    Have you ever met anyone who is like this?

4   How do mother and father get on with each other?

5   Trace carefully the way in which the rabbit becomes acclimatized (i.e. gets used to the household).
    What effects does he have on those who live in the house?

6   In what ways is it possible to compare the way of life of the father and of the rabbit?

7   What do the children feel about the departure of Adolf?
    Talk about any pet you've lost and how you felt about it.

8   Using the story and your discussion as a basis, try to consider and analyse your own attitude towards pet animals or wild animals.
    Has this attitude changed over the last few years? Are girls different from boys in this respect? What are the attitudes of your parents?

9   You might like to act out the short story, with each member of the group playing the part of one of the characters.

In my experience, a teacher-less small group operating in this manner can often achieve a high degree of understanding if the participants attend closely to the text and work in a mutually supportive way. This won't always happen but it should happen often enough for the method to be used without undue anxiety.

I want to end this chapter with two examples of different groups of average fifth year pupils, grappling with data unaided by either teacher or questions. The first group, consisting of Colin, Jane, William and Kay, had, along with sixty other pupils, seen a thirty minute Canadian film, *Phoebe*, which is concerned with the breakdown in communication which occurs when sixteen year old Phoebe discovers she is pregnant by her boyfriend, Paul. The group's twenty minute discussion, which followed their viewing of the film, and was monitored only by the tape recorder, fell into the following divisions:

1   Parental attitudes towards pregnancy
2   Paul's maturity
3   An analysis of a surrealist part of the film
4   An attempt to understand Phoebe's situation
5   The problem of communication
6   Consideration of what Paul would and should have done when he learnt the news
7   Parental attitude and behaviour
8   Paul's sense of responsibility
9   Relationship between Paul and Phoebe
10 The problem of whether Phoebe should tell her parents immediately
11 Consideration of one scene in the film which the group found baffling.

The transcript which follows is of section 7, 'Parental attitude and behaviour'. I've added punctuation so as to make reading easier. The numbers refer to the sequence of comments made.

159 J. I think if our mom told me not to hitch-hike, I wouldn't hitch-hike.
160 K. No. I wouldn't.
161 J. Because your mom and dad know best.
162 C. Mind you, they probably in the situation, that it's perhaps the only thing to do.
163 W. That's . . . that's another reason though, isn't it? Sp . . . spoilt children. They all, you know, people of our . . . they don't really really take much notice of their mother. They think, 'Oh, I'm old enough. I can do what I like.' (C. don't you do that?) But if . . .
164 C. Don't you think, 'I'm in a, I'm old enough to

look after myself', and do things against your
mom's word or . . .

165 K.   No, not usually. You know, I always, I think
I (C. If she said, say . . . J. if I strongly . . .)

166 C.   If she says, 'Now be back at half-past ten,
because it's school tomorrow', and you were
out with all your friends and that, wouldn't
you, would you make sure you went off at the
right time and, you know, not be in after your
mom told you to be in and, you know . . .

167 K.   I think I would go back (J. yeah). I mean,
when I was on me holidays, you know, I met
this kid and, er, we goes out, we went out,
erm, about fifteen miles to this place, you
know, inn, and, like, there was these mates
and they got a car. They was ever so nice,
you know (C. yeah), very friendly like.
Anyway, we went out and, on the way back,
we ran out of petrol (C. *laughs*). Oh! I could
have died (*laughing*) and I was really worried
about what our mom and dad would say, you
know, and I was thinking, 'Oh, I bet our mom
and dad are ever so worried' like (C. yeah . . .
J. yeah) and, er, I was expecting me dad to
punch Pete on the nose (*laughing*) or something, you know, and, er, when we get back
our dad says, 'Oh, that's alright' you know
and er . . .

168 W.   I bet . . . I bet . . .

169 J.   They'd think it was an excuse wouldn't they?

170 K.   No. And I realized, you know, I think it made
me realize, you know, I was thinking over all
these things about what mom and dad would
say and do, you know, and..

171 J.   Really, parents are very understanding,
aren't they? (K. yeah). Even though they
might not show it all the time.

172 K.   I think, like er, you feel at this age, like we
are, you think that they're nagging at you (J.
yeah) because they're making . . .

173 C.   You tend to feel, you know, some people with,

perhaps, older parents, they don't understand
you and they don't understand the way you
think and the way you dress and

174 J.   Although other parents aren't always
like . . . (*inaudible*) . . . your parents,
because my friend, she's got some horrible
parents. They really keep on at her.

175 W.   And does she go out, stay out of a night longer
than . . .

176 J.   No. She doesn't stay out.

177 W.   But (J. She likes) she's not spoilt, is she? (J.
She likes . . .)

178 J.   She likes other people to be with her all the
time because she doesn't like to be in the
house on her own with them, you know.
Arguments set in (K. No . . .) and that.

179 W.   That's what I was saying.

180 K.   Staying with our mom and day, you know, I
I don't think I'd swop, I wouldn't swop my
parents for the world, you know. I really love
them like.

181 J.   I wouldn't either.

182 K.   No. I think with our mom and dad you can
talk about anything with them. (C. mm.)

183 J.   Oh! I don't know about me dad. I couldn't talk
about anything to me dad.

184 K.   Erm . . .

185 J.   To me mom, yeah, but not me dad.

186 W.   I think if my sister got in a situation like that
I'd think my mom would fall down on her,
you know, and give her as much love as she
could, but I think dad would act a bit
ashamed, something like that.

187 C.   You know, when our Rob, you know, put his
wife in it, like, our mom went, er, you know,
she went a bit, er, mad at him cos she didn't
want him to get married at nineteen, like,
and, er, of course, he did it on purpose so that
they'd have to get married. And our mom
went furious but, and our dad just said his
bit and left it at that and helped them out,

you know, and our mom kept nagging (W. It's alright, it's alright) for a bit. She got to understand (W. if they want to get married isn't it?)

188 W.   But in that film, there was no thoughts of marriage. It's just like a normal boy and girl relationship, wasn't it?

189 K.   Yeah. Just like, you know, just a little court-ship that you get when you're about our age, you know. I mean, you don't think about usually landing up marrying them, do you, (C. *laughs*) you know?

190 C.   Seems a bit far fetched, don't it, when you think of, 'Well, wouldn't mind marrying her', you know.

191 J.   Didn't seem all that strong, you know, you know what I mean?

192 K.   No.

193 C.   What, the love for each other?

194 J.   Yeah. Oh, I think they had love for each other, but it wasn't, you know, absolute dire love really, you know what I mean?

In this short extract we see features which occur constantly throughout the discussion. Particularly interesting is the use of expressive, informal language, often of great honesty (notice that remarkable contribution 187), to interweave personal anecdote and experience on the one hand, with the experience which the film offers on the other. The group is successful in analysing personal relationships – their own and other people's – and I believe they are brought to a greater depth of realization (See 170, 171, 180, 186) of their own relationship with their parents than would have been achieved in other ways. Moreover, they manage to sustain exchanges of this kind throughout the whole twenty minutes, never flagging, and returning time and again to different parts of the film.

In my second example of what may be achieved by pupils operating without the teacher I want to cite the work of two fifth-year pupils, Christopher and Adrian. Christopher has read Philip Larkin's poem, *Mr Bleaney*, on his own and written about it. Then, after a discussion with Sandra, Ann and David, but without teacher or questions, has written a second time, thereby indicating his increase in understanding, particularly of the poem's structure. In an identical manner, Adrian has written about Yevtushenko's poem, *Schoolmaster*, and then written again after a discussion with Linda, Jayne and Malcolm, and testifies to the value of the intervening discussion although, as you will see from his first piece, he had achieved considerable understanding on his own. So much so that I was originally sceptical that he would have more to say. Hence my increased delight with what he produced. All four pieces are printed exactly as they were written and they speak for themselves without a commentary from me, showing that quite considerable learning can occur in small group *analysis* of the kind outlined.

Christopher's first piece on 'Mr Bleaney'

This poem is about a man moving into a room previously taken by a Mr Bleaney. But it concentrates far more on Mr Bleaney than the man. It discribes the room, probably in some city suburb, as an ill equiped and bare.

His second piece

This poem seems to be told by two people. Firstly the man who is coming to stay in Mr Bleaney's room and also the landlady who used to look after Mr Bleaney. The difficulty in understanding this poem is seeing who is speaking.

My impression of Mr Bleaney is an ageing man living on his own. It seems that he continually moved around, living off four groups of people untill they can take him no longer. Yet, the poet thinks that this small ill-equiped room is Mr Bleaney's home and that it show's how this man lives.

Adrian's first piece on 'Schoolmaster'

The powet is trying to portray the schoolmaster as a rather lonely lost kind of man wandering about in a dream. The schoolmaster has lost all his charecter his vigor for life. All the indiviguality has gone from the schoolmaster his mind has broken down murging with the background. The schoolmaster fails to stand out as he used to. He not only accepts his faults but worse still play them up. The schoolmaster feels lost he has been deserted by his wife he has lost confidence in his abbillity to teach. He is seen as a old and lonely figure fadeing into obscurity as so many have before him. While seeing his world colapsing around him he cannot think why, why he's forgot about long division, why his wife has left him, why he has forgot the ticket and worst of all why he lives at all. He is a man left without a perpose without a perpose or life to defend. Soon the schoolmaster will have faded further untill neither he or anyone else shall be able to pick him out of his obscure background. It is at this point the schoolmasters mind will die compleatly.

His second piece

The poet I think is still trying to put over the idea of the schoolmasters mind having to accept a reality he did not realise had existed. One appresiated the physical side of the poem more. In that less of it seems to be taken from the mind of the schoolmaster but more from the thoughts of the children. The children and the school have become more real after disscussion they become more important and not so much reference points for the schoolmasters mind. It has become clearer that he realy did get down and feel for his ticket rather than just a way of expressing how the schoolmaster sees himself as a stupid forgetfull man. Now it seems clearer that the schoolmaster is not only becoming obscurer himself but also as seen by the children (his pupils) It seems more that not only the schoolmasters mind is becoming old and worn out but his body itself this is shown by the reference to the clumsey walk of the schoolmaster. Everything has become more real the trees and the snow. The schoolmaster not only fades into obscurity but his physical person his body also clearly becomes covered with snow and inter-mingles with the white background. It seems that not only the mans mind is dying but his body also it is obvious what a poor, sick lonely figure this man is. The poem makes you more awear and feel more say for him.

APPENDIX I

Group work tasks

Many activities in English work can be carried out in small groups. Here are some of them. The tasks are numbered but the order is random.

1 Discussion of ideas, topics, books, plays, poems, short stories, television and radio programmes, films, photographs.
2 Preparation of improvisation/scripted plays to be acted. Other drama work, including dramatization of a passage or short story.
3 Writing of group play/dialogue/article/summary/ television or radio serial episode.
4 Preliminary discussion (possibly including note-making) before class discussion/writing.
5 Intensive study of texts.
6 Group reading of a play, short story, parts of a novel.
7 Project/theme work including research into, and production of, for example, a group newspaper, comic, magazine, advertisements, anthology; parts of these on paper; parts on tape.
8 Recounting a story and teaching one another in pairs.
9 Grammar exercises.
10 Compiling collections of personal and professional prose and poetry, factual and visual material, on particular themes and topics.
11 Word game exercises and crosswords.
12 Film and slide and photograph-essay production.
13 Decision-making, including games and simulations.
14 Story-making (possibly with pictures).

15 Sharing work cards.
16 Marking/discussion of pupils' written work.
17 Reading to each other and questioning each other on what has been read.
18 Planning for, and follow-up from, visits.
19 Preparing and executing surveys/questionnaires, including making use of cassette recorders.
20 Presentation/display/exhibition.

APPENDIX II

An example

To add flesh to some of the activities just suggested, here is a structure used by Trevor Wright, Head of the English Department in a Comprehensive School, with a class of 13 to 14 year olds working on the novel *To Sir With Love*, E. Braithwaite, and the topic of racial prejudice.

The class had been working on the book for a short while; all had read it and were about to embark on a reasonably substantial piece of work arising from it. The group tasks and compositon had been negotiated with the boys and girls and each pupil was now required to work with peers on one of the six group tasks. These tasks were briefly summarized on cards labelled A to G and intended to serve as a starter and a buffer while the teacher moved from group to group, helping to develop ideas.

A
Racial Prejudice
Option: Survey/Questionnaire

The aim of a survey or questionnaire is to find out the opinions of a group of people who represent a cross-section of the community. In your case, this group could be your own class in school, or people at home or in your neighbourhood.

Some questions which you ask may call for a yes/no answer; others may ask for reasons or opinions.

The exercise is in five parts:
1 Decide what you are trying to test, and with whom.
2 Work out a rough draft of the questions (and have a word with me before going any further).
3 Duplicate your question sheets (I will help you with this, if you need it), and carry out the survey.
4 Show your results either as statistics, or a block graph, or a descriptive commentary.
5 Give your conclusions and say what you have learnt from the exercise.

Notes:
You will have a chance to tell the class your findings, and hear their reactions.

B
Racial Prejudice
Option: Research Project

A lot of things are said without any basis in fact. This project requires you to find out some facts and figures.

You must limit your research to a specific area. Here are some suggestions:
1 The Irish in England.
2 Non-Christian religions in Britain.
3 Immigration over the last twenty years.
4 The West Indian community in Britain.

You may choose another topic if you wish, but check with me first.

The emphasis in this is on *facts* and *figures*. Find these from newspapers, books, libraries. (Ask me if you get really stuck). When writing up your information, organize it in some logical way that will make sense to a reader who is not familiar with the topic, and indicate where you found the information.

Notes: See me after rough planning of project and layout. Final copy in exercise book.

C
Racial Prejudice
Option: Radio Play

1 First, decide on the general story. The play should show some attitudes to prejudice – as many different attitudes as possible. At least one character should be non-British born.
2 Next, script the play. Each actor must have a copy. Each member of the group must play one part. A good way to write the play is to take one scene each, *all writing at the same time.* Before you can do this, you must have discussed each character, and exactly what will happen in each scene, so that the scenes carry on naturally from each other.
3 When the play is written, decide on a title.
4 Rehearse the play. Read it with as much expression as possible, discussing your performance, and adding simple sound effects until the production is perfect.
5 Borrow a cassette recorder from me and make the final recording.

Notes: The play should last at least 10 minutes.
Write final copy in your exercise book. Remember layout – for example:
    JAMES (whispering): 'Look at him! Come over here.'

D
Racial Prejudice
Option: Short Story

You have written stories before, so you do not need much help with layout. Remember these points:

1 Plan the outline of the story before starting. Discuss your plan with me.
2 Your story should centre around an incident involving racial prejudice. It should have a gradual

build-up. The incident itself should be realistic – not too extreme or violent.

3   Don't forget to write about feelings and events *after* the incident.

4   While planning, write some notes on the different characters and their personalities. Their different attitudes to prejudice should be revealed by their actions in the story, and by conversation, if you have any.

5   A story works through *detail*. Describe people and places so that I can *see* them.

Notes: Write final copy in exercise book, after rough planning.

Use sentences, paragraphs and, perhaps, direct speech. The story should be long.

E
Racial Prejudice
Option: Free Drama (Improvisation)

Prepare a piece of group drama showing racial prejudice actually happening. At least one of the actors will play a foreigner of some sort. The play should lead up to the main incident, and end by showing what happens to the characters as a result.

See me for help with ideas.

Notes: Every member of the group must act.

No script is written, but a summary of the story is written in exercise book.

The standard of the play, which will be shown to the class, must be high. The best way to achieve this is to arrive at a basic idea, and make the rest up as you go along. Try to involve the audience in your play.

See me at all stages of your preparation.

F
Racial Prejudice
Option: Speech or Newspaper Article

Your aim is to produce a piece of writing expressing your own *feelings* and *opinions*. The purpose of this speech or article is to *persuade* others to agree with you.

The piece will only work if it is thoughtful, logical and entertaining. You must back up your opinions with sensible arguments and, where possible, facts and figures. Bring in your own experiences where you can. Think carefully, and use as many arguments as possible to support your views.

Notes: Prepare in rough. Show me before final copy in exercise book.

G
Racial Prejudice
Option: Poster

The purpose of the poster is to encourage *racial harmony*, that is, to persuade people to get on well with others from a different background.

First, plan the poster in rough.

It needs to be eye-catching and attractive. You can use:
- paint;
- felt-tip pens;
- collage (i.e. pictures cut out from magazines and suitably arranged).

See me for other ideas on this.

The poster will carry a message in words as well. This might include some suggestions as to *how* people should react to each other; *why* people should try harder; *what* the advantages of a multi-racial society are. The writing should be clear, persuasive and punchy, with a slogan. (Ask me if you do not understand this.)

The finished poster will be on a large sheet of paper.

Notes: See me for materials. Bring in anything which may be useful.
Show me your planned poster before beginning the final copy.

Part Three: Materials

The intention in this last part of the book is to list, in what I hope is a convenient form, some of the books, and other materials which I believe worth considering by English teachers. While some will be well known, others may be brought to your attention for the first time.

7 Plays, Poetry, Prose

RICHARD MILLS

Section 1: Scripted drama

Most children seem to enjoy reading plays in small groups, and a number enjoy studying the texts in depth and doing a variety of assignments on them. Many enjoy writing their own scripts, and it's a rare boy or girl who doesn't take to improvisation. In other words, we start with a built-in advantage; drama is one of those marvellous activities that doesn't seem to constitute 'real work'.

We can strongly recommend the forty or so plays now listed and have indicated the age range they might be used with. There seems little suitable scripted drama for first- and second-year level and perhaps this is just as well since improvisation may be more appropriate anyway for eleven and twelve year olds. However, there is, in our view, no weighty reason why the two activities shouldn't be pursued side by side at any age.

ADLAND, D. *Group Approach to Drama*, 1–3 Longman (11–14 years)
ALBEE, E. *The American Dream*, French (15–16)
ANON *The Shepherds' Play*, Penguin (11–13) ·
(P. 137 *Voices 1*, SUMMERFIELD, G.)
ANON *Christmas Mummers' Play*, Penguin (11–13)
(P. 167 *Voices II*, SUMMERFIELD, G.)

ARDEN, J. *Sergeant Musgrave's Dance*, Eyre Methuen (15–16)

AYCKBOURN, A. *Ernie's Incredible Illucinations*, Hutchinson (11–13) (in *Playbill One*)

BEHAN, B. *The Hostage*, Eyre Methuen (15–16)
The Quare Fellow, Eyre Methuen (15–16)

BOLT, R. *The Thwarting of Baron Bolligrew*, Heinemann (11–12)
A Man for All Seasons Heinemann (15–16)

BRECHT, B. *The Good Woman of Setzuan*, Penguin (14–16)
Galileo, Eyre Methuen (15–16)
Mother Courage, Eyre Methuen (15–16)
The Caucasian Chalk Circle, Penguin (14–16)

BRIGHOUSE, H. *Hobson's Choice*, Heinemann (13–14)

CHAMBERS, A. *The Chicken Run*, Heinemann (12–13)
Johnny Salter, Heinemann (12–13)
The Car, Heinemann (12–13)

COOPER, G. *Unman, Wittering and Zigo*, Macmillan Dramascript (13–16)

DELANEY, S. *A Taste of Honey*, Eyre Methuen (14–15)

FUGARD, A. *Sizwe Bansi is Dead*, Oxford (15–16)

GALTON, R. & SIMPSON, A. *Steptoe and Son*, Longman (13–16)

HALL, W. *The Long and the Short and the Tall*, Heinemann (15–16)

HUGHES, T. *The Coming of the Kings and Other Plays*, Faber (12–14)

JENKINS, R. *Five Green Bottles*, Macmillan Dramascript (12–14)

LATIMER, J. *Maria Marten*, (ed. M. Slater) Heinemann (13–15)

LAWRENCE, D. H. *A Collier's Friday Night*, Penguin (14–15)
The Daughter-in-Law, Penguin (14–15)
The Widowing of Mrs Holroyd, Penguin (14–15)

LITTLEWOOD, J. *Oh What a Lovely War*, Eyre Methuen (14–15) (Theatre Workshop)

MARLAND, M. (ed.) *Conflicting Generations* (Five plays), Longman (14–15)
Scene Scripts, Longman (13–14)
Z Cars (Four television scripts), Longman (14–15)

MILLER, A. *The Crucible*, Penguin (15–16)
  Death of a Salesman, Penguin (15–16)
  A View from the Bridge, Heinemann (15–16)
MILNE, A. A. *Toad of Toad Hall*, Methuen (11–12)
NAUGHTON, B. *Spring and Port Wine*, Heinemann (14–16)
NICHOLS, P. *A Day in the Death of Joe Egg*, Faber (15–16)
OBEY, A. *Noah*, Heinemann (12–14)
PICK, J. *Carrigan Street*, Macmillan Dramascript (12–14)
PINTER, H. *A Slight Ache and Other Plays*, Eyre Methuen (14–15)
  A Night out, French (14–15)
PLATER, A. *Excursion* (in *Playbill Three*) Hutchinson (14–16)
SELF, D & SPEAKMAN, R. (eds.) *Act 1* (4 plays), *Act 2* (3 plays), *Act 3* (4 plays), Hutchinson (14–16)
SHAW, G. B. *Androcles and the Lion* (extracts), Penguin (11–12)
  Pygmalion Penguin, (13–14)
TERSON, P. *Zigger Zagger*, Penguin (14–15)
  The Apprentices, Penguin (14–15)
THOMAS, D. *Under Milk Wood*, Dent (13–15)
WATERHOUSE, K. & HALL, W. *Billy Liar*, Blackie (14–15)
WILDE, O. *The Importance of Being Earnest*, Heinemann (13–14)
WILDER. T. *Our Town*, Penguin (14–15)

Section 2: Poetry

Some useful anthologies
ALLOT, K. *The Penguin Book of Contemporary Verse.*
BECKETT, J. *The Keen Edge*, Blackie.
BENTON, M. and P. *Touchstones; Poetry Workshop; Watchwords* (3 vols), Hodder & Stoughton.
BLACK, E. *Nine Modern Poets*, Macmillan.
COSMAN, C and WEAKER, K. *The Penguin Book of Women Poets.*
DAWE, B. *Sometimes Gladness*, Longman.
FINN, F. *The Albemarle Book of Modern Verse* 1, 2, Murray.
FINNEGAN, R. *The Penguin Book of Oral Poetry.*
GIBSON, J. *Let the Poet Choose*, Harrap.

HARRISON, M and STUART-CLARK, C. *The New Dragon Book of Verse*, OUP.

HEANEY, S & HUGHES, T. *The Rattle Bag*, Faber.

HEWETT, S. *This Day and Age*, Arnold.

HUGHES, T. *Here Today*, Hutchinson.

JOHNSON, L. K. *Dread Beat and Blood*, Bogle L'Ouverture.

MANSFIELD, R. and ARMSTRONG, I. *Every Man Will Shout*, OUP.

MAYBURY, B. *Wordscapes; Thoughtshapes; Bandstand; Bandwagon; Wordspinners; Thoughtweavers*. OUP.

McGOUGH, R. *In the Glassroom*, Cape; *Strictly Private*, Puffin.

ROSEN, M. *I See A Voice*, Hutchinson; *Mind Your Own Business*, Deutsch.

SERRAILLIER, I. *The Windmill Book of Ballads*, Heinemann.

STYLES, M. *I Like That Stuff*, CUP.

SUMMERFIELD, G. *Voices* (3 vols); *Junior Voices* (4 vols); *Worlds*, Penguin.

WEBB, K. *I Like This Poem*, Penguin.

WILLIAMS, E. *Dragonsteeth*, Arnold.

WOLLMAN, M. *7 Themes in Modern Verse; Ten Twentieth Century Poets*, Harrap.

Some popular modern poets

W. H. Auden	Patricia Beer	James Berry
John Betjeman	E.K. Brathwaite	Bertolt Brecht
Charles Causley	Lewis Carroll	e. e. cummings
Bruce Dawe	Emily Dickinson	T. S. Eliot
Robert Frost	Seamus Heaney	Adrian Henri
Ted Hughes	Elizabeth Jennings	Lynton Kwesi Johnson
Philip Larkin	D. H. Lawrence	Edward Lear
Roger McGough	Spike Milligan	Adrian Mitchell
Edwin Morgan	Ogden Nash	Wilfred Owen
Brian Patten	Peter Porter	Michael Rosen
Carl Sandburg	Vernon Scannell	Stephen Spender
Dylan Thomas	Edward Thomas	R. S. Thomas
Kath Walker	W. B. Yeats	

Poems

We offer now these twenty or so poems for each year, not as a 'common core', but merely as material which we have either used with children or which, we feel, is particularly suitable to be read aloud, or to be studied, as part of theme or literature work.

11–12 years

BLAKE, W. 'The Tyger'
CARROLL, L. 'Jabberwocky'
GIBSON, W. 'Flannan Isle'
HUGHES, T. 'My Father'
LEE, L. 'Apples'
LINDSAY, V. 'Daniel'
LOGAN, J. 'A Portrait of the Foot'
MARE, W. de la 'The Listeners'
MASEFIELD, J. 'Cargoes'; 'Reynard the Fox'
MORGAN, E. 'The Computer's First Christmas Card'
MORLEY, C. 'Smells'
NASH, O. 'Children's Party'
OWEN, G. 'The Fight'
ROETHKE, T. 'Child on Top of a Greenhouse', 'My Papa's Waltz'
ROSEN, M. 'Alone', 'In the Daytime'
SANDBURG, C. 'Arithmetic'
SCANNELL, V. 'Hide and Seek'
SONG, 'The Big Rock Candy Mountain'
STONE, G. 'Snaily House'

12–13 years

AUDEN, W. H. 'Night Mail', 'The Quarry'
CAUSLEY, C. 'Timothy Winters'
FIELD, H. 'Sad Story of a Motor Fan'
GRAVES, R. 'The "Alice Jean" '
HARDY, T. 'The Oxen'
HEANEY, S. 'Blackberry Picking'
HUGHES, T. 'My Brother Bert'
MANIFOLD, J. 'The Death of Ned Kelly'
MILLIGAN, S. 'The ABC'; 'Soldier Freddy'
NOYCE, W. 'Breathless'
SERRAILLIER, I. 'Beowulf'

STALLWORTHY, J. 'The Postman'
THOMAS, E. 'Digging'
WALSH, J. 'The Bully Asleep'
YEVTUSHENKO, Y. 'On a Bicycle'
YOUNG, A. 'Hard Frost'

13–14 years

ALEXANDER, M. 'The Seafarer' (translation)
AUDEN, W. 'Roman Wall Blues'
cummings, e. e. 'in Just-spring'
DALY, T. 'Mia Carlotta'
ENDICOFF, M. 'The Excavation'
ENRIGHT, D. 'The Rebel'
HOBSBAUM, P. 'The Place's Fault'
HOLUB, M. 'A Boy's Head'
HUGHES, T. 'Pike'; 'Wind'
KELL, R. 'Pigeons'
LAWRENCE, D. H. 'Kangaroo'; 'The Mountain Lion'; 'Snake'
MITCHELL, J. 'Holiday'
NASH, O. 'Will Consider Situation'
PICKETT, L. 'The One that Got Away'
SCANNELL, V. 'Gunpowder Plot', 'Autobiographical Note'
SPENDER, S. 'My Parents Kept Me from Children who were Rough'

14–15 years

AUDEN, W. H. 'Refugee Blues'; 'Let Me Tell You a Little Story'
BERRY, J. 'Batsman-With-Music Sobers'
BETJEMAN, J. 'Death in Leamington', 'Christmas'
BROCK, E. 'Song of the Battery Hen'
CAUSLEY, C. 'Ballad of the Bread Man'
FROST, R. 'Death of the Hired Man'
HEANEY, S. 'Mid-term Break'
HUGHES, T. 'Hawk Roosting'; 'View of a Pig'; 'A Dream of Horses'
LARKIN, P. 'Toads'
LAWRENCE, D. H. 'Last Lesson of the Afternoon'
MARQUIS, D. 'Warty Bliggens the Toad'
MORGAN, E. 'In the Snack Bar'
SASSOON, S. 'Falling Asleep'

SMITH, E. 'The Lesson'
SOUSTER, R. 'The Man who finds that his Son has become a Thief'
YEVTUSHENKO, Y. 'Lies'; 'Schoolmaster'

15–16 years
AUDEN, W. H. 'The Unknown Citizen'
BEER, P. 'The Fifth Sense'
BETJEMAN, J. 'Cricket Master'
BRECHT, B. 'A Worker Reads History'
BROCK, E. 'Five Ways to Kill a Man'
CAUSLEY, C. 'Ten Types of Hospital Visitor'
ELIOT, T. S. 'Journey of the Magi'
FROST, R. 'The Road Not Taken'; 'Mending Wall'; 'Out Out'
HENRI, A. 'Love is'
LARKIN, P. 'Mr Bleaney'; 'Whitsun Weddings'
LAWRENCE, D. H. 'Bat'
MACNEICE, L. 'Prayer Before Birth'
MCGOUGH, R. 'My Busconductor'
MUIR, E. 'The Horses'
OWEN, W. 'Dulce et Decorum Est'; 'Anthem for Doomed Youth'; 'Strange Meeting'
PORTER, P. 'Your Attention Please'
SCANNELL, V. 'Incendiary'
SOYINKA, W. 'Telephone Conversation'
STALLWORTHY, J. 'The Almond Tree'
TESSIMOND, A. 'The Man in the Bowler Hat'
THOMAS, D. 'The Hunchback in the Park'
THOMAS, R. S. 'Affinity'
WEBSTER, H. 'Street Gang'

Section 3: Teachers' books

Assessment
CHATER, P. *Marking and Assessment in English*, Methuen, 1984.
DUNSBEE, T. and FORD, T. *Mark My Words*, Ward Lock and NATE, 1980.
JOHNSTON, B. *Assessing English*, St Clair Press, 1983.

STIBBS, A. *Assessing Children's Language*, Ward Lock, 1979.

WILKINSON, A. M. *Assessing Language Development*, OUP, 1980.

Computers

CHANDLER, D. and MARCUS, S. *Computers and Literacy*, Open University, 1984.

CHANDLER, D. (Ed.) *Exploring English With Microcomputers*, Council for Educational Technology (CET), 1983.

CHANDLER, D. *Young Learners and the Microcomputer*, Open University, 1984.

HOLMES, B. et al *The Child, the Teacher and the Micro –* Using simulations in the classroom, Cambridge Scholastic Services, 1985.

MOORE, P. *Using Computers in English: a practical guide*, Methuen, 1985.

ROBINSON, B. *Microcomputers and the Language Arts*, OUP, 1985.

TERRY, C. *Using Micro-Computers in School*, Croom Helm, 1984.

Language

BARNES, D. et al *Language, the Learner and the School*, Penguin, 1969.

BRITTON, J. *Language and Learning*, Penguin, 1972.

DOUGHTY, P. *Language in Use*, Arnold, 1971.

EDWARDS, V. *The West Indian Language Issue in British Schools*, Routledge and Kegan Paul, 1979.

HALLIDAY, M. A. K. *Explorations in the Functions of Language*, Arnold, 1973.

HOULTON, D. *All Our Languages:* A Handbook for the Multilingual Classroom, Edward Arnold, 1985.

HOULTON, D. & WILLEY, R. *Supporting Children's Bilingualism*, Longman for Schools Council, 1983.

KHAN, V. et al *Linguistic Minorities Project*, Routledge & Kegan Paul, 1985.

MARLAND, M. (Ed.) *Language Across the Curriculum*, Heinemann, 1977.

OPEN UNIVERSITY *Every Child's Language*, Multilingual Matters Ltd, 1985.

STRATTA, L. et al *Patterns of Language*, Heinemann, 1973.

TORBE, M. (Ed.) *Language Policies in Action*, Ward Lock, 1980.

TRUDGILL, P. *Accent, Dialect and the School*, Edward Arnold, 1975.

TRUDGILL, P. (Ed.) *Language in the British Isles*, CUP, 1984.

WADE, B. (Ed.) *Language Perspectives*, Heinemann, 1982.

WADE, B. (Ed.) *Talking to Some Purpose*, Educational Review, 1985.

WELLS, G. *Language Development in the Pre-School Years*, CUP, 1985.

WILKINSON, A. M. *The Foundations of Language*, OUP, 1971.

WILKINSON, A. M. *Language and Education*, OUP, 1975.

Method and Philosophy

ADAMS, A. (Ed.) *New Directions in English Teaching*, Falmer Press, 1982.

ALLEN, D. *English Teaching Since 1965*, Heinemann, 1980.

BARNES, D. *From Communication to Curriculum*, Penguin, 1976.

BARNES, D. & D. *Versions of English*, Heinemann, 1984.

BARNES, D., TODD, F. *Communication and Learning in Small Groups*, Routledge and Kegan Paul, 1977.

BULLOCK, A. *A Language for Life* (The Bullock Report), HMSO, 1975.

DIXON, J. *Growth Through English*, OUP for NATE, 1967.

EVANS, T. *Teaching English*, Croom Helm, 1982.

GULLIFORD, R. *Teaching Children with Learning Difficulties*, NFER-Nelson, 1985.

HORNER, S. (Ed.) *Best Laid Plans: English Teachers At Work*, report by NATE Secondary Committee, Longman for Schools Council, 1983.

JACKSON, D. *Continuity in Secondary English*, Methuen, 1982.

KLEIN, G. *Resources for Multicultural Education – an Introduction*, Longman, 1984.

KNOTT, R. *The English Department in a Changing World*, Heinemann, 1984.

MARTIN, N. et al *Understanding Children Talking*, Penguin, 1976.

MEEK, M. & MILLER, J. (Eds) *Changing English* Essays for Harold Rosen, Heinemann, 1984.

PEARCE, J. *The Heart of English* Nine to Fourteen, OUP, 1985.

RALEIGH, M. *The English Department Book*, ILEA English Centre, 1982.

Reading

BENTON, M. & FOX, G. *Teaching Literature* Nine to Fourteen, OUP, 1985.

BRENNAN, W. K. *Reading for Slow Learners* A Curriculum Guide, Evans/Methuen, 1978.

FRY, D. *Children Talk About Books:* Seeing themselves as readers, OUP, 1985.

GUNNER, E. *A Handbook for Teaching African Literature*, Heinemann, 1984.

HAYHOE, M. & PARKER, S. *Working with Fiction*, Edward Arnold, 1984.

JACKSON, D. *Encounters with Books*, Methuen, 1983.

LEESON, R. *Reading and Righting*, Collins, 1985.

LUNZER, E. & GARDNER, K. *Learning from the Written Word*, Schools Council, Oliver & Boyd, 1984.

LUNZER, E. & GARDNER, K. (Eds.) *The Effective Use of Reading*, Schools Council, Heinemann, 1979.

McVITTY, W. (Ed.) *Guide to Children's Literature*, PETA, 1985.

MEEK, M. (Ed.) *The Cool Web:* The Pattern of Children's Reading, Bodley Head, 1977.

MEEK, M. et al *Achieving Literacy* – Longitudinal Studies of Adolescents Learning to Read, Routledge & Kegan Paul, 1983.

MOSS, E. *Picture Books for Young People 9–13*, Signal Bookguides, 1985 2nd Edition.

PROTHEROUGH, R. *Developing Response to Fiction* Open University, 1983.

TAYLOR, B. & BRAITHWAITE, P. (Eds.) *The Good Book Guide to Children's Books*, Penguin, 1985.

SMITH, F. *Reading*, CUP, 1978.

SOUTHGATE, V. et al *Extending Beginning Reading*, Heinemann, 1981.

WADE, B. *Story at Home & School*, Educational Review, 1984.

WATSON, K. (Ed.) *Reading Is Response*, St. Clair Press, 1980.

WHITEHEAD, F. *Children and their Books*, Macmillan, 1977.

YOUNG, P. & TYRE, C. *Dyslexia or Illiteracy?* Open University, 1983.

Writing

BEARD, R. *Children's Writing in the Primary School*, Hodder & Stoughton, 1984.

BLISHEN, E. (Ed.) *The Thorny Paradise*, Kestrel Penguin, 1975.

BRITTON, J. et al *The Development of Writing Abilities 11–18*, Macmillan, 1975.

BURGESS, T. et al *Understanding Children's Writing*, Penguin, 1973.

DIXON, J. & STRATTA, L. *Achievements in Writing at 16+* and other pamphlets, Schools Council, 1981.

GRAVES, D. M. *Writing: Teachers & Children at Work*, Heinemann, 1983.

HARRISON, B. T. *Learning Through Writing*, NFER-Nelson, 1983.

KRESS, G. *Learning to Write*, Routledge and Kegan Paul, 1982.

MAYBURY, B. *Creative Writing for Juniors* 2nd edition, Batsford, 1981.

PROTHEROUGH, R. *Encouraging Writing*, Methuen, 1983.

SMITH, F. *Writing and the Writer*, Heinemann, 1982.

TORBE, M. *Teaching Spelling*, Ward Lock, 1977.

TURNBULL, J. *Now We Want To Write*, PETA, 1983.

WALSHE, R. D. *Every Child Can Write*, PETA, 1981.

WILKINSON, A. M. *The Quality of Writing*, Open University, 1986.

WILKINSON, A. M. (Ed.) *The Writing of Writing*, Open University, 1986.

Periodicals

Children's Literature in Education (international quarterly), Agathon Press Inc., 111 Eighth Avenue, New York, NY10011.

Critical Quarterly, Manchester University Press, Oxford Road, Manchester M13 9PL.

Educational Review (three times a year), Birmingham University Faculty of Education, PO Box 363, Edgbaston, Birmingham B15 2TT

English in Education (three times a year), The NATE Office, 49 Bromgrove Road, Sheffield S10 2NA.

Multi-ethnic Education Review (bi-annually), ILEA Learning Resources Branch, Production Division, Highbury Station Road, London N1 1SB.

Reading (three times a year), UKRA, Basil Blackwell Ltd, 108 Cowley Road, Oxford OX4 1JF.

School Librarian (quarterly), The School Library Association, Victoria House, 29–31 George Street, Oxford OX1 2AY.

Signal, Approaches to Children's Books, (three times a year), The Thimble Press, Lockwood, Station Road, South Woodchester, Stroud, Glos GL5 5EQ.

Support for Learning (formerly *Remedial Education*) (three times a year), Longman Group Ltd, Subscriptions (Journals) Department, Fourth Avenue, Harlow, Essex CM19 5AA.

Teaching London Kids (bi-annually), TLK, 20 Durham Road, London SW20.

Times Educational Supplement, and *Times Literary Supplement* (weekly), Priory House, St John's Lane, London EC1M 4BX.

Times Educational Supplement (Scotland), 56 Hanover Street, Edinburgh EH2 2DZ.

Use of English (three times a year), Scottish Academic Press (Ref. U/E), 33 Montgomery Street, Edinburgh EH7 5JX.

Section 4: Class libraries

We hope that the following lists will be of particular use to new teachers but also to experienced staff who may not be familiar with the age/interest/ability ranges contemplated here.

None of the age compartments should be regarded as

watertight. They merely indicate the points at which we've found material to be appropriate and which we would be confident in recommending to others. Some books, as we are all aware, can span an enormous range.

Almost all the literature in our lists is modern, not because only modern literature is accessible or appropriate for today's pupils but because such material may be less familiar to an English teacher trained in the discipline. Teachers who have followed college or university courses in English literature will be well aware of the vast riches to be mined with pupils. Certainly, none of us would wish to rule out great literature which is part of our cultural heritage; we must first ascertain its appropriateness for our boys and girls. I have heard the choice of a book (*Middlemarch*, in fact) justified to a third-year class with the words, 'You've got to do it because it's one of the classics'. This is not sufficient, great a book as *Middlemarch* is.

Some of the material in the lists which follow would be highly appropriate for detailed study either with the teacher or in small groups. Shirley Hoole gives information about this in her chapter on literature, but teachers must decide such a matter for themselves, when they have studied the books and know their children well. So we haven't been prescriptive and indicated which books, in our opinion, are suitable for detailed work. However, we have asterisked material for weaker readers, not to determine who should read what, but to make the teacher's initial choice a little easier.

For additional books in the easy reading range we would refer you to the publishers' catalogues for Longman *Knockout* and *Tempo* series; Macmillan *Topliner* and *Nippers* books and, at a higher level, Heinemann *Windmill* series and Longman *Imprint* books. A collection of all publishers' current catalogues is extremely useful.

Class Library 11–12 years
ALEXANDER, L. *The Book of Three*, Fontana;
   The Black Cauldron, Fontana.
ANDERSON, J. *The Vikings*, Penguin.
ASHLEY, B. *A Kind of Wild Justice*, Puffin;
   Your Guess is as Good as Mine, Puffin.

BARRY, M. *Tommy Mac*, Viking Kestrel;
  Tommy Mac Battles On, Viking Kestrel;
  Tommy Mac on Safari, Viking Kestrel.
BAWDEN, N. *The Witch's Daughter*, Penguin.
BENJAMIN, F. *Why the Agouti has no Tail*, Hutchinson.
BLUME, J. *Tales of a 4th Grade Nothing*, Piccolo;
  Otherwise Known as Sheila the Great, Piccolo.
BOND, R. *Tales and Legends from India*, Julia MacRae.
BREENBURG, *One Day, Another Day*, Macmillan.
BRIGGS, R. *Fungus the Bogeyman*, Hamish Hamilton.
BYARS, B. *TV Ki*, Macmillan;
  Another Day, Macmillan;
  The Eighteenth Emergency, Puffin;
  The Two Thousand Pound Goldfish, Puffin.
BURNETT, F. *The Secret Garden*, Penguin.
CARR, J. *The Red Windcheater*, Macmillan.
COCKETT, M. *The Lost Money*, Macmillan.
COOPER, L. *The Strange Feathery Beast and Other French
  Fables*, Carousel.
COOPER, S. *Dawn of fear*, Puffin.
CRESSWELL, H. *John's First Fish*, Macmillan.
DAHL, R. *Charlie and the Chocolate Factory*, Penguin;
  James and the Giant Peach, Penguin.
DEADMAN, R. *The Pretenders*, Macmillan.
DE LARRABEITI, M. *The Borribles*, Piccolo;
  The Borribles go for broke, Piccolo.
EDWARDS, D. *A Strong and Willing Girl*, Magnet.
ELKIN, J. *The New Golden Land Anthology*, Puffin.
ELLIS, A. Williams *The Story Spirits*, Piccolo.
ENRIGHT, E. *Thimble Summer*, Penguin.
FURNEAUX, R. *On Buried and Sunken Treasure*, Penguin.
GARNER, A. *The Stone Book Quartet*, Fontana;
  Elidor, Fontana;
  The Moon of Gomrath, Fontana.
GARNETT, E. *The Family from One End Street*, Penguin.
GILROY, B. *Knock at Mrs Herb's*, Macmillan.
GORDON, J. *The Giant under the Snow*, Penguin.
GREEN, R. *The Tale of Troy*, Penguin;
  Myths of the Norsemen, Penguin;
  Tales of the Greek Heroes, Penguin.
GREENE, B. *Philip Hall Likes Me, I Reckon Maybe*, Penguin.

GRICE, F. *Folk Tales of the West Midlands* (eight more folk story anthologies in this series), Nelson.

GRIFFITHS, T. **Tip's Lot*, Macmillan.

HESLETINE, M. **Bri's Accident*, Macmillan.

HUGHES, T. *The Iron Man*, Faber.

KÄSTNER, E. *Emil and the Detectives*, Penguin;
Lottie and Lisa, Cape.

KAYE, G. *Comfort herself*, Deutsch;
Nowhere to Stop, Brockhampton.

KING, C. *Stig of the Dump*, Penguin.

KIPLING, R. *Just So Stories*, Macmillan;
The Jungle Book, Macmillan.

LEESON, R. *Grange Hill Rules OK?*, Penguin.

DAY LEWIS, C. *The Otterbury Incident*, Heinemann.

LEWIS, C. S. *The Lion, the Witch and the Wardrobe*, Fontana;
The Magician's Nephew, Fontana;
Prince Caspian, Fontana;
The Voyage of the Dawn Treader, Fontana;
The Last Battle, Fontana.

LIVELY, P. *The Ghost of Thomas Kempe*, Heinemann.

McNEIL, J. **The Family Upstairs*, Macmillan.

MANKOWITZ, W. *A Kid for Two Farthings*, Heinemann.

MARK, J. *Hairs in the Palm of the Hand*, Puffin.

MILLIGAN, S. **A Book of Milliganimals*, Penguin;
Silly Verse for Kids, Penguin.

MORRIS, M. *About Dinosaurs*, Penguin.

NEEDLE, J. *My Mate Shofiq*, Fontana;
Wild Wood, Magnet;
Behind the Bike Sheds, Methuen.

OATES, A. **Meet Harry King*, Macmillan;
The Bet, Macmillan;
The Milk Round, Macmillan.

PEARCE, P. *The Battle of Bubble and Squeak*, Puffin;
Tom's Midnight Garden, Penguin;
Return to Air, Penguin.

PICKERING, P. **Uncle Norman*, Macmillan.

ROBERTSON, S. **The New Pet*, Macmillan.

ROBINSON, B. *The Worst Kids in the World*, Hamlyn.

ROSEN, M. *Quick Let's Get Out of Here*, Fontana.

SERRAILLIER, I. *I'll Tell you a Tale*, Viking Kestrel;
The Way of Danger, Heinemann.
SMITH, D. *The Hundred and One Dalmatians*, Heinemann;
The Starlight Barking, Penguin.
STORR, C. *Marianne Dreams*, Penguin.
STREATFEILD, N. *Ballet Shoes*, Penguin.
SUTCLIFF, R. *Brother Dusty-Feet*, OUP;
Dragon Slayer, Penguin;
*The Chief's Daughter, Piccolo.
TATE, J. **The Crane*, Heinemann.
TOWNSEND, J. *Gumble's Yard*, Penguin.
TREECE, H. *Viking's Dawn*, Penguin;
Viking's Sunset, Penguin;
The Road to Miklagard, Penguin;
Horned Helmet, Macmillan.
WARNER, R. *Men and Gods*, Heinemann.
WILLIAMS, J. *The Practical Princess*, Scholastic.
WILLIAMSON, H. *Tarka the Otter*, Penguin.

Class library 12–13 years
ADAMSON, J. *Born Free*, Fontana.
ALCOCK, V. *The Haunting of Cassie Palmer*, Fontana.
ALLEN, E. *The Latchkey Children*, OUP.
BACH, R. *Jonathan Livingston Seagull*, Pan.
BALDWIN, M. *Grandad with Snails*, Hutchinson.
BAWDEN, N. *Carrie's War*, Heinemann;
On the Run, Penguin.
BLUME, J. *It's Not the End of the World*, Piccolo;
Are you There God, it's Me, Margaret, Piccolo.
BRENNAND, S. *Gold and Granite*, Penguin.
BROWN, M. *A Book of Sea Legends*, Hamilton.
BUSH, H. *Mary Anning's Treasures*, Heinemann.
BUTLER, W. **The Riddles of the Yojok Rocks*, Macmillan.
BYARS, B. *The Pinballs*, Puffin;
The Cartoonist, Puffin.
CHRISTOPHER, J. *In the Beginning*, Longman;
The Guardians, Puffin.
CLEARY, B. **Ramona the Pest*, Penguin.
COOKSON, C. *The Nipper*, Penguin.
COOPER, S. *The Dark is rising quintet*, Puffin;
The Grey King, Puffin.

DARKE, M. *A Question of Courage*, Penguin;
   The First of Midnight, Penguin.
DeJONG. M. *The House of Sixty Fathers*, Penguin.
DICKINSON, P. *The Weathermonger*, Penguin;
   The Devil's Children, Penguin;
   Heartsease, Penguin.
DOORLY. E. *The Radium Woman*, Heinemann.
DOYLE, A. C. *Memories of Sherlock Holmes*, Penguin;
   Hound of the Baskervilles, Pan.
DRAKE, T. *Playing it right*, Puffin.
FITZHUGH, L. *Nobody's Family is Going to Change*, Fontana.
FOSTER, J. **My Friend Cheryl*, Macmillan.
GARNER, A. *The Owl Service*, Fontana;
   The Weirdstone of Brisingamen, Fontana.
GARFIELD, L. *Mister Corbett's Ghost and Other Stories*,
   Penguin.
GODDEN, R. *The Diddakoi*, Penguin.
HARNETT, C. *The Wool Pack*, Penguin.
HOLM, A. *I am David*, Magnet.
KAY, S. *Digging into the Past*, Penguin.
LEESON, R. *Third Class Genie*, Fontana;
   Genie on the Loose, Fontana.
LEGUIN, U. *Wizard of Earthsea*, Heinemann.
LINGARD, J. *Maggie and Sequels*, Penguin.
MAGORIAN, M. *Goodnight Mister Tom*, Puffin.
MARK, J. *Thunder and Lightnings*, Penguin.
MARSHALL, J. *My Boy that Went to Sea*, Heinemann.
MONTGOMERY. L. *Anne of Green Gables*, Penguin.
MORPURGO, M. **It Never Rained* (short stories), Macmillan.
MORROW, H. *The Splendid Journey*, Heinemann.
NAUGHTON, B. *My Pal Spadger*, Heinemann.
NEEDLE, J. *A Game of Soldiers*, Fontana.
NESBIT, E. *The Railway Children*, Heinemann.
OATES. A. **Tests and Things*, Macmillan;
   *Meet Linda King, Macmillan;
   *The Leather Jacket Boys, Macmillan.
O'DELL, S. *Island of the Blue Dolphins*, Penguin.
PEARCE, P. *A Dog So Small*, Penguin.
PICARD, B. *One is One*, OUP.
PLATER, A. **Trouble with Abracadabra*, Macmillan.
POINTON, B. *Michelle* (4 stories), Macmillan.

READ, R. *The Living Sea*, Penguin.
ROCKET, B. *Whales and Dolphins*, Penguin.
ROGERS. *The Playing Field Horses*, Abelard;
    The Magnolia Tree, Abelard.
ROWE, A. *Lone Wolf*, Macmillan.
RYAN, P. *The Ocean World*, Penguin.
SALKEY, A. *Earthquake*, OUP;
    Hurricane, OUP;
    Drought, OUP.
SERRAILLIER, I. *The Clashing Rocks*, Heinemann;
    The Silver Sword, Penguin;
    There's No Escape, Heinemann.
SLATER *Hamburger's House of Horrors*, Abelard.
SMITH, L. *The New House*, Macmillan.
STEVENSON, R. L. *Treaure Island*, Penguin.
STREATFEILD, N. *Growing Summer*, Penguin.
STUCLEY, E. *Magnolia Buildings*, Penguin.
SUTCLIFF, R. *Warrior Scarlet*, OUP.
TOLKIEN, J.R. *The Hobbit*, Allen & Unwin.
TREASE, G. *Cue for Treason*, Penguin.
TREECE, H. *The Dream Time*, Heinemann;
    Legions of the Eagle, Penguin.
TWAIN, M. *Tom Sawyer*, Penguin;
    Huckleberry Finn, Penguin.
UNDERHILL, R. *Antelope Singer*, Penguin;
    Beaverbird, Ward Lock.
WALSH, G. *The Dolphin Crossing*, Penguin.
WESTALL, R. *The Machine Gunners*, Penguin.
WHITE, T. *The Sword in the Stone*, Fontana.
WILDER, L. *Little House on the Prairie*, Puffin.

Class library 13–14 years
ADAMS, R. *Watership Down*, Penguin.
ARMSTRONG, W. *Sounder*, Penguin.
ASHLEY, B. *A Kind of Wild Justice*, Puffin.
BANKS, L. *One More River*, Penguin.
BLISH, J. *Star Trek*, Corgi.
BOYERS, B. *Lost and Found*, Evans;
    Two Sides to Everything, Evans.
CARTER, B. *The Bike Racers*, Longman.
CATE, D. *On the Run*, Macmillan.

CHAMBERS, A. **Don't Forget Charlie*, Macmillan;
*The Vase, Macmillan;
*Ghosts (short stories), Macmillan;
*Ghosts 2, Macmillan.
CHILTON, I. **The Hundred*, Macmillan.
CHITTY, S. & PARRY, A. *The Puffin Book of Horses*, Penguin.
CHRISTOPHER, J. *The White Mountains*, Hutchinson.
CLARKE, A. C. *Of Time and Stars* (short stories), Penguin.
COOKSON, C. *Joe and the Gladiators*, Penguin.
CROSS, G. *The Dark Behind the Curtain*, OUP;
On the Edge, OUP.
DEJONG, M. *The Tower by the Sea*, Hutchinson.
DICKENSON, C. **Siege at Robins Hill*, Macmillan.
DICKINSON, P. *The Seventh Raven*, Puffin.
FITZHUGH, L. *Harriet the Spy*, Fontana.
FOX, P. *Blowfish Live in the Sea*, Penguin.
GALLICO, P. *The Snow Goose*, Penguin.
GARDAM, J. *The Hollow Land*, Puffin.
GARFIELD, L. *Smith*, Penguin.
GLANVILLE, B. *Goalkeepers are Different*, Penguin.
GOODBODY, J. **Topliner Book of Football*, Macmillan.
GREEN, B. *Summer of my German Soldier*, Penguin.
GREEN, J. **The Six* (short stories and cassette), Longman.
GRICE, F. *The Bonny Pit Laddie*, OUP.
GUY, R. *The Friends*, Puffin.
HILDICK, E. **Birdy Jones* (and others in the series),
Macmillan;
*Louie's SOS, Macmillan;
Louie's Lot, Macmillan.
HAUGAARD, E. *The Little Fishes*, Heinemann.
HITCHCOCK, A. *Ghostly Gallery* (short stories), Reinhardt.
HOWKER, J. *Badger on the Barge*, Julia MacRae.
HOY, L. *Your friend, Rebecca*, Sparrow.
HUDDY, D. **The Mini Prize*, Macmillan.
JONES, D. *Charmed Life*, Puffin,
The Homeward Bounders, Magnet.
KENNEMORE, T. *Wall of Words*, Puffin.
KITCHING, J. **One From Three Makes None*, Macmillan;
*Anyway (short stories), Macmillan.
LAYTON, G. **A Northern Childhood. The Balaclava Story
and Other Stories*, Longman.

LEESON, R. *It's My Life*, Fontana.
LEGUIN, U. *The Farthest Shore*, Heinemann;
Tombs of Atuan, Heinemann.
LESTER, J. *A Taste of Freedom*, Longman.
LINGARD, J. *The Twelfth Day of July*, Penguin.
LIVELY, P. *A Stitch in Time*, Piccolo.
LONDON, J. *White Fang*, Heinemann.
MADDOCK, R. **Sell Out*, Macmillan;
*Dragon in the Garden, Macmillan.
MARSHALL, A. *I Can Jump Puddles*, Penguin.
MARSHALL, J. *Walkabout*, Penguin.
MAXWELL, G. *Ring of Bright Water*, Penguin.
MAYNE, W. *Earthfasts*, Hamilton.
MORSE, B. **The Ring*, Macmillan.
NAUGHTON, B. *The Goalkeeper's Revenge* (short stories),
Penguin.
NEEDLE, J. *A Sense of Shame*, Fontana.
O'BRIEN, R. *Z for Zachariah*, Fontana.
OWEN, E. **Freestyle Champ*, Evans.
PARK, R. *Playing Beattie Bow*, Puffin.
PATERSON, K. *Bridge to Terabithia*, Puffin,
The Great Gilly Hopkins, Puffin.
POPE, R. **Is It Always Like This?* Macmillan;
*The Drum, Macmillan.
RAWLINGS, M. *The Yearling*, Heinemann.
RHUE, M. *The Wave*, Puffin.
RUDGE, K. **The Mud Scene*, Macmillan.
RYAN, P. *Journey to the Planets*, Penguin;
UFOs and Other Worlds, Penguin;
Planet Earth, Penguin.
SERRAILLIER, I. *Fight for Freedom*, Heinemann.
SCHAEFER, J. *Shane and Other Stories*, Penguin.
SHERMAN, D. *Old Mali and the Boy*, Heinemann.
SHERRY, S. *A Pair of Jesus-Boots*, Heinemann.
SHYER, M. *Welcome home, Jellybean*, Dragon.
SOUTHALL, I. *Josh*, Penguin.
SPERRY, A. *The Boy Who Was Afraid*, Heinemann.
STEINBECK, J. *The Red Pony*, Heinemann.
STEWART, M. **Orange Wendy*, Macmillan.
STRACHAN, I. *Moses Beech*, OUP.

SUTCLIFF, R. *Eagle of the Ninth*, OUP;
  The Outcast, OUP;
  Mark of the Horselord, OUP.
SWINDELLS, R. *Brother in the land*, Puffin.
TATE, J. **Tad*, Heinemann;
  *Ginger Mick (and cassette), Longman;
  *The Rabbit Boy, Heinemann;
  *The Next Doors, Heinemann.
TAYLOR, T. *The Cay*, Heinemann.
TOWNSEND, J. *Goodnight Prof. Love.* OUP.
TOWNSEND, S. *The Secret diary of Adrian Mole aged 13¾*,
  Methuen;
  The Growing Pains of Adrian Mole, Methuen.
ULYATT, K. *The Day of the Cowboy*, Penguin;
  The Time of the Indian, Penguin.
URE, J. *A Proper Little Nooryeff*, Puffin.
WALSH, J. P. *A Parcell of Patterns*, Puffin.
WATERHOUSE, K. *There is a Happy Land*, Longman.
WELLS, H. G. *War of the Worlds*, Heinemann;
  The First Men in the Moon, Longman.
WILSON, J. *Nobody's Perfect*, Puffin.
WILSON, R. **All for the Rovers*, Macmillan.
WRIGHTSON, P. *I Own the Racecourse*, Penguin.
ZINDEL, P. *The Pigman*, Macmillan;
  Pardon Me You're Stepping on My Eyeball, Fontana.

Class library 14–15 years
ABSE, D. *Ash on a Young Man's Sleeve*, Penguin.
ACHEBE, C. *Things Fall Apart*, Heinemann.
AIKEN. J. **Night Fall*, Macmillan.
ALLINGHAM, M. *Tiger in the Smoke*, Penguin.
ANDERSON, L. & SHERWIN, D. *If* (Film script), Plexus.
ANDERSON, R. *The Poacher's Son*, Fontana.
ARKLEY Ed. **Gangs and Victims*, Nelson;
  In Fear and Dread, Nelson;
  Ends and Escapes, Nelson;
  Far Out, Nelson.
ARUNDEL, H. **The Girl in the Opposite Bed*, Macmillan.
AVERY, V. *London Morning*, Arnold-Wheaton.
BARSTOW. S. *Joby*, Heinemann.

BATES. H. E. *The Good Corn and Other Stories* (Ed. G. Halson), Longman;
  My Uncle Silas (short stories), Cape.
BECKMAN. G. **19 is Too Young to Die*, Macmillan.
BLISHEN, E. *The School that I'd Like*, Penguin.
BOULLE, P. *The Bridge on the River Kwai*, Heinemann.
BRADBURY, R. *Fahrenheit 451*, Hart-Davis.
BRAITHWAITE, E. *To Sir, With Love*, Heinemann.
BRANFIELD, J. *The Fox in Winter*, Fontana.
BRATSTROM, I. **Since That Party*, Macmillan.
CHAMBERS. A. **I Want to Get Out*, Macmillan.
CHESTERTON, G. K. *The Incredulity of Father Brown* (short stories), Penguin;
  The Wisdom of Father Brown, Penguin;
  The Innocence of Father Brown, Penguin;
  The Secret of Father Brown, Penguin.
CHRISTOPHER, J. *The Guardians*, Heinemann;
  The City of Gold and Lead, Hutchinson;
  The Pool of Fire, Hutchinson.
CLEARY, B. *Fifteen*, Penguin.
COLE, G. *Gregory's Girl*, Fontana.
DARKE, M. *Comeback*, Puffin;
  A Long Way to Go, Puffin.
DAVIES, M. & MARLAND, M. *Breaking Away* (extracts), Longman.
DHONDY, F. *Come to Mecca*, Fontana;
  East End at Your Feet, Fontana.
DICKINSON, P. *Tulku*, Puffin.
FOSTER, J. **That's Love*, Macmillan.
FRANK, A. *The Diary of Ann Frank*, Pan.
GARNER, A. *Red Shift*, Fontana.
GUY, R. *Edith Jackson*, Puffin.
HANLEY, C. *A Taste of Too Much*, Blackie.
HAUTZIG, D. *Hey Dollface*, Fontana;
  Second Star to the Right, Fontana.
HEMINGWAY, E. *The Old Man and the Sea*, Heinemann.
HERRIOT, J. *It Shouldn't Happen to a Vet*, Pan.
HEYERDAHL, T. *The Kon-Tiki Expedition*, Allen & Unwin.
HINES, B. *A Kestrel for a Knave*, Penguin.
HINTON, N. *Buddy*, Puffin.

HINTON, S. *That Was Then, This is Now*, Fontana.
  The Outsiders, Fontana;
  Tex, Fontana;
  Rumble Fish, Fontana.
HITCHMAN, J. *The King of the Barbareens*, Penguin.
HOLM, A. *I Am David*, Magnet.
INNES, H. *The White South*, Fontana;
  The Wreck of the 'Mary Deare', Fontana.
JONES, T. *Go Well, Stay Well*, Fontana.
KAMM, J. *Young Mother*, Heinemann;
  Out of Step, Heinemann.
KAYE, G. *Marie Alone*, Heinemann.
KELLER, H. *The Story of My Life*, Collier-Macmillan.
KNOWLES, J. *A Separate Peace*, Heinemann.
LAYE, C. *African Child*, Fontana.
LEACH, C. *Decision for Katie*, Macmillan;
  Answering Miss Roberts, Macmillan.
LEE, L. *Cider with Rosie*, Penguin.
LEESON, R. *It's my Life*, Fontana.
LEGUIN, U. *Rocannon's World*, Star.
LINGARD, J. *Across the Barricades*, PENGUIN.
LIPSYTE, R. *The Contender*, Macmillan.
LOWRY, L. *A Summer to Die*, Dragon.
McGRATH, P. *The Green Leaves of Nottingham*, Hutchinson.
MADDOCK, R. *The Pit*, Macmillan.
MARLAND, E. & M. *Friends and Families* (extracts), Longman.
MARLAND, M. *Loves, Hopes and Fears*, Longman;
  The Experience of Work, Longman;
  The Experience of Sport, Longman;
  (all extracts)
MARSHALL, J. *The Children*, Methuen.
MORPURGO, M. *Long Way Home*, Macmillan.
NEVILLE, E. *It's Like This Cat*, Heinemann.
ORWELL, G. *Animal Farm*, Penguin.
PEYTON, K. *Flambards*, Oxford.
PIERCE, M. *The Dark-angel*, Fontana.
SANDFORD, J. *Cathy Come Home*, Boyars.
SCHLEE, A. *The Vandal*, Magnet.
SHOLOKHOV, M. *Fierce and Gentle Warriors* (short stories), Heinemann.

SHUTE, N. *A Town Like Alice*, Heinemann.
SMITH, C. *Ten Western Stories*, Longman.
STEINBECK, J. *The Pearl*, Heinemann.
STORR, C. *Thursday*, Penguin.
TATE, J. *Sam and Me*, Macmillan;
   Clipper, Macmillan;
   Whizz Kid, Macmillan;
   The Silver Grill, Heinemann;
   The Tree, Heinemann.
TAYLOR, M. *Let the Circle be Unbroken*, Puffin;
   Roll of Thunder, Hear My Cry, Puffin.
TOYNBEE, P. *A Working Life*, Penguin.
URE, J. *See You Thursday*, Puffin.
WALSH, J. *Fireweed*, Penguin.
WATSON, J. *Talking in Whispers*, Fontana.
WILLIAMS, E. *The Wooden Horse*, Collins;
   Great Escape Stories, Penguin.
ZINDEL, P. *My Darling, My Hamburger*, Fontana;
   I Never Loved Your Mind, Fontana;
   Confessions of a Teenage Baboon, Fontana.

Class library 15–16 years
ANTHONY, M. *Green Days By the River*, Heinemann.
ASIMOV, I. *I, Robot*, Panther.
BALDWIN, J. *Go Tell it on the Mountain*, Corgi.
BARSTOW, S. *A Kind of Loving*, Corgi;
   The Human Element (short stories), Longman;
   A Casual Acquaintance and Other Stories (Ed. M. Davies,
   with cassette), Longman.
BATES, H. E. *The Triple Echo*, Penguin.
BECKMAN, G. *Mia*, Longman.
BRADBURY, R. *Golden Apples of the Sun* (short stories),
   Panther.
BUCHANAN, P. *The Marco File*, Longman.
CHAMBERS, A. & N. *World Zero Minus* (short stories),
   Macmillan;
   In Time to Come (short stories), Macmillan.
CRISPIN, E. *The Stars and Under* (short stories), Faber.
FACEY, A. B. *A Fortunate Life*, Penguin.
GOLDING, W. *Lord of the Flies*, Faber.
GORKI, M. *My Childhood*, Penguin.

GRAVES, R. *Goodbye to All That*, Penguin.
GREENE, G. *Brighton Rock*, Penguin;
  The Power and the Glory, Penguin.
HALEY, A. *Roots*, Picador.
HARTLEY, L. P. *The Go-Between*, Penguin.
HELLER, J. *Catch–22*, Corgi.
HERSEY, J. *Hiroshima*, Penguin.
HEWINS, A. *The Dillen*, OUP.
HOLT, J. *How Children Fail*, Penguin.
HUGHES, R. *High Wind in Jamaica*, Panther.
HUXLEY, A. *Brave New World*, Panther.
JOYCE, J. *Dubliners* (short stories), Panther;
  Portrait of the Artist as a Young Man, Panther.
KAFKA, F. *Metamorphosis and Other Stories*, Penguin.
KAMM, J. *Young Mother*, Heinemann.
KAUFMAN, B. *Up the Down Staircase*, Pan.
KOHL, H. *36 Children*, Penguin.
KOZOL, J. *Death at an Early Age*, Penguin.
LASKI, M. *Little Boy Lost*, Heinemann.
LAWRENCE, D. H. *Selected Tales*, Heinemann;
  Sons and Lovers, Penguin;
  The Rainbow, Penguin.
LAWRENCE, L. **Andra*, Macmillan.
LEE, H. *To Kill a Mockingbird*, Heinemann.
LEGUIN, U. *Lathe of Heaven*, Panther.
LESSING, D. *Nine African Stories*, Longman;
  The Habit of Loving, Panther.
LONDON, J. *Twelve Short Stories* (ed. J. Tillett), Arnold.
McCULLERS. C. *The Heart is a Lonely Hunter*, Penguin;
  The Member of the Wedding, Heinemann.
MALAMUD, B. *The Assistant*, Penguin.
MEAD, M. *Growing Up in New Guinea*, Penguin.
NAIPAUL, V.S. *Miguel Street* (short stories), Penguin.
NAUGHTON, B. *One Small Boy*, Longman;
  Late Night on Watling Street, Longman.
O'BRIEN, E. *The Country Girls*, Penguin.
O'CONNOR, F. *My Oedipus Complex and Other Stories*,
  Penguin.
ORWELL, G. *Nineteen Eighty-Four*, Penguin;
  Down and Out in Paris and London, Penguin;
  The Road to Wigan Pier, Penguin.

PATON, A. *Cry, the Beloved Country*, Penguin.

REMARQUE, E. *All Quiet on the Western Front*, Heinemann.

SALINGER, J.D. *The Catcher in the Rye*, Penguin.

SILLITOE, A. *A Sillitoe Selection*, Longman;
Saturday Night and Sunday Morning, Longman;
The Loneliness of the Long Distance Runner, Longman.

SOLZHENITSYN, A. *One Day in the Life of Ivan Denisovich*, Penguin.

STEINBECK, J. *Of Mice and Men*, Heinemann;
The Grapes of Wrath, Heinemann.

UPDIKE, J. *Pigeon Feathers and Other Stories*, Penguin.

VONNEGUT, K. *Slaughterhouse Five*, Panther.

WATERHOUSE, K. *Billy Liar*, Penguin.

WATTS, S. *The Breaking of Arnold*, Macmillan.

WINDSOR, P. *The Summer Before*, Macmillan.

WOODHAM-SMITH, C. *The Reason Why*, Penguin.

WRIGHT, R. *Black Boy*, Longman;
Native Son, Penguin.

WYNDHAM, J. *The Chrysalids*, Penguin;
The Kraken Wakes, Penguin;
The Day of the Triffids, Penguin.

8 Useful Addresses

RICHARD MILLS

Section 1: Publishers

It's useful to have in each school an up-to-date collection of catalogues from the main educational suppliers. Most publishers will provide free catalogues on request and many include Heads of English Departments in schools on their regular mailing lists. In addition, the majority offer an inspection copy service which permits books to be assessed for a limited period on a sale/return/retain and requisition basis. Some beginning teachers may be unaware of this facility and the following addresses may prove helpful not only to them but to all staff.

Allen (George) & Unwin Ltd, Ruskin House, 40 Museum Street, London WC1A 1LU. Tel. 01 405 8577.
Arnold-Wheaton Ltd, Parkside Lane, Leeds LS11 5TD. Tel. 0532 772112.
Arnold (Edward) (Publishers) Ltd, 41 Bedford Square, London WC1B 3DQ. Tel. 01 637 7161.
Associated Book Publishers Ltd, 11 New Fetter Lane, London EC4P 4EE. Tel. 01 583 9855.
Batsford (B.T.) Ltd, 4 Fitzhardinge Street, Portman Square, London W1H 0AH. Tel. 01 486 8484.
Bell & Hyman Ltd, Denmark House, 37–39 Queen Elizabeth Street, London SE1 2QB. Tel. 01 407 0709.

Black (A & C) (Publishers) Ltd, 35 Bedford Row, London WC1R 4JH. Tel. 01 242 0946.

Blackie & Son Ltd, Bishopsbriggs, Glasgow G64 2NZ. Tel. 041 772 2311.

Blackwell (Basil) (Publisher) Ltd, 108 Cowley Road, Oxford OX4 1JF. Tel. 0865 724041.

Bodley Head, 30 Bedford Square, London WC1B 3EL. Tel. 01 631 4434.

Brodie (James) Ltd, 15 Queen Square, Bath BA1 2HW. Tel. 0225 22110.

Cambridge University Press, The Edinburgh Building, Shaftesbury Road, Cambridge CB2 2RU. Tel. 0223 312393.

Cape (Jonathan) Ltd, 30 Bedford Square, London WC1B 3EL. Tel. 01 636 3344.

Cassell Ltd, 1 Vincent Square, London SW1P 2PN. Tel. 01 630 7881.

Chambers (W & R) Ltd, 43/45 Annandale Street, Edinburgh EH7 4AZ. Tel. 031 557 4571.

Chatto & Windus Ltd, 40 William IV Street, London WC2N 4DF. Tel. 01 379 6637.

Collins (William) plc, 8 Grafton Street, London WC1X 3LA. Tel. 01 493 7070.

Croom Helm, Provident House, Burrell Road, Beckenham, Kent BR3 1AT. Tel. 01 658 7813.

David & Charles (Holdings) Ltd, Brunel House, Newton Abbot, Devon TQ12 4PU. Tel. 0626 61121.

Dent (J.M.) & Sons Ltd, Aldine House, 33 Welbeck Street, London W1M 8LX. Tel. 01 486 7233.

Deutsch (André) Ltd, 105 Great Russell Street, London WC1B 3LJ. Tel. 01 580 2746.

Educational Explorers Ltd, 11 Crown Street, Reading RG1 2TQ. Tel. 0734 873103.

Evans Brothers Ltd, 2A Portman Mansions, Chiltern Street, London W1M 1LE, Tel. 01 935 7160.

Faber & Faber Ltd, 3 Queen Square, London WC1N 3AU. Tel. 01 278 6881.

French (Samuel) Ltd, 52 Fitzroy Street, London W1P 6JR. Tel. 01 387 9373.

Ginn & Co. Ltd, Prebendal House, Parson's Fee, Aylesbury, Bucks HP20 2QZ. Tel. 0296 88411.

Gollancz (Victor) Ltd, 14 Henrietta Street, London WC2E 8QJ. Tel. 01 836 2006.

Hamilton (Hamish) Ltd, Garden House, 57–59 Long Acre, London WC2E 9JZ. Tel. 01 836 7733.

Harper & Row Ltd, 28 Tavistock Street, London WC2E 7PN. Tel. 01 836 4635.

Harrap Ltd, 19–23 Ludgate Hill, London EC4M 7PD. Tel. 01 248 6444.

Heinemann Educational Books Ltd, 22 Bedford Square, London WC1B 3HH. Tel. 01 637 3311.

Her Majesty's Stationery Office, Publicity Department, (P9D) Freepost, Norwich NR3 1BR.

Holmes McDougall Ltd, Allander House, 137–141 Leith Walk, Edinburgh EH6 8NS. Tel. 031 554 9444.

Hutchinson Educational Ltd, Hutchinson House, 17–21 Conway Street, London W1P 6JD. Tel. 01 387 2811.

Jackdaw Publications Ltd, 30 Bedford Square, London WC1B 3EL. Tel. 01 636 3344.

Ladybird Books Ltd, PO Box 12, Beeches Road, Loughborough, Leics LE11 2NQ. Tel. 0509 268021.

Longman Group Ltd, Longman House, Burnt Mill, Harlow, Essex CM20 2JE. Tel. 0279 26721.

Lutterworth Press, 7 All Saints' Passage, Cambridge CB2 3LS. Tel. 0223 350865.

Macdonald & Evans Ltd, Estover, Plymouth PL6 7PZ. Tel. 0752 705251.

Macmillan Education, Houndmills, Basingstoke, Hampshire RG21 2XS. Tel. 0252 29242.

Mary Glasgow Publications, Brookhampton Lane, Kineton, Warwick CV35 0JB. Tel. 0926 640606.

McGraw Hill, McGraw Hill House, Shoppenhangers Road, Maidenhead, Berks SL6 2QL. Tel. 0628 23432.

Methuen & Co. Ltd, 11 New Fetter Lane, London EC4P 4EE. Tel. 01 583 9855.

Murray, John (Publishers) Ltd, 50 Albemarle Street, London W1X 4BD. Tel. 01 493 4361.

Nelson (Thomas) & Sons Ltd, Nelson House, Mayfield Road, Walton-on-Thames, Surrey KT12 5PL. Tel. 0932 246133.

NFER (National Foundation for Educational Research), Nelson, Darville House, 2 Oxford Road East, Windsor, Berks SL4 1DF. Tel. 075 35 58961.

Nisbet (James) & Co. Ltd, Digswell Place, Welwyn, Herts AL8 7SX. Tel. 070 73 25491.

Oliver & Boyd, Robert Stevenson House, 1–3 Baxter's Place, Leith Walk, Edinburgh EH1 3BB. Tel. 031 556 2424.

Open University Press, Open University Educational Enterprises Ltd, 12 Cofferidge Close, Stony Stratford, Milton Keynes MK11 1BY. Tel. 0908 566744.

Oxford University Press, Walton Street, Oxford OX2 6DP. Tel. 0865 56767.

Pan Books Ltd, Cavaye Place, London SW10 9PG. Tel. 01 373 6070.

Paternoster Press Ltd, Paternoster House, 3 Mount Radford Crescent, Exeter, Devon EX2 4JW. Tel. 0392 50631.

Penguin Books Ltd, Bath Road, Harmondsworth, Middlesex UB7 0DA. Tel. 01 759 1984.

Pergamon Press Ltd, Headington Hill Hall, Oxford OX3 0BW. Tel. 0865 64881.

Pitman Publishing Ltd, 128 Long Acre, London WC2E 9AN. Tel. 01 379 7383.

Primary English Teaching Association, (PETA), PO Box 167, Rozelle, N.S.W. 2039, Australia.

Routledge & Kegan Paul, 14 Leicester Square, London WC2H 7PH. Tel. 01 437 9011.

Robert Royce Ltd, 93 Bedwardine Road, London SE19 3AY. Tel. 01 771 2496.

Schofield & Sims Ltd, Dogley Mill, Fenay Bridge, Huddersfield HD8 0NW. Tel. 0484 607080.

St Clair Press, PO Box 314, Epping, N.S.W. 2121, Australia.

Temple Smith (Maurice) Ltd, Gower House, Croft Road, Aldershot, Hants GU11 3HR. Tel. 0252 331551.

Transworld Publishers Ltd (Corgi, Bantam, Carousel, etc.), Century House, 61/63 Uxbridge Road, London W5 5SA. Tel. 01 579 2652.

University Tutorial Press Ltd, 842 Yeovil Road, Trading Estate, Slough SL1 4JQ. Tel. 0753 29844.

Virago Press, 41 William IV Street, London WC2N 4DE. Tel. 01 379 6977.

Ward Lock Educational Ltd, 47 Marylebone Lane, London W1M 6AX. Tel. 01 486 3271.

Section 2: Visual aids

See also the appendix of Gordon Taylor's chapter giving details of film distributors.

Athena International, PO Box 13, Raynham Road Estate, Bishops Stortford, Herts. Tel. 0279 56627.
  Small charge for catalogue of prints, posters, cards and blocks of fine art reproductions.
Audio Visual Productions, Hocker Hill House, Chepstow, Gwent NP6 5ER.
  Free catalogues. Materials on English language, social studies, literature.
BBC Publications, 144–152 Bermondsey Street, London SE1 3TH.
  Teachers' notes and pamphlets.
EAV Ltd (Educational Audio Visual), c/o Mary Glasgow Publications Ltd, Brookhampton Lane, Kineton, Warwick CV35 0BR.
Educational Productions, 89 St Fagan's Road, Fairwater, Cardiff CF5 3AE. Tel. 0222 554760.
  Film strips, slides, wall charts, cassettes, including material in Welsh.
EFVA (Educational Foundation for Visual Aids. Also NCAVAE, National Council for Audio Visual Aids in Education), The George Building, Normal College, Holyhead Road, Bangor LL57 2PZ. Tel. 0248 355155.
  Hire of films and sale of multimedia kits, OHP transparencies, filmstrips, slides, tapes. Teacher-training courses arranged.
Independent Broadcasting Authority (IBA), Education Officer, ITCA, Knighton House, 56 Mortimer Street, London W1N 8AN. Tel. 01 636 6866.
  Annual programme sent to all schools.
Pictorial Charts Educational Trust, 27 Kirchen Road, London W13 0UD. Tel. 01 567 5543.
  Free catalogue of charts on English literature, theatre, library, punctuation, as well as social studies.
Slide Centre Ltd, 143 Chatham Road, London SW11 6SR. Tel. 01 223 3457.
  Free catalogue of slide folios and filmstrips.

Theatre Association, 9 Fitzroy Square, London W1P 6AE. Tel. 01 387 2666.
Over 5000 sets of plays, drama research information etc for library subscribers. Quarterly theatre review. Dialect records for sale.

Visual Publications, The Green, Northleach, Cheltenham, Gloucestershire GL54 1BR. Tel. 04516 518.
Free catalogues.

Woodmansterne Ltd, Greenhill Crescent, Holywell Industrial Estate, Watford, Hertfordshire WS1 8RD. Tel. 0923 28236.
Free catalogue of materials for sale, including tape-slide sequences and slide books.

Section 3: Computers

Fear of robots taking over the world is mirrored in the teacher's nightmare of computers ruling the classroom. Perhaps our real fear is of being left behind, of not knowing what computers can do, how we can use them and where we can get suitable programs. Since many programs presently on the market are the equivalent of poor quality cut-up text books, we need to be on the look-out for the more open-ended variety which give pupils real choices and develop real skills. We can also (i.e. the masochists among us) write our own.
Useful sources include:

Acorn-CES, c/o Victor Marketing Ltd, Denington Estate, Wellingborough, Northamptonshire NN8 2RL. Tel. 0933 79300.

Advisory Unit for Computer Based Education (AUCBE), Endymion Road, Hatfield, Herts AL10 8AU. Tel. 07072 65443.

Cambridge Language Arts Software Services Ltd, 197 Henley Road, Caversham, Reading RG4 0LJ.

Cambridge Micro Software, CUP, The Edinburgh Building; Shaftesbury Road, Cambridge CB2 2RU. Tel. 0223 312393.

CET (Council for Educational Technology), 3 Devonshire Street, London W1N 2BA.

COIC, Sales Dept, Room W1 101, Manpower Services Commission, Moorfoot, Sheffield S1 4PQ. Tel. 0742 704563.

Computer Concepts, 16 Wayside, Chipperfield, Herts WD4 9JJ. Tel. 09277 69727.

Ed.soft, 76 Woodville Road, Exmouth, Devon EX8 1SW. Tel. 0395 275741.

4 mat Educational Software, Linden Lea, Rock Park, Barnstaple, Devon EX32 9AQ. Tel. 0271 45566.

Ginn & Co Ltd, Prebendal House, Parsons Fee, Aylesbury HP20 2QZ. Tel. 0296 88411.

H & H Software, Dept E, 53 Holloway, Runcorn, Cheshire WA7 4TJ. Tel. 09285 65566.

Learning and Training Systems Ltd, Haydon House, Alcester Road, Studley, Warwickshire B80 7AP.

Melbourne House, 131 Trafalgar Road, London SE10.

MEP (Microelectronics Education Programme), Cheviot House, Coach Lane Campus, Newcastle-upon-Tyne NE7 7XA. Tel. 091 266 4716.

Addresses of Regional Centres on application.

System Software, 12 Collegiate Crescent, Sheffield S10 2BA. Tel. 0742 682321.

Tecmedia Ltd, 5 Granby Street, Loughborough, Leics LE11 3DU. Tel. 0509 230248.

Toxteth Tecs, 15 Berbice Road, Liverpool L18 0HU. Tel. 051 734 0786.

Tressell Publications, 139 Carden Avenue, Brighton, Sussex BN1 8NH. Tel. 0273 561464.

Section 4: Multicultural material

More schools in all areas are now providing courses and materials which reflect a variety of ways of life and thought. This may be a response to the presence of many children, in certain schools, from culturally diverse backgrounds, or it may be part of a general move towards widening horizons and learning to appreciate the richness and variety of other cultures. Geographers have clearly had this objective all along but it's only recently that English stock cupboards outside the major cities have begun to acquire in any quantity literature from Asia, Africa, the Caribbean and the Americas.

What follows now is a list of sources for those who wish to extend their interest in this area. The list excludes publishers given elsewhere, and it excludes addresses of embassies, high commissions and tourist offices, all of which could be useful. Some indication is generally given of what each agency has to offer.

All Faiths for One Race (AFFOR), 173 Lozells Road, Lozells, Birmingham B19 1RN. Tel. 021 523 8076.
Translations, resources, library, publications.

All London Teachers Against Racism and Fascism (ALTARF), Room 216, Panther House, Mount Pleasant, London WC1. Tel. 01 278 7856.
Meetings, publications.

Africa Resource Centre, 38 King Street, London WC2. Tel. 01 836 1973.
Also at this address: The Association for the Teaching of Caribbean and African Literature (ATCAL).
Teachers' association to promote Afro-Caribbean writing. Journal *Wasafiri*.

African Arts in Education Project, c/o 101 Odhams Walk, London WC2. Tel. 01 836 2103.
West African artists/musicians for school visits.

African and Asian Resource Centre (AARC), Newman College, Bartley Green, Birmingham B32 2NT. Tel. 021 476 1181.
Reference material, consultancy, courses on Afro-Caribbean literature and multicultural matters.

African and Caribbean Educational Research Project Library, Centre for Learning Resources, 275 Kennington Lane, London SE11 5QZ. Tel. 01 582 2771.
Material, including children's literature, on black experience in Britain and the United States.

Birmingham Development Education Centre (DEC), Selly Oak Colleges, Birmingham B29 6LE. Tel. 021 472 4231.
Bookshop, packages of material on development education, study tours.

British Council, 10 Spring Gardens, London SW1A 2BN. Tel. 01 930 8466.

Information on aspects of English education for overseas consumption and on education in Commonwealth countries.

Catholic Fund for Overseas Development (CAFOD), 2 Garden Close, Stockwell Road, London SW9 9TY. Tel. 01 735 9041.

Resources catalogue, speakers, material on South Africa.

Centre for Contemporary Cultural Studies (CCCS), Faculty of Arts, University of Birmingham, PO Box 363, Birmingham B15 2TT. Tel. 021 472 1301 ext. 3549.

Independent research and post-graduate centre.

Centre for Information on Language Teaching (CILT), Regent's College, Inner Circle, Regents Park, London NW1 4NS. Tel. 01 486 8221/2/3/4.

National centre with information about all aspects of modern languages (including 'community' languages).

Centre for World Development Education (CWDE), 128 Buckingham Palace Road, London SW1W 9SH. Tel. 01 730 8332/3.

Funded largely by ODA (Overseas Development Administration).

Centreprise Bookshop, 136 Kingsland High Street, London E8. Tel. 01 254 9632.

Books on African, United States and Caribbean life and literature and black British material.

Commission for Racial Equality (CRE), Education Department, Elliott House, 10–12 Allington Street, London SW1E 5EH. Tel. 01 828 7022.

Commonwealth Institute, Library and Resource Centre, Kensington High Street, London W8 6NQ. Tel. 01 603 4535.

Materials for reference and loan, including reading lists and bibliographies on all Commonwealth countries.

English Centre, Ebury Teachers' Centre, Sutherland Street, London SW1V 4LH. Tel. 01 828 8560.

English magazine and other publications reflecting culturally diverse society. Reference collection.

Harriet Tubman Bookshop, 27–29 Grove Lane, Handsworth, Birmingham B21 9ES. Tel. 021 554 8479.

Afro-Caribbean fiction and non-fiction.

ILEA Learning Materials Service Publishing Centre, Highbury Station Road, Islington, London N1 1SB. Tel. 01 226 9143.

Free catalogue for wide range of multimedia materials for sale, not hire, including books, simulations, drama packs, booklets and broadsheets.

Institute of Race Relations, 2–6 Leeke Street, London WC1X 9HS. Tel. 01 837 0041.

Reference library and quarterly journal.

National Anti-Racist Movement in Education (NAME), Avon Multicultural Education Centre, Bishop Road, Bristol BS7. Tel. 0272 427636.

Journal, newsletter, publications, conferences.

National Council for Mother-Tongue Teaching (NCMTT), 4 Rutland Terrace, Stamford, Lincolnshire PE9 1QD.

Overseas Development Administration (ODA), Abercrombie House, Eaglesham Road, East Kilbride, Glasgow G75 8EA.

Oxfam, Education Department, 274 Banbury Road, Oxford OX2 7DZ. Tel. 0865 56777.

Race Relations Board, 5 Lower Belgrave Street, London SW1W 0NR. Tel. 01 730 6291.

Regional R.E. Centre, Westhill College, Selly Oak, Birmingham B29 6LL. Tel. 021 472 7245.

Major religions and third world materials.

Royal Anthropological Society, 36 Craven Street, London WC2N 5NG. Tel. 01 930 6328.

Teachers' resources guide for sale, with bibliographies, addresses, films for anthropology/humanities courses.

Runnymede Trust, 37A Gray's Inn Road, London WC1 8PS. Free list of publications on race relations, including a monthly bulletin.

School of Oriental and African Studies, Malet Street, London WC1E 7HP, Tel. 01 637 2388.

No loan system. Visits welcomed for information on all aspects of Africa, Asia, Latin America and the Caribbean.

Soma Books (Independent Publishing Company), 38 Kennington Lane, London SE11 4LS. Tel. 01 735 2101.

Books from Indian sub-continent and Afro-Caribbean material.

Third World Publications, 151 Stratford Road, Birmingham
B11 1RD. Tel. 01 773 6572.
Catalogue available.

Walter Rodney Book Shop, (formerly Bogle L'Ouverture
Bookshop), 5a Chigwell Place, London W13 0TJ. Tel. 01
579 4920.
Caribbean school books and Afro-Caribbean and U.S.
material.

Hans Zell Publishers Ltd, PO Box 56, Oxford OX1 3EL.
Tel. 0865 40512.

9 Postscript

RICHARD MILLS

The intention of this book is a very practical one. It is to offer some possibilities for the pragmatic activity of teaching English across a wide age and ability range. Now, towards the end of the book, it seems appropriate to pause for a moment and try to identify some of the issues with which English teaching is going to be concerned over the next decade. All these concerns will have been touched on already for the seeds of the future are with us here and now. It is, thus, not idle star-gazing; decisions taken presently will affect us for years to come.

Accordingly, I have tried to sort out in my own mind some of the key issues and since, as any writer of fiction knows, the gaps are as important as the text, I have left plenty of spaces for you to fill in from your own perceptions.

One of those spaces, more a grand canyon, concerns the nature of the subject itself. What is English? What is distinctive about it? What is the relationship between English and language? Is literature its only unique aspect? In terms of a journey, does English represent the destination, or the road itself, or the street lighting, or a service station for other vehicles? Certainly, this debate is not a new one (and not confined to English) but it seems currently to be very keen. On the one hand, the line between English and certain other curriculum areas such as media studies and communications courses is by no means clear. On the other hand, one attempt to be more precise about the nature of English (I refer to the HMI document *English 5–16*, HMSO 1984) has outraged many English teachers by its cold and bloodless prescription, its disturbing omissions, and its tunnel vision. So the confusion is widespread.

However, at the risk of being accused of dealing in aspirins with a terminally ill patient, I intend for present purposes to avoid that fundamental debate. Instead, I want to touch on certain other concerns.

Exam assessment

One of these (which has been partly considered in the appendix to chapter one) is the stress on assessment. As a stress, it is reasonable; as a stranglehold, it is not. Certainly, it makes sense to measure what is done, but that must not mean doing only what is measurable. That would merely produce a restricted, functional, utilitarian curriculum.

The move away from norm referenced testing, where pupils were judged against each other, to criterion referenced testing where, in theory, pupils are measured against objectively established criteria, is to be welcomed. However, no one should underestimate the problems involved in first devising, then applying, those criteria in a subject like English. The General Certificate of Secondary Education (GCSE) English grade criteria (See *The National Criteria*, DES, HMSO, 1985) require, in some areas, slide rule techniques yet to be invented if they are to be applied fairly. Present proposals for the exam itself are for an English Certificate including a compulsory assessment of oral communication (but separately assessed and appearing as an endorsement on the Certificate). An English Literature Certificate will also be available, based on assessment of written responses to novels, poetry and drama. It is recognized that course work is particularly appropriate in English and, depending on local conditions and examining boards, there will be varying amounts of it, possibly ranging from 20 per cent to 100 per cent. (For current information, application could be made to the relevant address given in Appendix I of this chapter).

The concept of one examination is surely right and can promote many desirable features such as the opportunity for more negotiation of task between teacher and taught; greater choice within the curriculum; more individualization of approach, alongside collaborative enterprises; and a greater range of media and skills (particularly oral) through which English material is presented and assessed.

Alongside the GCSE move is the interest shown in modular courses with assessment by means of profiles and, in some areas, with an element of pupil self-assessment. Such a development not only places more responsibility with the learner, leading to greater autonomy, it is also less divisive. In other words, both GCSE and modular courses / profiling can promote those very features which have been argued for in the early part of this book.

Special needs

The developing individualization of approach just mentioned finds its expression strongly in the area of special needs. The pejorative term 'remedial education' based, as it was, on a deficit medical model, is now being replaced by something much more wide ranging and positive. Such a move, encouraged by the Warnock Report, is reflected in many ways, not least the change of two labels or titles. One is the journal *Remedial Education* (of the National Association for Remedial Education) which now has the title *Support for Learning*. This is a much warmer and all embracing notion and is reflected increasingly in the practice of providing that 'support for learning' within the classroom itself, rather than in some segregated annexe.

The other label in process of being changed, although less dramatically, is that of the learning of English as a second language (E2L). Increasingly, such children are now being referred to not as 'E2Ls' but as 'bilingual', thereby promoting a positive image of mother tongue languages other than English and stressing children's attainments

rather than their deficiencies. It is unfortunate that, in the minds of many, 'E2L' children have been thought of as 'remedial' children. How much better to regard 'bilingual' children as requiring, in the same way as many others, 'support for learning'. This is not merely a matter of semantics but of attitude and approach and practice, as chapter one asserted in respect of all children.

Multicultural matters and language texts

Mentioning mother tongues and bilingualism inevitably reminds us of the wealth of material of all kinds from many of the world's cultures which ought to be reflected in our English curriculum. (See the earlier appendix on Multiculture Matters, page 267). This is a notion that some teachers have supported for a long time and, increasingly, more are recognizing that the world is small and interdependent; that understanding of, and appreciation for, other cultures is not only educationally desirable, but could even be thought crucial to survival; that there is a richness in variety which, despite the tensions, needs to be endorsed and celebrated. In the past we have had our classics in translation, now some of us have story-telling in Punjabi and Gujarati; drama improvisation in Creole; a literature theme comparing black experience in Britain and the United States; a project on marriage across cultures; an anthology of parents' and grandparents' personal anecdotes, compiled by pupils from tape recordings and printed in a school booklet with the mother tongue version and the English translation juxtaposed.

Such a broadening of outlook keeps us on our toes in scrutinizing whatever we do and whatever materials we use, as part of an anti-racist policy, and asking ourselves if what is done is appropriate for all our children, not only as pupils in their school, but also as citizens of their country and dwellers on planet Earth. That may sound a bit grand but it does focus down to something quite specific and manageable. We have all been encouraged over the last few years, through the insights of sociological and linguistic study, to look very carefully at all written text used in school, from work sheets and work cards, to text books and source books and works of literature, to public notices and letters sent home from school. Such scrutiny of new English course books should occur not only from a multicultural standpoint but from other viewpoints, too, such as:

(a) Aims and tasks
(b) Presentation
(c) Language
(d) Cultural background.

Some of these are familiar concerns; others are of fairly recent origin, and Appendix II to this chapter offers a checklist of questions.

Technology

Many of the questions asked of course books could, with slight modification, be asked of the hardware and software being used in English classrooms, since a major concern for all of us is the rapidly expanding world of technology and the extent to which it might change the nature of English teaching (and of all other teaching too), as well as other aspects of our lives. The overwhelming view of a panel of English, American and Canadian English-teaching educators (unpublished 1985 survey, University of Connecticut) is that, despite problems of finance, teacher attitude, and availability of software, technology will play an increasingly positive role in English teaching.

This would be seen, for example, in the development of more open-ended computer programs to replace the more easily produced low-level drill exercises analogous to those de-contextualized language 'exercises' which merely contain children. Such a rich, open-ended program is that of the *Mary Rose* which is being used very successfully with 10 to 12 year olds. The program, which is in two parts, concerns first the location, and then the contents recovery, of Henry VIII's flagship, the *Mary Rose*. All manner of language and other skills are involved as the children simulate diving to locate the ship and identify the artefacts, and as they work collaboratively to research historical records, to investigate the functions of particular objects, and to understand the whole nature of the enterprise. Such programs (and there are now increasing numbers of them) help to bring alive a simulated activity, offering children a unique way into the imaginative experience.

The positive role of technology may also be envisaged in the ultimate use of classroom word processors as a means by which written text may be manipulated easily and conveniently, to the advantage of both pupil author (in terms of drafting, editing, revising) and pupil critic (in terms of analysis and transformation from one genre to another).

It will also be seen, when finances permit, in the use of interactive video where the advantages of both video and computer complement each other. The Department of Trade and Industry, together with two major producers of video-discs (Thorn-EMI and Philips), are presently working to establish the use of videodiscs in United Kingdom schools.

To quote the Connecticut survey:

'It is a strongly positive and optimistic vision that sees a future English classroom in which integration and collaboration crowd out mindless drill and isolated acquisition of fact, in which technology serves, not dominates, in which the thrust is humanistic not mechanical.'

English for real purposes

All this would be in keeping with the notion of English for real purposes, a concept which takes English outside the textbook-bound world and moves it into the community, into 'reality'. As Frank Smith observes in his book *Writing and the Writer* (Heinemann, 1982):

Writing should be used to tell stories and to produce artefacts – books to be published; poems to be recited; songs to be sung; plays to be acted; letters to be delivered; programmes to be consulted; newspapers to be distributed; advertisements to be displayed; complaints

277

to be aired; ideas to be shared; worlds to be constructed and explored.

In such a workshop, based on such a philosophy, all pupils of all ages and abilities can find a role which is both respected and relevant. Such a philosophy is not based on a system of hurdles designed to hinder; it is inclusive and enabling, and in keeping with all the approaches which my colleagues and I have described throughout this book. Appendix III to this chapter outlines some 50 plus suggestions for English for real purposes.

APPENDIX I

GCSE information

Details concerning the General Certificate of Secondary Education examinations may be obtained from any GCE or CSE examination boards. The addresses of the present GCE boards are as follows:

London Group: University of London School Examinations Board, Stewart House, 32 Russell Square, London WC1B 5DN.

Midland Group: University of Cambridge Local Examinations Syndicate, Syndicate Buildings, 1 Hills Road, Cambridge CB1 2EU.

Northern Group: Joint Matriculation Board, Manchester M15 6EU.

Southern Group: Associated Examining Board, Wellington House, Aldershot GU11 1BQ.

Welsh Group: Welsh Joint Education Committee, 245 Western Avenue, Cardiff CF5 2YX.

APPENDIX II

Course book checklist

Aims and tasks
1 What are the intentions of the book or series?
2 Do those intentions suit you and your school and your pupils?
3 Do they fill a gap in your present provision?
4 Do they cover the appropriate range of literacy and oracy skills?
5 Are the tasks clearly distinguished and is there a sufficient number for classroom and follow-up work?
6 Are too many tasks silly or illogical or unrealistic?
7 Is choice and/or negotiation of task encouraged?

Presentation
1 Is the book attractive and durable?
2 Is the size and style and range of print appropriate?
3 Is there a variety of visual material (e.g. photographs, designs, cartoons etc) and how is this related to the written text?
4 Is colour used and how?
5 Is the page layout pleasing and effective? Is there space for the eye to rest?
6 Is there a variety of appropriate stimuli?
7 What is the overall structure and sequence behind the book?
8 Does the book offer value for money?

Language
1 Is the language of the extracts pitched at an appropriate level for your pupils?
2 Is the language of the tasks 'user friendly' (i.e. warm and inviting, without being patronising or mawkish)?
3 Is the tone heavy or light?
4 Is the humour successful?
5 Are difficult words and phrases included and explained or translated?
6 What range of genres is represented?

7   Is there reinforcement of understanding within the text?
8   Are questions closed or open?

Cultural background
1   What kind of world is presented? Is it appropriate?
2   Is there opportunity for readers to identify with characters and/or situations in the text?
3   Are all groups in the community fairly represented?
4   Is the book non-sexist and non-racist and non-classist?
5   Does it deal with matters of current and sensible concern?
6   Does it promote a positive intention to celebrate cultural diversity?

APPENDIX III

English for real purposes

This section offers over fifty possibilities for classroom work to have a real purpose. Some of the ideas may appear sensible, others dotty. But let us hope that the former predominate, for there is plenty of evidence that, where students are involved in an activity with real outcomes and real consequences, then their motivation and quality of work increases substantially. Simulations have an important part to play in language development, but the activities listed here go beyond simulation. They involve discussion, planning, writing, re-drafting (rehearsing), proof reading, polishing, with a view to publication of some sort or public display for a real audience. In some cases, public response and involvement ought to lead to more sustained communication and negotiation between students and those outside the school, so that the relationship may have its own impetus and dynamic. The order of the activities is random, and the degree of involvement of the teacher would depend on the age and capability of the class.
1   Students are encouraged to scrutinize each other's work and to suggest improvements and assist in the re-drafting process, taking care to stress ideas for

raising the interest level, in addition to merely indicating punctuation and spelling errors.

2 Regular exchanges take place of written, visual, and taped information between two classes in different schools at home or abroad (e.g. about aspects of school life, surrounding area surveys, opinions on a variety of issues). Where feasible, this might build up to a real physical exchange between students for a day or so.

3 Students prepare written, taped, visual material and/or exhibition of work and/or drama happening for another class, or others, in the same school. An exhibition would need posters, tickets for entry, a programme, individual cards describing each object, and ushers or guides to explain items. (Appropriate exhibition themes include: Space Film Paraphernalia, Toys from around the World, War Objects, Stamps, Pop Music Today and Yesterday, Video Release, Painting, Family Photographs, Local History.) Classes working on a particular book or play might devise an exhibition of photographs and objects designed to put the book in a context and/or illustrate special episodes or characters or events.

4 Students invite local writers/actors to school to talk about their work and perform. Studying the writer's or actor's work prior to the visit could be expected to improve subsequent discussion.

5 Students investigate the various schemes for having a 'Writer-in-Residence' at their school for a term or so. This would involve finding out about Arts Council-type subsidies, reading and discussing the work of some contenders, selecting appropriate possibilities, negotiating with relevant people.

6 Students scrutinize the language, appearance and layout of several dust jackets and then produce one, tailor-made, for a book in the school, or class, or local library. The jackets could be used initially within the school to promote reading and/or advertise a bookshop or bookfair, and, later, they could be placed permanently around appropriate books in the library. The same principle would apply to record sleeves and video tape covers.

7   Students keep a log book of English lessons to monitor for their own interest the work they've been doing. Or a personal diary or jotting book, for their own scrutiny only.

8   Older students develop self-initiated activities, as part of a Personal Achievement Record. (For example, one student telephones the managing director of a computer firm and arranges to visit; one student starts a science club for younger students.)

9   Older students write stories (either individually or in small groups) to be read, or told by them, to younger students. The stories may be in English, or any mother tongue language, as appropriate.

10   Older students develop board games (e.g. Monopoly-type) for younger students to play for enjoyment (and, incidentally, develop their reading and number skills). They also develop computer programs and simulation games for the same purpose.

11   Students in pairs teach each other a board or card game, first by explanation and demonstration and playing, then with joint writing out of rules in careful sequence. Ideally, the game is either original, or new to the partner. Variations on this theme could be tried, drawing up the rules for any competitive sport, or the sequence for any physical exercise.

12   One class begins a story, then sends it off to another class for the second part, and so on round the school, as appropriate. When it's finished and checked, or when everyone is exhausted, a parent types two copies, one to tour relevant classes and the other for the school library.

13   Older students are paired with younger students, or able with less able, to assist in developing reading skills and other 'English' abilities.

14   A whole-class council, or members of a School Council, are responsible for drawing up agendas, conducting meetings, reproducing minutes, conveying views, estimating response.

15   The annual internal post system for Christmas cards is extended to encourage other internal exchange of letters and information.

16   Students provide their classmates with reviews and comments on: a film, a play, an exhibition, a motor show, an agricultural show, a carnival, a circus, a pop concert, a flower show, a dog show, a wedding, a religious festival In short, any notable event which they have witnessed.

17   A class or group of students devises a programme for school or class assembly to commemorate the birth or death of a famous writer or artist or musician, or to mark a particular event or anniversary or special day, or merely on a particular theme.

18   The traditional scripted school play is replaced, on occasions, or supplemented, by documentaries or plays devised by the pupils themselves. In some cases, they may include television-type advertisements.

19   Schools develop annual drama festivals where class plays are performed (with some productions even going on local tour); or weekly film society meetings; or lunch-time music/poetry/prose reading sessions each fortnight. Such happenings can be advertised by many means devised by students, including some walking round the school carrying sandwich boards/cards.

20   Students take new staff round the area of the school and introduce them to the local sights/sites. The same could be done around the school itself for new students, with a questionnaire devised for the purpose by present students.

21   Students are partly responsible for organizing class visits to films, plays, buildings etc. This would include scrutiny of what is available, buying tickets, hiring transport, liaising with all relevant people and agencies. If the visit were to a place associated with an author, then time could be spent prior to the visit researching the background. If the visit were to a Youth Hostel, then log books could be kept and a report made on the amenities and the local area (and the dormitory ghost stories) for the group due to visit the following year.

22   Students participate in the setting up, organization, and running of a school bookshop and/or book buying

scheme and/or new and secondhand book fair (to include records, audio cassettes, videos).

23 Students help with scrutiny of inspection copies, ordering of books and other stock (including records and tapes), labelling and stamping of new books, repair of older books, termly or annual stock-taking.

24 On occasion, students proof-read handouts and work sheets produced by teachers, before final duplication.

25 Students produce booklets of information about their school and its curriculum. These may be distributed by primary schools to their neighbouring senior schools, and by senior schools to their feeder primary schools. Such booklets can back up visits in both directions.

26 Students develop a file of information on themselves and their school, to be sent to local colleges and university departments of education and to be available for prospective student teachers on practice in the school or, in scaled down form, for visitors to the school. Photographs of people and places, with brief commentary, might be appropriate.

27 Liaising with relevant staff, and using appropriate photographs, students produce brief biographies of all school staff to accompany the photographs which are mounted on boards (behind glass?) in the foyer, for the benefit of visitors, new students, and others. Staff identified would include all people who work in the school and the biographies would be compiled from interviews organized by students. Something similar could be done for any group of students and mounted in the classroom (preferably protected!).

28 Students provide sign boards for strangers to the school, wall notices (e.g. of rules or processes or explanations), instructions for the care of animals or equipment, welcome notices in school entrances (preferably in several languages), brief cards to accompany photographs or paintings hanging on the school walls.

29 Students devise classroom decorations appropriate to a particular topic (e.g. animal shape mobiles with poems on them, or descriptions of the scene outside, written on transparencies and stuck on windows.)

30 Students produce regular, up-to-date guides to the best

shops (e.g. for clothing, music, video films); to discos; groups; sporting activities, amateur and professional. Such guides to be on display in the school library.

31 Students undertake surveys to build up knowledge of local activities (i.e. addresses, phone numbers, range of provision) of: community and youth organizations; drama societies; theatre; film; libraries and bookshops; local history and civic societies; manufacturing and service industries; museums and art galleries; sites, farms and canals; religious buildings and resources.

32 Students produce a local trail (as a booklet and/or on audio tape) for residents, highlighting places of historical, geographical, industrial, cultural, architectural interest. Such a guide can be on display, or for sale, in local libraries and community centres and shops, along with regular displays of other work.

33 Students regularly prepare a miscellany of material for outside groups (e.g. fortnightly radio programmes for a local hospital; exhibitions of work at a local supermarket, library, theatre, community centre; drama or documentary or musical or poetry reading at an Old People's Home.)

34 Students collect anecdotes and personal experience accounts from parents and relatives and friends about the area they live in (or their own upbringing and schooldays, or their own cultural traditions), and the resulting anthology (including, in some instances, material in languages other than English) can become a source book for use with other students.

35 Students collect material for anthologies consisting of adult views on topics of local concern (e.g. services provided by roads, shops, the council); national issues (e.g. capital punishment, health service); eternal issues (e.g. existence of God). Such anthologies may be placed in the school library and be used as source books by other students. Schools may produce such anthologies for each other's library.

36 Students produce material for a wall display, or for a project folder, to be placed in the library (e.g. a collection of gardening hints, or jokes, or problem pages, or recently used cross-cultural recipes).

37 Classes annually produce selections of their work done throughout the preceding terms for an end-of-year anthology, to be adequately bound and catalogued into the school library. Such a publication would involve the class in skills of discrimination, balance, organization, production, negotiation.

38 A classroom bulletin board is maintained with regularly changing items of school, local, national, international concern.

39 Students occasionally make an entry in the school log book, or report to the Governors or Managers, or to Heads of Department.

40 A suggestions box is made available in the classroom for students to put forward ideas for improving their school life. Such suggestions may be passed on for comment by Headteacher, Caretaker, Cooks, Cleaners, Local Education Authority, and others.

41 Students contact local teachers' organizations (e.g. unions; National Association for the Teaching of English; United Kingdom Reading Association) with suggestions for topics to be covered at their meetings, or offers of help with sessions, or requests for information.

42 Light entertainment books can be compiled by individuals or groups, using original material, and given as Christmas or birthday gifts, or on other suitable occasions. Humorous topics include: How To Pretend To Be Ill And Miss School; How To Make Parents/Teachers Mad; Schemes for Money Making; How to Torment My Brother/Sister; Neat Ways to Avoid Washing; How Not To Eat Crusts; A Book of the World's Weakest Jokes.

43 Students are encouraged to write for, and be involved in, the organization, production, and distribution of: class newspaper; school magazine; parents' newsletter; anthologies of short stories/poetry.

44 Students produce a series of anthologies for the school library of transcribed extracts of tape-recorded conversations with people around the school, such as caretaker and cleaning staff, secretarial and ancillary staff,

lollypop persons, medical and technical helpers, visitors.

45 After appropriate testing of a product, students produce a consumers' type report (e.g. on tapes, computer games, sports equipment, fizzy drinks, hamburgers etc). Such regular reports may be on sale in school and, perhaps, sent for comment to the manufacturers, or to an appropriate journal.

46 Occasionally when a government department or university or research agency calls for views and evidence on a particular topic (e.g. cigarette smoking, glue sniffing, drug taking, the state of literacy or numeracy, the attitude of girls towards engineering) it may be appropriate for a class to submit its views or the results of a survey it has conducted.

47 Journal articles written by teachers describing particular English projects might occasionally include commentary by students on the project from their point of view.

48 Students mount an advertising campaign:
(a) to raise money for charity;
(b) for those in distress after a disaster;
(c) for any school fund raising activity.
There can be advertising campaigns, too, without collection of funds, to promote a school club or visit, or a cause within the local community.

49 A class undertakes the sponsorship of an overseas project (e.g. the sinking of a well, the buying of a tractor), raises funds and contributes to regular exchange of information.

50 Students discuss and devise a time capsule to illustrate the age and locality. The capsule is then placed inside a biscuit tin, or whatever, and sealed. It is then buried ceremoniously in or near the school grounds. Alternatively, there could be individual time capsules to be buried less publicly, thereby preventing easy detection. They would then be left forever!

52 Occasionally, individual students, or groups of students, will want to enter national poetry competitions and/or submit a television play or radio programme manuscript to a producer and/or send a

novel manuscript to a publisher and/or short stories to
magazine editors and/or articles to specialist period-
icals and/or items for newspapers.

53   Students who are good readers read short stories and
even short novels, or extracts from novels, onto audio
tape, to be placed in the school library for the benefit
of weak readers.

53   There are many occasions when students can write real
letters (and get replies), for example:

(a) to a singer/actor/dancer/playwright, whose work is
known;

(b) to an agency or an individual (perhaps MP or Coun-
cillor) asking for information;

(c) inviting a visitor; thanking a visitor for coming;

(d) to an author, publisher, bookshop, librarian;

(e) thanking a guide or other expert for services
rendered;

(f) to a student or teacher in hospital, or one who has
just moved away;

(g) to a newspaper or specialist magazine or comic;

(h) to the public, via a newspaper, inviting views and
information on a topic being studied in school;

(i) congratulating an individual or group on some
achievement;

(j) to people well known locally or nationally asking
which novels influenced them when they were young,
and in what ways. Students then follow-up by reading
some of the books mentioned.

(k) to past students asking about their new lives at
different schools or colleges, or in work, or
unemployment.

Index